Why
People Change
the psychology
of influence

William C. Lewis

University of Wisconsin
Medical School

Why
People Change

the psychology
of influence

HOLT, RINEHART AND WINSTON, INC.
New York Chicago San Francisco Atlanta
Dallas Montreal Toronto London Sydney

To Katherine
and
Willy, David, Tim, Jon,
Steve, Ben, Pete

Preface

"I'm sick of feeling as if I were in a straitjacket," he said quietly, turning his palm up in a gesture of defeat. Then he told of his early years and of his grim parents, who, he observed wryly, might well have served as models for Grant Wood's "American Gothic." Not only had beatings been commonplace events, but they had been uncommonly severe and had been administered by his father with an inexorable righteousness.

He, a young doctor, said that he not only felt a severe constriction of his emotional life, but that he also suffered periodic constriction of the blood vessels of his lower arms and hands, a symptom as closely tied to emotions as blushing is to embarrassment, but called "Raynaud's Disease." He had not wept since childhood. He hardly ever let his feelings show, whatever their nature.

One short question transformed this composed, restrained man. He began to weep, wracked by soundless sobs. He was asked, concerning his father's beatings, "Did you ever want to hit back?" An emotional explosion and the answer, "I *wanted* to *kill* him!" followed.

The reasons why this young doctor suddenly changed his ways and reversed long-established habits of restraining his feelings are what this book is about. Although this encounter took place in a medical setting where the young doctor had labelled himself as a "patient" seeking "psychotherapy," the factors guiding what took place are not limited by these labels. The material to be presented applies just as well in other settings to persons labelled "clients," "employees," "students," and so forth. The information in these pages pertains to all the efforts people make to change themselves and others.

Acknowledgments

The tradition of naming one's relatives, friends, and colleagues who have contributed to the complex operation of creating a book is an honored one, recognizing an enterprise which cannot be a solo flight except in the case of unusually gifted individuals. This volume profited enormously from the readings and commentaries of:

Bert Boothe, Ellen Dohman, my wife Katherine, my sons Jonathan and Timothy, my brother Samuel Lewis, Jane Seegal, Ellen Terrill, and Charles Totto.

Professors Aristotle Alexander, Lorna Benjamin, David Graham, Norman Greenfield, Seymour Halleck, and Richard Wolman.

Doctors Nancy Cain, Paul Cotton, Ronald Furedy, and Fred Silvers.

The author wishes to express thanks to those who remain to him and to the reader anonymous. Unless the reader has had the pleasure of the assistance of an excellent publishing firm he can scarcely realize the helping concern of a veritable army of expert professionals. Several are known to the writer: Professor Theodore Sarbin spent untold hours sympathetically and painstakingly reading and commenting on the manuscript; Miss Jan Hughes, Miss Deborah Doty, and Mr. Thomas Davies supplied meticulous care in the many stages of preparing it for publishing.

No writer can proceed without the hard work, often frustratingly repetitious, of those who type his scribbled manuscript over and over again, shaping and interpreting his sometimes obscure revisions. Miss Mary E. White was in charge of this whole operation and has my deepest gratitude. She was assisted by Lynn Gessler, Vicki Gessler Lashua, and Gail Katagiri, who share my thanks.

The Macmillan Company, Cambridge University Press, and the Milwaukee Journal graciously gave permission to quote portions of published works.

My friend Sy Halleck has often commented that life with someone writing a book is hell, because one inevitably becomes preoccupied, petulant, irritable, unavailable, and narcissistically isolated, plus showing a host of other unpleasant personality traits. One's family deserves the most heartfelt thanks, and to mine this small work is dedicated with love.

Contents

Why
People Change
the psychology
of influence

1

The Mother-Child Dialogue

the first roots of interpersonal influence

Infants are popularly supposed to be impressionable creatures. This characterization comes from equating infants with such malleable substances as sealing wax. But in recent years the plot has thickened: Babies, innocent creatures though they seem, now are known to possess quite remarkable powers to influence their parents. Their influence is far more sophisticated than simple signals of need arising from biological necessity: Recent discoveries have penetrated the "cover identity" of the little innocents and have shown them to be as clever and as devious as the secret agents some of them will grow up to be.

Experienced mothers and their pediatricians have known for a long time that the first few days of a baby's life—even the first few hours—can make important and lasting differences in the way the child relates to the world. Some years ago it was standard practice to keep newborns in a hospital nursery, separated from their mothers. The babies were brought to their mothers at intervals to be fed, but much of their care, including some of their feedings, was given by the nursing staff. In recent years many hospitals have adopted the policy, called "rooming-in," of keeping the mother and baby together from the start. The mother does all the feeding of and caring for the newborn almost from birth. Ask mothers of several children, who have experienced both regimes, which they prefer and most will say that rooming-in is greatly preferable in accomplishing a smooth "locking-on" of infant to mother. The mutual adaptation of schedules—of nursing, sleep-wakefulness, production and consumption of milk, and the like—proceeds more smoothly in the absence of outside interference. When mother and child have been separated, it may be weeks after leaving the hospital before they achieve the level of mutual adaptation and influence they obtain when kept together from the first day on. It is as if both needed to explore each other, negotiate agreements, and consolidate contracts.

This would not surprise mothers from so-called primitive societies, who practice rooming-in naturally as part of their culture. Eskimo mothers or Balinese mothers would probably be aghast at the idea of letting a hospital nurse take care of their babies. The comparison of this age-old pattern with the routine of modern hospitals seems to show clearly the rule that keeping mother and child together works best.

Superiority of the practice of keeping mother and child together is apparent not only to mothers, but also to experienced fathers, who appreciate the gain in hours of sleep which comes from smoother mother-child

2

transactions. So also with the nursing staff of the maternity ward and even with medical students—all can detect subtle differences in the mother-child relation when the rapid adaptation of rules between mother and child has occurred within the first few days.

This is one of those remarkable phenomena whose virtually constant presence lulls us into blindness. *Naturally* mothers understand babies. *Naturally* babies turn to their mothers. When one considers the enormous number of transactions that occur in the first week of the acquaintanceship of the newborn with its mother, one is awed by the complexity of the implicit dialogue between the two. But how, really, does it come about? Those not immediately involved in the process find it mysterious. Those in past years who have watched the mother-child interaction have had to give very general explanations relying heavily on postulated forces, drives, and affinities.

Until recently the behavior of the newborn was inaccessible to testing of any precise nature. Theorists had only data coming from rather fragmentary and imprecise observations of the mother-child interaction. This led to the assumption that the behavior of the newborn was guided by unknown mechanisms centering around feeding, which were loosely collected under the rubric of "the oral drive."

There can be no doubt that infants are interested in sucking and swallowing. But this is an observation which is at a level comparable to the observation which some extraterrestrial creature might make when observing two Frenchmen in heated discourse; if he reported that they seemed to have a need to use their mouths in relation to each other he would be correct, but from the Frenchmen's point of view he would miss what really took place. This is the position of anyone who watches the early interchanges between mother and child, nurse and child, father and child. Something is going on; clearly the infant needs food, makes noises and gestures interpreted by the mother as signaling his need—but the intricacy of the communication is as lost to the human observer as it would be to a Martian visitor observing a Frenchman.

Baby cries, mother responds. Skilled mothers develop an ability to sense whether their babies are hungry, wet, bored, or sick, which, though not without its flaws and confusions, is remarkably accurate. Remarkable, that is, to those nonmothers who watch the process and are partially deaf and blind to the sound and sign language of the dialogue. For this dialogue to be possible, both mother and baby must possess intricate signal sending and signal receiving apparatuses. On the part of the mother these apparatuses and their operations have long been lumped under the general name of "the maternal instinct," corresponding to the similarly general name for the infant's equipment, "the oral drive." In this first attempt at explanation the infant's oral drive and the mother's maternal instinct were assumed to lock together to produce a successful interaction, but how this operated was mysterious. Since babies can't talk, the older view argued, we can't expect to understand the workings of the baby's brain—that is, what signals he's able to perceive, organize, and act upon. But ways have recently been developed to convert what babies do into something approximating talk. They don't have words to tell us what they like or dislike, yet they seem to be able to tell their mothers what they want. They can't give a word picture of how the world appears to them, but speech is only one form of behavior, one of the many behaviors that convey meaning from one human to another. A handshake with a smile says something; so does a frown accompanied by a threatening gesture. The trick is to be able to convert the signals babies give out into something intelligible. The required ingenuity has been developing rapidly.

The Language of the Newborn

Lacking a developed verbal language, babies must influence and be influenced in turn by some means combining sound and gesture. Though it is common knowledge that some mothers seem able to pick up their babies' signals better than other mothers, and better than do baby sitters, what are the signals mothers pick up? In 1959, investigators obtained some objective evidence that people who are around babies a good deal of the time (mothers, doctors, nurses, investigators) develop the ability to translate the baby's early communications into conventional language and can describe different messages they receive. These messages can be gauged roughly—but only roughly. Investigation faltered when it came down to questions of how much or exactly what kind of cry means this or that in the infant. About the same time Swedish and American investigators began to record the cries of infants using an instrument called a sound spectrograph, which transforms sounds into visible and measurable records. Since it has been common knowledge among those who work with children that sick children cry differently than healthy children, these researches were aimed at developing tools which might aid in the early diagnosis of brain injuries. The team of investigators, Bosma, Trudy, and Lind (Lind, 1965), proceeded to record the cries of babies from the moment of birth, right in the delivery room, even before the umbilical cord was cut—and for several weeks thereafter. They also recorded the babies' vocal movements, using X-ray movies of the larynx and also recordings of air intake and expulsion from the respiratory tract and esophagus (procedures called spirometry and esophageal catheterization, respectively) at times when babies were crying spontaneously. In subsequent weeks they recorded the babies' response to pinching the skin of the babies' wrists.

If there ever was doubt that babies arrive in the world equipped with a sizable repertoire of signaling capacities, these studies settled the question. Babies have recognizable types of cries, as one can see from the recordings—three basic sorts have been described thus far from these studies. These investigators can recognize at least nine distinct stages of infant crying. The investigations show not only recognizable crying and swallowing patterns, supplemented exceptionally by gasping, coughing, and larger body movements, but also show considerable individual variations on the basic types, characteristic for each baby. (Newborns also momentarily use the respiratory methods of the frog—these studies revealed that they swallow air both into the lungs and into the stomach, inflating both respiratory and intestinal tracts. This finding explains why the standard maneuver of putting a baby over one's shoulder and patting his back until he regurgitates air—burping—is so necessary.)

This beginning may prove to be the Rosetta stone which will open up the language of babies to translation and understanding. No doubt careful examination of such records will reveal more and more about the patterns of vocal influence babies bring with them into the world. These studies offer a tantalizing promise of removing some of the mystery of child-mother communications. When a mother has become attuned to her infant's routine crying patterns, she is ruled in part by them. She can recognize standard patterns associated with hunger or with other needs, and, once having learned the rule, she can recognize any variation. These can be powerful, well-nigh automatic, influences in childhood emergency situations. One example will make the point: An experienced mother's child, at the crawling-toddler stage, went exploring in an older brother's room while his mother was working on the floor below. The sound of a faint, unusual gurgle instantly recalled to his mother that the older brother had been painting in oils the night before. Before she realized what she was doing, she was up a flight of stairs and had seized a small glass of turpentine the baby had begun to drink. The child was sick but unharmed, rescued because of her practiced ear. This practiced ear is like that which therapists develop—Theodore Reik called it the "third ear" (Reik, 1948).

Does "Someone Get the Message"?

Babies, then, are signal senders from day one, but it does not necessarily follow that the slight variations in their cries will be received, noted, and responded to appropriately. Such signal reception requires the near-constant presence of a good mother—one who has her heart in the job and is consistently working to improve her understanding, just as a good therapist develops the ability to listen and observe attentively. When the mutuality of influence, the dialogue of mother and child, fails for any reason, the result is not as trivial as an awkward pause in a drawing room conversation: Serious consequences ensue. To make this point vivid, two dramatic instances will be described in a subsequent chapter. For the moment, let us consider some of the less obvious consequences of faulty dialogue between mother and child.

René Spitz, in studies now well known (Spitz, 1965), found differences between two groups of infants in two different institutions. These differences were not merely different rates of development; they involved widely divergent sickness and mortality rates. The infants in one group were raised by the personnel of a foundling home, and the others were raised by their own mothers living in a home for unwed mothers. Those raised by their own mothers developed faster and had far lower morbidity and mortality than those raised by the staff of the foundling home.

Spitz attributed these differences to inadequate mothering in the first group, since in all other respects the care of the two groups was comparable. The dialogue could not develop between infants and a nursing staff working on shifts, caring for many babies, and changing personnel frequently. Experts in child development who have observed infants being raised away from their mothers at the present time in large institutions in the Soviet countries have expressed alarm at the widespread stunting of development they saw (for example, Dale Meers [Meers, 1968], who visited the USSR in 1967). As for our primate cousins, anyone who sees a monkey raised in total isolation from other monkeys from birth on is touched by the spectacle of an animal whose capacity to relate to the world is shattered. These animals cower pitifully, rocking to and fro, picking at themselves, biting at their fingers or toes. As Harry Harlow showed, they are cut off permanently from normal monkey pursuits and pleasures (Harlow & Harlow, 1969).

Dialogue with an infant depends not only on perceiving his signals, but also on being able to signal back to him. How can a mother know for sure whether her baby is getting *any* message? In the first few weeks his obvious responses are limited to turning his head toward her body, rooting, and finding the nipple. This activates the whole pattern of sucking and swallowing.

In the first two months he shows various other patterned responses, such as the different varieties of crying recorded in Sweden. These patterns indicate that newborns have some ability to discriminate signals. Records of their voices show specific patterns linked to the different crude messages sent them. A touch on the cheek produces a different vocalization than a pinch on the leg. A loud noise evokes a different crying pattern than does deprivation of food. These differentiations scarcely suggest the kind of message reception and processing which would lead to a complex dialogue between mother and child, resembling the sort used with patients in psychotherapy. Given only such evidence, the exchanges of signals seem crude.

There are, however, indications that babies can process more complicated signals coming from the world than those which trigger simple reflexes. For example, present a human face to a baby and the baby will smile. But it has been known for many years that babies don't smile at all objects shaped like a human face. Their discrimination between such objects and the real face, beginning as early as two months of age, suggests an ability to process more complex signals.

Mothers respond to babies at many levels, some of which are out of awareness but have powerful effects on the baby. We, the observers, infer that there are many levels of response on the part of the baby in his dialogue with his mother, but these have been hard to document. If one waits until some fairly complicated pattern of behavior like smiling appears spontaneously, then one can test whether the baby will smile only at his mother's appearance or whether he will smile at a mask of a face—or even a representation of part of a face. As early as 20 years ago, two researchers in child development (Spitz and Wolf, 1946) mapped out the way smiling appears in children. At three to four weeks infants respond to the human face in motion by following it with their eyes. Babies of one to two months of age fix their gaze on the face of whoever is feeding them, but about this age a few begin to smile when they see the human face presented straight-on, nodding and smiling at them. Most babies of three or four months show this response. After about six months they stop smiling at just anyone—up to this age they are very democratic, smiling at every face regardless of sex or color. As they develop, they limit their smiles to a smaller and smaller circle of intimates. Strangers are excluded from the circle of those who merit the smile.

Spitz and Wolf went further: They found that babies respond to masks of faces just as well as to real faces, but in both cases they stop smiling if the presentation is in profile rather than in full-face.

The smiling response is even more specific: By covering parts of the face-mask they presented to the babies, Spitz and Wolf were able to show that the crucial area that sets off the pleased smile in babies is the area of the face surrounding the eyes. Babies will not smile for less—one eye won't do. They will smile if the mouth part of the face-mask is covered, but this apparently doesn't mean that they are indifferent to the mouth, because when Spitz and Wolf opened their mouths wide, as if baring their fangs to devour the baby, they provoked even more smiling (perhaps this response has roots in the responses of other primates to threats from dominant animals—they grimace in smiling submission). A nodding motion seemed to be a necessary part of the ensemble. This avenue of influence leads directly to the consulting room—psychotherapists do a great deal of nodding and smiling as they talk with patients (though a devouring grimace does not seem to have become the cornerstone of any school of psychotherapy to date).

The sequences in which ever-more-complex patterned dialogue appears between baby and mother provoke much interest these days. Researchers are trying various ways to get inside the infant's view of the world. Those interested in exploring such matters, researchers and theorists of child development (see Mussen, 1967, for a summary), have tended to divide on the nature-nurture issue. There are those who are inclined to assume that a child greets the world at birth equipped with minimal rules—he is essentially, as John Locke wrote in the seventeenth century, an unmarked page —a *tabula rasa*. This group—those researchers strongly influenced by psychoanalytic theory—takes the view that almost everything about the world and its ways must be learned, beyond the baby's inborn knowledge of how to solve the problems of keeping alive by such housekeeping functions as feeding and breathing. This group holds William James' view of the infant's world—he imagined it to be an unanalyzed bloom of confusion. There is a growing camp of theorists, however, who favor the idea that babies have much greater capabilities than was ever before suspected.

One might leave such controversies to the experts interested in them (in an effort to inquire into the nature of psychotherapy), if the therapists' view about early influence didn't directly affect how one goes about conducting the dialogue of psychotherapy. But it does: Any therapist influences his patient by using the patient's capacity to *be* influenced, which consists of the total influenceability he was born with, that which developed in maturation, and that which he learned by experience.

The therapist may protest that he cares not a fig about when a baby acquires a particular modality of influence, so long as that modality is there to be used in his adult patient. Many therapists call themselves "ahistoric," stressing that attempts to reconstruct and speculate about a patient's past are irrelevant to therapy: For them, the here-and-now encounter is all that matters (for example, "Existentialists"[1] or "Transactionalists"[2]). We all can grant that the past is exquisitely irrelevant except as it affects the present: but affect the present it does. It is only when one looks at what therapists of differing stripes *do* that the importance of their implicit or explicit models of the infant's world becomes apparent. For example, behavior therapists engage in a kind of training resembling Pavlovian conditioning. The most militant of this group concentrate on what influencing signals they send to patients and many of them tend to ignore the influencing signals patients send to them, the therapists.[3] This myopia may stem from a standpoint which originated in a laboratory where experimental animals were to be manipulated—not loved, feared, or hated. Even in the laboratory these emotions occasionally erupt in spite of the effort scientists make to be objective and detached. They can even threaten to disrupt experiments. They complicated Harry Harlow's attempts to raise monkeys in total isolation—young lady lab assistants had an irresistible attraction to the "poor little babies" and tended surreptitiously to mother them, a practice directly defeating to the experiment.[4] Conditioning experiments hinge on signals given to the animals, not on how the experimenter feels or how the animals influence the experimenter. (There is an old joke in which one rat comments to another, "I sure taught that man in the white coat to feed me, didn't I?") Those therapists who follow the conditioning model frequently leave out of account the whole complex of emotional reactions in the therapist which Freud called countertransference. This concept refers to the archaic, irrational, rigid attitudes, the inappropriate demands and expectations and involvements stemming from old relations with the important figures of the therapist's childhood which intrude into relations with his patient. These easily contaminate the thera-

[1] See the writings of Boss, 1958, and May, 1958.
[2] See the writings of Haley, 1963.
[3] See the writings of Wolpe, 1958.
[4] Personal communication.

peutic process, for patients experience the countertransference of the therapist and are influenced by it at a secondary level. In turn, the therapist responds to the patient's secondary reactions. Behavior therapists often seem to ignore these phenomena. Not only do they follow much the same maneuvers with patients as experimenters use with experimental animals, but they also act as though they think their patients as babies had been passive objects of conditioning, rather than active participants in a complex dialogue in which their mothers were influenced reciprocally.

Levels of Dialogue

Any mother knows her side of the mother-child dialogue and can describe its many levels. Once underway it is so continuous and circular that it is hard to find the pattern of what leads to what. Consider a single feeding sequence: Baby cries, mother picks him up. She next observes his satisfaction, which makes her feel more adequate as a mother in her own eyes. Next time he cries, her approach to him is surer, less uncertain. Her assurance calms her baby. So it goes over the weeks, as the baby develops increased responsiveness, begins to watch his mother's face, smile at her, reward her attentions with an increasing repertoire of signals. For her, much more is involved than a simple pattern of stimulus and response (though that is present: one cry at feeding time from the crib will start the flow of milk—even the thought of nursing will, for many a nursing mother, produce a steady stream from the breast). But she evaluates her performance in many ways which go far beyond such a simple response—competence today compared with yesterday, with this baby as compared to another, competence compared to her sisters, satisfaction in the process at home as compared to traveling in the car, ability to discriminate the cry of hunger as compared with the cry of being cold and wet, and so on. This cry occurs in the context of her life with all its competing demands, and her response is determined not only by the cry but also by these other demands.

So also, it appears now, with babies. Newborns influence back: They have precise tracking apparatuses, comparable in precision to radar-tracking devices, which allow them to sense a touch somewhere on their cheeks, and then to make active movements, finely coordinated, to reduce the distance of their mouths from the touching object. One can easily miss the reciprocal aspect of this "homing behavior"—homing on the nipple, ensuring a meal—but careful observers have shown[5] that this rooting and searching elicits accommodative behavior from the mother or other adult feeding the baby, via adjustments of the breast or a bottle to assist the babies' homing on the nipple. Typewriter keys don't reach for the hunt-and-peck finger of the typist, but babies not only reach for the nipple, they also influence the feeding person to be more competent. Experienced

[5] Blauvelt & McKenna, 1961.

therapists have noticed a parallel phenomenon; they say that learning to be a competent psychotherapist is often assisted by the patient, who reaches to the therapist for help and reinforces the efforts made by the therapist to reach him.

Individual Dialects of the Dialogue

The capacity of babies to influence the influencer is itself not a standard item of equipment. Babies are very different at birth, as any parent of a large family knows, and they show stable differences from one another as they mature. Physical growth patterns, patterns of psychophysiological response, activity and reactivity of various types—styles—all vary from baby to baby, and these variations are now known to remain stable. Nurses, pediatricians, and parents of more than one child have been saying this from time immemorial. The question of native differences in babies is particularly poignant to one segment of the population, namely parents. Parents tend to feel that their children have come into the world as totally malleable little creatures, and that they, the parents, are of course responsible for whatever problems of adjustment a child has. This is also an insidious prejudice among psychotherapists (which they try to control), which leads them to concentrate upon the malfunctions of parenthood in their patient's childhood as compared with the endowment, and the limitations of endowment, which the patient brought with him into the world at birth. This prejudice tends to underscore the guilt of parents and to perpetuate the blaming of nurture rather than nature for the maladjustments of psychiatric patients.

There is now scientific evidence to bolster common experience that children *are* different at birth.[6] There are studies providing evidence that differences in the newborn's style of coping with the world persist long past babyhood.[7] The repertoire of responses a baby brings with him into the world influences the mother. Phlegmatic babies can disappoint volatile mothers; placid mothers can frustrate babies who want to find out where the action is. The situation between mother and child is not unlike that of dancing partners: It takes two to tango and two whose styles of action mesh well, tango well. For at least the last 20 years, researchers have studied the intricacies of this terpsichorean type of mesh between mother and child. What is it that makes for beautiful dancing and the consolidation of a team capable of making a living by dancing—or in the parallel instance, a viable mother-child relationship? Is it the child's equipment? The mother's? Or the actual experience of relating together? There is a parallel matching of therapist and patient in the mutual influence in psychotherapy: Patients shop around when they don't find a rapid meshing

---

6 See the studies of Thomas et al., 1963, and Bell, 1965.
7 Papousek, 1965.

with their therapists, and experienced therapists find all sorts of reasons to refer a patient to someone else after the first interview, if prospects for mutually rewarding interaction seem dim.

One student of the mother-child interaction, Sybille Escalona, assembled and published in 1969 data gathered over 20 years of close observation of such interactions, both in the clinic and in the baby's home. She thinks that the best way to guess how the dance will turn out is not to study either mother or child alone, but to see how they actually get along *together.* Perhaps, in some Orwellian future, some pediatrician or government official of 1984 may feed computers data about the temperaments and physiological endowments of mothers and babies separately. He may ask the computer to match mother and newborn to decide whether they belong together (after all, even now dating is so matched on many college campuses). This Brave-New-World pediatrician might decide whether to place the child with another mother, rather than with his own mother, on the basis of such matching. For Escalona this would be a monstrously inadequate choice—the battle is the payoff, and what makes for success or failure of development is neither the child's nor the mother's equipment but what actually happens between them—their experience of each other at all levels.

Relatively inactive babies need more stimulation from the world in order to develop normally than do active ones. If inactive babies have relatively inattentive mothers, or if they are raised in institutions, a vicious cycle tends to develop. If those who are caring for the babies operate on the principle that infants should be approached when they appear to be in need, which is the rule rather than the exception in institutional care, the very ones who need stimulation most often get it least. Inactive babies respond to hunger less than active ones and tend to turn to thumbsucking or rocking to overcome their distress. If inactive babies go to the hospital for some illness, they show a greater temporary loss of development than active babies. It is the old case of the squeaking wheel getting the grease. Inactive babies, unless blessed with active mothers, tend to develop into wallflowers.

Escalona was able to measure a fact known to every parent and teacher but which is neglected by those theorists who tie their theory of influence to any simple biological need, such as those clearly evident in the infant: Babies who are very hungry do *not* learn to perform well, but tend to become fretful and even more infantile than is usual for them. Anyone who has tried to influence a tired, hungry, or thirsty child knows that the child is not particularly amenable at such times. On the other hand Escalona's studies showed that continual satiation in all respects does not spur learning or maximal development: Even infants conform to the old rule that influence—parental, educational, or therapeutic—depends on a happy combination of frustration and satisfaction. The Swiss psychologist Piaget's maxim is that without a problem there is no learning, and Esca-

Iona's studies confirm this rule. If babies never meet challenge their behavior tends to freeze at babyish levels. If a mother always hands a rattle to her reaching baby, his Horatio Alger tendency to triumph over obstacles is slow to develop.

Implications of Dialects for Therapeutic Change

The way infants respond to influence reveals fundamental principles of human interaction. These principles have bearing on some old controversies among therapists even if one has reservations about comparing patients with babies (obviously there are differences). It is the process of influence, not the age of the person influenced, which counts for this inquiry. The stereotype of psychotherapy seen in movies and plays would lead one to think that therapists, and particularly psychoanalysts, behave as if abstentions in giving to patients were their cardinal rule. The image of the ungiving analyst runs through much of the written literature of psychotherapy, starting with Freud's papers on technique (1949), in one of which he recommends that so far as possible, analysis should be conducted in a state of abstinence from the satisfaction of instinctual needs. This dictum tends to guide beginners at psychotherapy, especially recent graduates from analytic institutes. Yet Freud's daily notes on his work with the patient known in psychiatric circles as the "Rat Man" (because of one of the patient's obsessions)—the only such notes of his daily work which have been preserved (Freud, 1955)—contain a notation that on arrival the patient "was hungry and was fed."

Freud, in contrast with some contemporary followers, honored the fact shown later by Escalona's studies. Being an experienced father, he knew that with patients, as with children, first things came first; little analytic work is possible when the patient is starved. On the other hand, a smothering therapist who tries to satisfy all the dependent needs of his patient is like the mother who blights the unfolding tendency her baby shows toward discovery and exploration by satisfying all his needs whenever he is frustrated mildly. Escalona's studies suggest that moderate and varying states of need-satisfaction go with the best progress. Neither abstention nor satisfaction maximizes influence and development. The babies who develop best are those who experience periodic variation of arousal, including moderate deprivation, even though this brings about the temporary loss of the most advanced patterns of which they are capable. Escalona suggests that this intermittent loss prevents a premature stabilization of behavior which would be resistant to change if maintained over long periods. Placid babies who seldom experience strong excitation like real hunger tend to maintain simple, bodily focused behavior patterns. Babies who are continually in a high state of excitement (whether because of stimulation from within their own bodies or from the environment) also fail to develop optimally. High arousal leads to primitive behavior in babies, not toward the development of coordinated, finely tuned patterns of response. Any parent who has dealt with a hungry, tired, overstimulated baby knows this. A prolonged party—the family gathering at Christmas time—does not bring out the best in a baby.

Something similar is seen in the consulting room in the form of psycho-therapeutic stalemates. Both patient and therapist may get stuck in a therapeutic rut, having learned each other's rules so well that challenge is lost. Psychotherapeutic movements stop when patient and therapist pose no problem to each other. Therapy can also grind to a halt when there is no mutual stimulation and satisfaction. Withdrawn patients are analogous to the wallflower babies Dr. Escalona studied—they need out-side stimulation to develop. But, both in the consulting room and in hos-pital situations, such patients are least likely to receive it. Escalona's studies, if extrapolated to adults in psychotherapy, would indicate that more stimulation and reaching out is in order with withdrawn, inactive patients. And indeed this seems to have been borne out in clinical prac-tice: Though experiments in clinical technique have ranged from the most passive stratagem—sitting beside a catatonic patient for months, demanding no response[8]—to the most active type of intervention—in-cluding wiping the patient's nose, feeding him, fighting with him, and so on, in a sort of free-for-all,[9]—it appears at this point that the activists get more rapid results in working with withdrawn patients than the pas-sivists. Granted that patients are often afraid of active attempts to reach them, and may withdraw further from a barrage of stimuli, by-and-large they get nowhere when ignored. The large number of chronic patients in mental hospitals who seem marooned on the island of their own quan-daries, ignored by the staff execpt for creature functions, seems to sup-port Escalona's observations about babies.

Summary

Primitive cultures and recent hospital practices recognize the impor-tance of establishing the mother-child dialogue as early in life as possible. Study of the mechanisms by which the dialogue takes place has only re-cently become feasible. Interactions which have been lumped together under the terms "the oral drive" and "the maternal instinct" now appear to involve complex information-processing operations between mother and child. This dialogue is reciprocal, has many levels, and has vital signif-icance. Recent studies show "individual dialects" of the dialogue, which relate to differing rates and kinds of later development in the child. This new knowledge applies to efforts to work change in many other inter-personal settings, such as the nurse-patient, teacher-student, or employer-employee relation. The psychotherapeutic relation was singled out to demonstrate some implications of this knowledge.

8 Fromm-Reichman, 1958, or Sechehaye, 1951.
9 Rosen, 1953, or Wexler, 1951.

2

Newborn Scientists,
Mature Gamblers

Recent technical refinements in methods of studying children have produced evidence which requires a revision of our ideas of the infant's world. No longer need the investigator wait for a spontaneous behavior, like the smiling response, to develop in order to test how a baby relates to the world. Some recent studies involve measuring physiological responses to the presentation of various types of stimuli, others measuring eye movement or fixation in a precise fashion, and still others teaching active manipulations to babies within their limited repertoire. With these methods it is now possible to "converse" with an infant in ways never before available. One can discover how infants perceive and process the information coming from their sense organs—how they think—and how one can influence their thoughts. The rules of behavior they bring with them into the world have become more accessible, and the potentiality for therapeutic altering of those rules, even in earliest life, is at hand.

The most dramatic studies involve the visual apparatus. This most potent of the perceptual systems brings to the brain more fibers than all other sensory systems combined—more than a million. Its structure and function have been worked out in considerable detail. A great deal is known about the retina, the optic nerve, the way-stations and offshoots from them, and the visual cortex. This whole system, called the visual analyzer by the Russians, is better understood anatomically and physiologically than are many other sensory systems—one is on much less uncertain ground with the visual analyzer than with the analyzer for smell, for example. The precision of the visual analyzer makes it possible to study its function in detail and to arrive at a much better understanding of infant behavior than could be obtained from study of the gustatory analyzer—the apparatuses involved in feeding—which, after all, serves a creature as primitive as a worm quite well without the help of anything like the complicated apparatus of the human brain. In early Freudian theory the gustatory analyzer provided the model for the way babies perceive and know, mainly because feeding is the most obvious channel of interaction between mother and child during the earliest periods of life.

But human babies are natively curious creatures. Like their primate cousins, rhesus monkeys, they are fascinated with puzzle solving. Monkeys are moved by sheer curiosity; rewarding their efforts with prizes of food actually takes the edge off the monkeys' enthusiasm for puzzle solving, as long as they are reasonably well-nourished.[1] Human and monkey babies are hungry for all sorts of stimulation, not merely for food. This hunger for stimulation requires modification of two prevalent habits of thought regarding earliest mental life. One is what Freud called the constancy principle, which postulates that any rise in instinctual pressure, say hunger, gives rise to "unpleasure" and is therefore avoided. The other is the simple reflex-arc model in which an outside stimulus leads a relatively passive organism to respond. Neither can any longer be sustained as an adequate explanation of human, mammalian, or even lower vertebrate behavior. Instead it is now clear that babies are continually active, curious, and that they *seek* stimulation—a need almost as basic and early as their need for nutriment of the edible variety.

The Peekaboo Game: Nascent Science

Babies as young as two weeks old like to play peekaboo. From 2 to 20 weeks of age they respond as long as 20 minutes at a time, if someone will pop out, smiling and nodding from behind a screen, sometimes patting the baby on the tummy. They respond in obvious ways—a smile of pleasure, a lighting up of the face. Delight is hard to measure accurately, but the psychologist Bower and his colleagues at Harvard arranged a method of recording the baby's responses: Place a baby recumbent with his head between two yielding pads and hook these pads up to a microswitch, and the baby can signal his pleasure to the investigator by turning his head as little as half an inch to right or left. This gives him a way to say, in effect, "I want to play peekaboo." Bower reports that two-week-old infants can give 400 messages of this sort without getting tired. Given a way to call for the game, babies quickly learn to interpret a signal coming from their field of vision as an open invitation which only needs from them an acceptance—an R.S.V.P. of an infantile sort—consisting of a slight turn of the head in order to make the game begin. A dialogue, a kind of charade, becomes possible.

Bower first let the 50- to 60-day-old babies he was studying learn that a particular signal was an invitation to play. In one experiment it was a white cube, one foot long to a side, placed a certain distance away. Whenever a removable screen dropped, revealing this cube on a table in front of a baby, the baby had only to move his head slightly to make the peekaboo game begin; a pretty young lady would pop up on command from her hiding place below his line of vision.

The next step Bower took was extraordinarily ingenious: By varying the size of the signaling cube and also its distance from the baby, and then by counting the number of times the baby signalled back his intention to play, he set a trap from which the baby could not escape. The

1 See Harlow, 1953, 1963.

baby could not fail to reveal the way he saw Bower's invitation. Was the near, small cube (or the big, far cube) the reliable invitation?

It turned out that babies' responses are influenced by real size and real distance, not by contrived cues which might be expected to fool the baby's eyes. Similar studies by Bower's group indicate that at eight weeks of age babies discriminate depth and the orientation of planes in space, and they grasp the constancy of an object's size and shape. Babies can register and sort correctly most of the visual information an adult can. They have binocular vision, which gives them what astronomers call parallax—the perception of the distance of a star via two observations from different points in space (as from two positions on the earth's orbit). Babies can also use motion parallax: By moving their heads slightly they can judge by the relative motion of near and far objects which one is closer. They have a surprising ability to use these combined observations in sensing accurately how objects are formed and how surfaces are tilted—an ability which has obvious survival value for them.

This, no doubt, is interesting information in its own right, but Bower's work casts even more light on the newborn's capacities for making guesses and testing them. He took the sort of triangular metal object used in orchestras and schoolrooms to produce a musical tone and partially covered it with a rectangular bar-shaped card across the middle of the triangle. He then trained 50-day-old babies that this combined triangle-and-bar was an invitation to play peekaboo. He could then investigate how the child sees the triangle. Does he respond to the whole ensemble as a unit? Or can he ignore the bar (obscuring part of the triangle), and fill out the triangle image to make it an imagined complete triangle? To settle these questions, Bower constructed metallic alternatives to a complete triangle: △   △̲   △̲   or △ . He then tested the babies, comparing their R.S.V.P.'s to these altered invitations to play peekaboo; in effect, he gave them a research problem. The complete triangle was a hands-down favorite, winning out by twice as many responses as any of the variations. In other words, the babies were able to take the ensemble apart, process its components separately, test various hypotheses, and ignore the bar-card selectively. Respectable research for a two-month-old baby!

But, present to the baby *pictures* of cubes, triangles, or other invitations to play and then pictures of alternative invitations, and babies are out of business. They seem not to have the capacity adults possess to suppress some of the evidence of their senses. If babies see a picture, their parallax-sensing capacity tells them that the picture is a flat piece of paper with various marks on it. Their ability to fill out the triangle as an imaginary complete form vanishes. When deprived of the slight cues coming from the round form of the metal and the slightly different distance of the triangle itself from the distance of the card occluding part of the triangle, they lose their capacity to imagine a complete triangle.

Newborn and Mature Gamblers

Adult humans have far greater ability than babies to ignore sensory cues. Their selective inattention sometimes reaches well-nigh incredible levels. The father of a severely disturbed soldier, himself a Protestant minister, once wrote me (I was his son's psychiatrist) as follows: ". . . I want my son to get every ~~hell~~ help . . . ." Not only had he ignored the evidence of his own senses, the sight of his crossed-out original message (showing some glimmer of how he really felt about his son), but he had also ignored what I would see, and had not bothered to erase or obliterate the word "hell." This ignoring capacity of adults appears daily in clinical settings as well as in everyday life. It occurs moment by moment in psychotherapy.

> (*Couples therapy—husband and wife and two co-therapists*)
> *1st therapist:* (*To wife, who looks ghastly*) "You look like someone out of Belsen today."
> *Wife:* "I didn't hear what you said—"
> *Husband:* "You know—Buchenwald—"
> *2nd therapist:* (*Chuckling wryly*) "Would you believe it?"
> *Wife:* "What did you say?"
> *1st therapist:* (*Louder*) "Belsen, Buchenwald, Dachau—"
> *Wife:* "I really didn't hear you—"
> (*Her hearing was not only very acute but she was closer to the first therapist than to either her husband or the second therapist.*)

If babies have weaknesses, as Bower's studies indicate, they also have strengths. These are the strengths used in psychotherapeutic influence: In playing peekaboo, the baby sees, attends to, and gives significance to a signal, a visual pattern, in this case. He connects the signal with the subsequent game. He can become bored (Bower reports this as a limiting factor in his studies), but he is also curious and enjoys playing—he will work at keeping the game going. His curiosity is sufficient to make him experiment with variations on rules—the variations on the bar-triangle theme elicit responses which in adult life might be accompanied by the statement "Let's give it a whirl." Even at this early age, he makes forecasts and has expectations of what should happen if this or that signal appears.

The baby is not merely influenced, he influences the experimenter by pushing a switch to make the game begin again. He then experiences the experimenter's reaction to his influence. It is as if a 50-day-old baby had a theory about the nature of the world—what is real, how it works, and how to gain some control over it. And he seems not only to create a theory but also to have ways to handle variations and exceptions to his theory. Give him reason to think that the bar-triangle means you'll play with him and he'll behave as though he had made up an hypothesis for himself: Variations on the bar-triangle theme make him behave like a scientist in miniature. He handles the variations as if he had compared them with his hypotheses about the nature of the triangle: The one most like his theoretical triangle gets the most plays, but *other* variations get some trials too—he acts as if they thought his theory of the complete triangle might be in error. And the baby's theory shows various levels of abstraction: He shows that he can define the situation as one in which it is safe to play; he does not withdraw and freeze, but recognizes the smile of the researcher and smiles in return. It is as if both players recognize each other's basic premise of safety and acceptance, and recognize the vital role of context.

Both players of the peekaboo game have plans[2] (variously called rules, sets, beliefs, transferences), both influence each other (they keep the game going), and both introduce variations on each other's plans, which then change the plans of both. A 50-day-old baby already shows the special human talent for categorizing and functioning at various levels. The baby in Bower's laboratory learns a lot about the game—its rules, exceptions, and variations—and about what goes on in laboratories of psychology. The experimenter learns a lot he didn't know about how babies perceive the world and also how they process the information contained in their perceptions: How babies abstract ("I'll bet there is a triangle shape behind that bar") and fail to abstract ("All I see is a piece of paper with some marks on it"). The researcher's expectations were changed, through playing with the babies, to include a new respect for an infant's capacities.[3]

The intricacy of reciprocal influence in the peekaboo game touches on one of the central problems humans struggle with all their lives. This is the problem of our fantasies of omnipotence—our own, or another being's, whether it be the Deity, or some human authority such as a parent, a judge, or a doctor. After an infant has experienced his capacity to guide the world around him and has learned to trust it, he must then gradually learn to relinquish the heady wine of feeling all-powerful. When he cries, mother appears; when he moves his head, he starts the peekaboo game as if by magic. No wonder children say "step on a crack, break your mother's back"! No wonder they impute magical powers to others and, as they grow to be adults, invent all manner of magicians possessing these powers—witches, devils, and demons beyond number. And when the hard-won learning of adulthood that tames our early omnipotence is bleached by overwhelming stress (or fever and toxins), we once more slip into grandiose delusions, or into horrifying terrors of the magically powerful forces before which we are helpless.

A Parallel Clinical Exchange

The reader might have difficulty applying laboratory studies of babies to efforts to effect change in the interpersonal relations of adults as, for example, the figures of the psychotherapeutic dance. An example may

2 See Chapter 17 for the difference between "plan" (small "p" and "Plan" (capital "P").
3 These and other studies are excellently described in a recent volume by Beadle, 1970.

help show a parallel between such adult exchanges and the peekaboo game: In a seminar discussion of influence, a psychiatric resident raised objections as to the relevance of theoretical formulations concerning the roots of influence, including Bower's findings, to clinical problems in psychotherapy. In response to this challenge the seminar leader asked for current problems in the residents' clinical affairs. A first-year resident said he had a problem. He had made an appointment to see a college student, and when the appointed time came, the student didn't appear. After waiting ten minutes, the resident did a housekeeping chore away from his office for ten minutes. When he returned the student was in his office. In the half-hour remaining before the next appointment the patient gave the resident the impression that he was experiencing one of the garden-varieties of disenchantment with college, common among students these days. The resident made another appointment with the patient one week later. The next move was a telephone call from the patient, resulting in a written message to the resident that the student had entered the infirmary because of infectious mononucleosis.

In this seminar the resident raised the question of what his next move should be. Should he drop in on the student? Should he offer to see the student in his hospital room? Should he ignore the message, refusing to be manipulated into showing his commitment to treating the student? Should he adopt a middle course, acknowledging his receipt of the message, and have the ward nurse tell the student to call for an appointment when released from the hospital? He was in a position not unlike that of the baby in Bower's laboratory. Discussion of these alternatives revealed that these exchanges, brief though they were, involved mutual influence and questions of control and motivation. Many guesses were plausible concerning the rules of the "game": Was the student frightened? bent on confusing the resident? afraid of homosexual seduction? inviting same? testing the resident to show whether protocol or human need governed their exchange? The way the resident viewed and responded to the student's signal would begin to establish a rule—either confirming or disconfirming the plans both participants had brought to their exchanges.

Summary

Precise laboratory studies of a type of dialogue similar to that seen in "rooming-in" have revealed that very young babies possess intricate equipment to receive and sort information, and to influence as well as to be influenced. They can play games at 50 days of age which depend on much more complex abilities to guess and bet than anyone had previously imagined. They show great native curiosity, and this guides their behavior. The complex maneuvers of interpersonal relations among adults, which often resemble the peekaboo game, begin in the earliest weeks of life. Fantasies of omnipotence, so common in later childhood, might well have their earliest roots in such maneuvers. An example from an exchange between two adults showed the relation of the peekaboo game to interpersonal encounter in general.

3

Failure in the Parent-Child Dialogue and Parallels in Therapeutic Change

The work so far mentioned shows the intricacy of the dialogue between mother and child. As always, influence becomes most obvious when it is denied to the participants—that is, when either mother or child ignores the other's influencing signals.

René Spitz once filmed the interaction of a 12-month-old baby with a baby-sized doll. The baby first showed puzzlement and curiosity; then she approached the doll and butted it with her head. Finding no response, she retreated, cried, and appeared anxious. The baby could find no response from the doll acknowledging her existence. When this lack of response occurs in the mother-child dialogue, it can be lethal. Mothers who ignore their babies (who behave, were they in Bower's laboratory, as if they could not receive the R.S.V.P. the baby sent to the peekaboo message) influence them in a profoundly negative way. We take mother love for granted, and this is so powerful an influence that few instances of its outright abrogation come to light in ordinary social circumstances. Newspapers report horrendous examples of child beating or child mutilation, but these are the exceptions to the universal power of mother love. Even child mutilation or murder implies mutual influence; the child must have exerted some influence to be worthy of butchering.

A Dying Child

Occasionally physicians see babies who have been subjected to total disconfirmation via a kind of "natural experiment" which no one could bring himself to arrange. One such child came to the attention of Sydney Margolin,[1] a resourceful investigator and clinician of many talents, among which is expertise with movie cameras. One day at the medical center at the University of Colorado, Margolin received an urgent appeal from the pediatric unit of the hospital. An infant had been brought into the hospital, a child of Mexican-Indian parents. Though only 18 months old, he managed to dumbfound the nursing staff by masturbating continuously, using a scissor-like motion of his legs.

This unconventional infantile behavior might not have been so powerful in provoking anxiety on the part of the nursing staff if the baby had been healthy. The nurses might have been able to ignore it, or to chalk it up as being due to some type of faulty parental training. But the child was dying

1 Personal communication (see references).

of starvation. He looked like those ghastly walking skeletons from Belsen and Buchenwald who greeted their liberators when concentration camps were released from Nazi control at the end of World War II. He was skin and bones, mewing and squeaking out his last will and testament. The combination of desperate need with behavior they found abhorrent was too much for the nurses—they called for psychiatric first aid, and Margolin appeared. He brought his camera and recorded the extraordinary spectacle of the child at that moment, and recorded the child's behavior at intervals for months and years thereafter as the child's problem was gradually understood and solved.

Margolin found a dying child who was almost impervious to influence. No efforts to contact the baby moved him—he was indifferent to a bottle placed beside his face, even though he was starving. Shortly after birth, this baby had showed evidence of a congenital fault in the development of his esophagus. There was a narrowing at one point, called an atresia in medical parlance, which permitted the passage of only milk. Surgeons had corrected this immediately, but the baby had been taken by his mother to the mountain wilds of Colorado, which prevented any follow-up observations by the surgeons. Such narrowings frequently have a stormy postoperative course as the process of repair and scar formation takes place.

In the mountain wilds, sheepherders consider a child who cannot nurse, cries incessantly, and masturbates constantly to be bewitched. The mother concluded that some malevolent supernatural influence had hexed her, or her child, or both, and responded to this situation by ignoring her baby. The child's grandmother, a more practiced maternal agent, was able to surmount traditional folklore to the extent of keeping the baby alive. The child experienced constant pain from the spasms of his esophagus. He resorted to the anesthesia provided by pleasant sensory experience. One sees similar behavior occasionally on the wards of mental hospitals housing adult psychotic patients. Nursing staffs ask what to do, as they asked Margolin what to do about the baby. When a catatonic patient suddenly begins to masturbate openly, the answer is not to remonstrate with him, or to interview the family, or to apply negative conditioning techniques: It is to arrange for a physician to examine the patient physically. An abscessed tooth or appendix can activate a knowledge most of us repress or forget, which is that sexual pleasure is a potent anesthetic. This baby was too young to know that one mustn't assuage misery with that panacea, genital balm.

Margolin's first step was to instruct the nurses that the baby was behaving in this fashion because he was starving not only for food but also for mothering. Margolin demonstrated this fact by having a nurse place a rubber nipple containing sugar solution in the baby's mouth. As the baby gradually began to respond to this treatment over a period of hours, and then began to respond to more complicated stimuli like the bottle, given with tender loving care, the nurse's initial rejection of the baby vanished.

By giving the nurses a rationale for extending to the baby their capacities to influence him, and an excuse for what seemed to them disgusting behavior, Margolin helped them extend to the baby their maternal influencing tendencies. One nurse attached herself to the baby and became a kind of surrogate mother, supplying to this poor waif what he so desperately needed.

The film record starts with the initial frantic behavior of the infant, then skips six weeks from the time this young nurse began to try to reach him. The next film sequence shows a changed infant. The spidery, frantic, skeleton of a child was transformed in a period of six weeks into a normal, plump infant of 19 months.

In subsequent sequences of the film Margolin was able to record the regaining of the capacity for dialogue between child and adult and its therapeutic impact on the child. Margolin also showed that the baby was profoundly influenced by the periodic, unavoidable absence of the nurse surrogate-mother. The pain recurred because nonsurgical means failed to ameliorate his esophageal problem. In response to such stresses the baby regressed. In this regression, the outer world, including humans, once more lost meaning for the child. He ignored the surrounding world and could hardly be influenced at all. The film records a second winning of the baby to a belief in the worth of attaching himself to humans. Margolin reports that he has followed this child into adolescence. After a series of attempts to tinker with the child's social situation, he was placed successfully in a foster home. Surprisingly, the child is quite intact and functions within the range of normal children.

Regression in Psychotherapy

This baby's behavior gives a condensed example of phenomena that therapists, especially psychoanalysts, see in an attenuated form in the behavior of their patients. Patients, like the child Margolin studied, respond to *deprivation* of influence. The analytic situation is a depriving one, relative to ordinary social relations. The patient, lying on a couch, cannot use visual cues to calibrate his impressions of the analyst's reactions to his utterances. His requests are not directly gratified. He is neither praised nor is he scolded. Sooner or later, he shows a tendency to fall back on whatever coping capacities he possessed or learned in earlier years, and he uses these in the analytic situation. He stops talking *about* these patterns and begins using them behaviorally—for example, silence, sulking, withdrawal, late arrival, nonpayment of bills—in a disguised and watered-down version of the Indian baby's unhappy withdrawal. The regular occurrence of this movement led Freud to recognize it and to name it the "regressive transference neurosis." In the baby's case, nurses brought him back into contact with the world around him by direct provision of the supplies which anyone needs in infancy. In the analytic situation, the analyst supplies understanding, communicated predominantly by verbal routes—as Freud pointed out, for our deepest levels of feeling, to be understood is to be loved. Such a regressive movement occurs to some extent in any therapy, but in once-a-week, face-to-face therapy, it is much harder to see than when one uses the so-called classical technique. It is so hard to see that theorists of other than analytic schools tend to ignore it entirely or to give it only passing notice. Theorists debate whether regression in therapy is to be deplored, or whether it is essential: In either case this is another example of the ubiquitous tendency to take aspects of the process of influence and its effects for granted—here the deprivation of one's ability to influence one's therapist.

This child's desperate misery, his anxiety, his reaching out, and, when faced with deprivation, his use of autoerotic pleasure for relief—all show the underpinnings of analytic concepts. These concepts were derived from clinical observations of patients' behavior. While it is fashionable to take potshots at analytic theory these days (it is not hard to do), the behavior of patients returning day after day, only to act toward the analyst as though they were hungry babies instead of, say, the responsible professional persons they are outside the consulting room, makes a strong impression on the observer. Such behavior is a far cry from the behavior of rats running mazes. Those psychologists who study rats predominantly are understandably inclined to discount concepts like "transference neurosis." The anguished experience of helpless frustration on the couch makes anyone who has been in analysis credit the reality of inner sub-jective experience as a potent influence. While psychologists who observe rats or other captive subjects in experiments can afford in some instances to dispense with concepts concerning the unobservable events occurring within the head of the creature being studied (often called in professional jargon "the contents of the black box" or the "mediated response"), any-one who has been a patient in psychotherapy finds them indispensable.

A Subtler Instance of Failure of Dialogue

Failures in influence in the case of humans are often extremely subtle and hard to detect, as contrasted with the blatant effects the Margolin film shows. Everyone around the affected person senses that something seems to be lacking but is at a loss to say what it is. Such subtle lacks appear in many life situations: Many a young lady of quality takes piano lessons for ten to twelve years, without being influenced to grasp the moving essence of music. She is put to shame by the black pianist who makes a composition come alive, the notes of which he can barely de-cipher (as compared with Miss Astorbilt's easy reading and pedestrian playing). What is it that makes home-cooked food better than steam-table cafeteria food? Individual attention, timing, variation of seasoning and ingredients? But try to specify what a restaurant chef must do, precisely, to bring his food to the level of home-cooked food, and one is in trouble.

Subtle failure of influence can work marked change long past baby-hood. An 18-year-old girl entered the hospital because of excessive weight loss that could not be traced to some primary metabolic (or other) illness. The eventual diagnosis, following elaborate tests, was anorexia nervosa (meaning loss of appetite from nervous causes, or more bluntly, weight loss of unknown origin). A big girl, she hovered around 70 pounds in weight, making her look like a prison-camp victim. Part of the origin of her weight loss was not so unknown, it turned out, when her view of the world became better understood. Her father, the apparent pacesetter of the family, was not a man for all seasons, but more a Jekyll and Hyde combination of personalities. Though he was respected as a teacher in his field, a competent wage earner, provider, and pillar of the community, his daughter was lost to him. When she first began to lose weight he "treated" her by conditioning methods of considerable expertise (a tech-nique which has shown promise in many cases in which "insight" methods have failed). He kept daily records, describing her reactions moment by moment. He had compiled a dossier—a thick *volume* of detailed ob-servations—concerning her habits of eating and noneating, which would have been a credit to any Ph.D. candidate in mammalian psychology. He spoke a great deal of what "reinforced" and what "extinguished" her eating patterns. He was determined to eradicate the pathological behavior if the effort killed them both, and would have none of the professional suggestions offered until his daughter was not only at death's door, but had one foot across the threshold.

She described her plight—all the while talking in a fey, Ophelia fashion —as one of despair that anyone could ever understand her. People, she said (especially her father) listened—they walked, talked, and acted as if she had said something comprehensible—but failed to convey to her any message indicating that she had been understood. Pressed to elaborate, she described her daily life as resembling the situation of a rat running in a maze and coming up against an unanticipated insurmountable wall.

Her father impressed observers of his interaction with his daughter as being warm, devoted, superficially empathic, but as much out of touch with her, moment by moment, as are the legislators of Midwestern states who try to deal with long-haired, apparently unwashed, new-left students from Eastern communities. The father's world excluded his daughter's: hers, his. All his gestures, he took pains to see, were correct for the raising of blue-blooded collies. She felt herself not to be a human but to be, in fact, a blue-blooded collie. The mother's behavior during the inter-changes between the patient and her father confirmed this view.

Even in a short initial interview, the girl was able to bring up the feelings she had experienced when, at 12 or 13 years of age, she had first learned of cannibalism among primitive peoples. She had read about it and had been fascinated by it but it had also repelled and horrified her. She had needed what any baby needs in infancy, and like the Indian baby, failed to get it. The baby Margolin filmed withdrew from all human contact. This girl had advanced to a stage of her life at which some kind of oral contact and satisfaction was predictable and expected, and she struggled with an inability to make contact with her parents in other ways. She had learned to expect to be fed, but she also knew at some level of awareness that you can't bite the hand that feeds you. The deprivation of higher values, the disconfirmation of worth at the higher symbolic levels, led to an exaggeration of some primitive human impulses in the patient. These were the savage, biting attempts to make an impact on others that we owe to our mammalian heritage. All humans use these in desperate situations. Who has not wanted to bite—who has not, in some desperate or permissive circumstances, bitten? For this girl, devouring, primitive, incorporative attempts to make some sort of fleshy contact, free from intellectualizations, had been raised by her frustration to such an imperative level—such an intrusive preoccupation—that she had had to pull the three-alarm fire signal in order to combat such insane bents. Her solution to one of her problems, the intrusion into her thoughts of frightening impulses to bite, was to renounce eating.

Both these examples, the anorexic baby and the anorexic teen-ager, point to a canon of psychotherapeutic influence: One must be alert to the signs and symptoms of breakdown of a patient's dialogue with his world, and one must take action to restore it. Margolin was able to guide the nurses to repair the damage suffered by the baby in a matter of weeks or months. Eighteen years of damage is harder to repair. At this writing, the young lady is much improved.

Summary

Failure of the parent-child dialogue leads to a kind of starvation which is both literal and figurative. This chapter presented examples of such failure and its consequences. Stark, obvious, and near-lethal effects appeared in the behavior of an infant, studied and photographed by Sydney Margolin. This child demonstrated the vital role of the dialogue, not only by bizarre behavior in response to deficits of the dialogue, but also by returning to healthy development in response to renewed and enriched contact and dialogue with those who took care of him. More subtle but similar effects of deprivation occur in other interactions, such as psychotherapy, seen most strikingly in what psychoanalysts call "the regressive transference neurosis." Even subtle deprivation of parent-child dialogue has important effects on development, as shown in a case of anorexia nervosa.

4

To Notice or Not To Notice

Babies, then, are far better equipped to use the scientific method than was ever before suspected. They thrive on their own research efforts about what makes the world of people tick. They languish without it. "Publish or perish" rules much of academia; the appropriate counterpart for the babies' world is "Engage or die," or perhaps "*Play* or perish." No game of solitaire will do. Babies need active partners in an active game—so do patients in psychotherapy. Many a patient has come to me in the last twenty or so years, exasperated with another therapist, saying, "I just gave up—he doesn't say or do anything—he just *sits* there!"

Fortunately, we have more solid evidence than the conflicting opinions of therapists today concerning what makes therapeutic influence work. The studies of early influence already cited show some of the influence ability we bring with us into the world—the importance, subtlety, and richness of the reciprocal interaction between babies and their world— but not much about the finer details of its mechanisms. For such enlightenment one must look elsewhere. Other studies have shown two basic influences, present from birth onwards, which had not previously been recognized. These are, first the automatic and imperative influence of the orienting reflex, and second the censoring activity of the lower levels of the nervous system in modifying channels of influence (including orienting responses themselves).[1]

What Guides Attention?

In the first few months the smiling response gives a rough index of whether or not a baby is attending to and being influenced by certain features of the human face. More precise ways of exploring what it is that grabs a newborn's interest have been devised, and these are currently being used in many laboratories.[2] One group of studies showed that babies attend to clay masks of the human face, but they attend even more avidly to a mask of the human face which has been slightly distorted. This interest in the off-beat face (say, one in which one eye is

[1] Both orienting and censoring functions alter any attempt at interpersonal influence (for example, awareness in psychotherapy), and since information concerning these functions is not common knowledge, nor readily available to the general reader, a somewhat extended presentation seems in order. Those readers familiar with these functions may wish to proceed directly to Chapter 5.

[2] The studies of Kagan and his group, 1969 (see his bibliography); and F. Graham, 1970, for example.

missing) is not to be interpreted as an interest in the bizarre, the esoteric, or the perverted—as if babies shared the tastes of faded old roués. Babies are not as interested in masks of faces in which the features have been totally garbled as they are in masks which are only slightly different from faces with which they are familiar. They tend to ignore masks which are totally unfamiliar. Further refinements of measurement have disclosed that a general rule holds regarding newborns: They attend to movement, to contrast, and to any change in a familiar image provided the change is not too great. It is as if we arrive in the world equipped with a photo-montage image of the human physiognomy, labelled "this is what to look for."

Humanitarian concerns prevent experimental deprivation of human babies in order to study the details of the process of early influence and what happens when it is missing. There have been more instances than one would like to contemplate of "wolf children" like Mowgli of Kipling's *Jungle Books,* or children raised by parents (often psychotic) who confined them to closets or attics, but these occur so infrequently and sporadically that no controlled scientific study has been possible.

The smiling response and the peekaboo game show that babies come into the world with a potential interest in human faces which shows up very early in their behavior. This interest appears to come with the genes.

The response babies make to *distorted* masks is a special instance of a general mode of influence that, though an inescapable feature of the exchanges between therapist and patient, is scarcely mentioned in the literature of psychotherapy. Pavlov, in 1910, named it the orienting reflex. It is one of the pervasive "invisibles" of any form of therapy.

If one thinks of approaching a deer quietly grazing in a forest glade, the function of this basic mode of influence becomes obvious. Any change in the deer's surroundings instantly alerts the animal, be it a sound, a sight, a smell, or a heavy footfall. The deer's attention automatically fixes on the change. His ears turn toward the sound, his head raises. If one had attached recording instruments to the deer, one would find that regardless of the type of signal which had alerted the animal, a wide variety of automatic reflex adjustments had occurred in the deer. It is as if a general alarm had been sounded: Ears hear more acutely; eyes see better; the brain is more ready to signal the alerted muscles and blood vessels to start the escape maneuver. This is no flight of fancy —all of these responses have been measured in the laboratory. Even an animal's skin participates—the electrical conductivity changes as the animal's sweat glands activate.

If one continues to monitor various physiologic functions of the deer, the general form of the alarm reaction changes to a specific one. It is as if the first reaction were a kind of general reaction, like the reaction of the people of a city to the sound of a siren, after which a search for the nature and locale of the disturbance—police? fire? ambulance?—takes place. The citizens make phone calls, ask neighbors, reach for field glasses, turn on radios. When they can pin down the source of the siren noise, the citizenry make more specific moves. The generalized alarm recedes, but the specific areas involved provoke even more intense inquiry. If a fire, how near? Something similar occurs in the deer in the forest—a general alerting changes to a specific alerting of whichever sensory apparatuses had been stimulated. If the signal of change was an odor, the receptors and brain centers involved in smelling remain at battle stations. If it was a change in the visual field, retinal sensitivity and occipital lobe brain activity remain tuned up. Similar reactions to the "unexpected" occur every moment in therapy.

If a doctor, performing a neurological examination, taps the tendon below the kneecap of his patient, he activates a general orienting reflex which has widespread effects. He also sets in motion a local reflexive circuit which results in contracture of the large muscle-group in the front of the thigh, the quadriceps, which causes the leg to extend. The difference between the local and the general orienting reactions would become embarrassingly apparent should this same doctor, riding the subway, suddenly reach over and perform the same maneuver on the knee of an unknown lady passenger sitting next to him: Though the doctor might escape a face-slapping, he certainly would be made aware of an indignant general response. Every change in perceiving the world, every stimulus, produces two different effects: a general alarm, and then the local, specific orienting reflex.

The rapidity of orienting responses (in or out of the consultation room) can be made more vivid by an example: Let the reader visualize several birds of the species called budgerigars (or, more familiarly, love birds) flying about, one chasing the other in an enclosed greenhouse containing trees, columns, and people walking about. The birds never collide with obstacles and follow each other at high speeds separated only a foot or so from each other. Each change in the course of the lead bird produces a reflex change in his pursuers' course, but also a general orienting reaction, all with breathtaking rapidity.

Humans share such rapid responses with budgerigars. This rapidity is astonishing to watch, but it is easier to understand in the light of recent findings of engineers in communication science: They calculate that our brains receive in the neighborhood of 10,000 bits of information a second (a "bit" is defined as that least amount of information which would tip the scales of a 50-50 decision one way or the other). It is the reflex automaticity of the orienting response, rather than its extraordinary rapidity, that gives the thoughtful observer pause in contemplating human interactions like those of psychotherapy.

Granted that much human communication is nonverbal, there has been a prevalent assumption that humans are free to take it or leave it in regard to signals from another person. Research on the orienting reflex makes clear that we humans cannot avoid responding to a change in sensory inputs—our brains and our bodies take note of the change and automatically change their function whether we will them to do so *or not*—and this is the hooker. We have conscious control, to be sure, of the major events following this first reflex response—we can choose later to ignore or to respond in some fashion to the change in our world—but the first reflex orienting response is not any more optional than is blinking at a flashbulb.

The orienting reflex differs from the two other known families of reflexes (shortly to be described) in one important respect: It fades away rapidly when a signal is repeated again and again. The rule of this reflex is that familiarity breeds content. The deer in the forest will notice you if you wave your arm. He may bolt. If you are sufficiently far away and continue to wave in a monotonous fashion, he will soon return to his grazing until some new change—perhaps a shift in the wind bringing your scent to him—occurs. A sound which will lead him to prick up his ears will, if repeated, lull the deer into inattentiveness.

This habituation does not occur with other reflexes. When one blinks at a flashbulb, one blinks as much at the flash of the hundredth bulb as at the first. The eye-blink response, which protects against excessive stimulation, is one member of the family of reflexes Pavlov called "defensive." (One incidental finding from studies of the newborn's defensive reflexes was noted by Bridger: One can put a newborn to sleep very effectively by working his defensive reflex. Expose him to a loud continuous noise, and immediately he goes into a catatonic withdrawal and sleep. This helps explain the soporific effect of plane, car, or train travel on the very young—they are great travellers.)

The third family of reflexes (called by Pavlov and his students "specific adaptive reflexes") are connected with the direction of change of some stimulus. An example of a specific adaptive reflex is the response of blood vessels to warm or cold stimuli applied to the skin. Another example is the reaction of the pupil of the eye: the stronger the light, the smaller the pupil.

Both defensive and adaptive reflexes tend to persist, but the orienting reflex fades rapidly on repetition of the same signal. The former types can be molded gradually, as Pavlov showed with experiments of the type familiar to all—his salivating dog, responding to a bell in place of food—and it is this molding toward which behavior therapies especially, and other therapies implicitly, aim.

Novelty, exceptions to rules, variations on themes all activate the orienting reflex. This is what the studies of babies demonstrate. A baby who sees a triangular black image on a screen is reflexly oriented to the areas of the image in which contrast is maximal (the edges and corners of the triangle). Babies orient their attention toward masks which resemble faces but present some change from the expected.

Russian investigators, in particular, have studied the orienting reflex extensively for many years. Though this work is known to many American experimental scientists, it seems virtually unknown to psychotherapists, judging from the lack of reference to it in the literature of psychotherapy. Yet the relevance of this reflex to the moment-by-moment process of therapy is obvious: Every gesture, inclination, or change of facial expression of the therapist constitutes a new signal which is capable of evoking the reflex-guided attention of the patient—and of course this is also true concerning the patient's effect on the therapist. Millisecond by millisecond, each influences the other—tone, expression, gesture, and so forth. Responses of the orienting variety take place without conscious attention on the part of either patient or therapist.

Specific adaptive and defensive reflexes are especially prominent elements of therapeutic influence in all the behavior therapies. The patient's reflexive fear responses gradually quiet down ("extinguish") as, by one or another means, the therapist loosens the conditioned connection of defensive and adaptive reflex responses with persons, places, things, or thoughts. (The patient learns to relax, for example, in the presence of any imposing authority much in the fashion that White House personnel become accustomed to the President's presence.) Even therapies which lean heavily on insight and understanding can hardly avoid a gradual deconditioning of defensive and adaptive reflexes. Instance after instance of previously threatening thoughts and feelings come up in the safe situation of the consulting room. Defensive-adaptive reflex responses, learned in early childhood toward parents, those giants of the nursery, change in the process which is called "working through" by psychoanalysts—the gradual bleaching of maladaptive patterns of behavior by repeated corrective experience in the comfortable atmosphere of therapy. But the orienting reflex has somehow escaped the explicit attention of theorists of therapy and of clinicians alike. It is taken for granted, like the air we breath, or like gravity.

The orienting reflex has remarkable precision, as shown by just one example. The Russian psychophysiologist Sokolov (1963) exposed a human subject to a spot of light which made a tiny retinal image (only one degree in diameter compared to the total circumference of the retina). This activated the orienting reflex, as shown by brain and skin responses. The skin response disappeared rapidly when the light was presented repeatedly (the brain response was much more persistent). Moving the light as little as ten degrees again produced a generalized orienting reflex, with especially responsive brain activity. The same sort of precise tuning occurs with regard to sounds. And sound and light channels interact in setting off orienting responses. This is what makes rock-and-roll "light shows" so stimulating—even overwhelming—in their effect.

The orienting reflex sharpens general sensory awareness. It can lift to perceptible levels those events in the world which are otherwise imperceptible. An unusual noise in a quiet house brings wakefulness to the sleeping owner; thereafter for a few moments all sorts of squeaks and creaks in the house impinge on his awareness—sounds that had left him peacefully asleep, night after night. The sleeper's response shows another aspect of the orienting reflex: A general alarm reaction (reflex) occurs more readily when something unusual happens to a person who is in a relaxed, drowsy, sleepy, or partially anesthetized condition. When the person is alert or excited, the orienting reflex is far more precise and selective in its effect.

The orienting reflex does not depend on positive increases of stimulation. It is *novelty* that counts: A decrease of some sensation is just as potent in provoking the reaction as an increase. Anyone who lives beside a railroad track and becomes accustomed to sleeping through the noise of the 2 A.M. freight notices the absence of that train if it fails by some circumstance to come past one night. Mothers who are used to a certain level of noise from the playroom instantly notice a suspicious silence. Forest animals orient when the other animals fall silent. The same effect occurs if the stimulus is shortened or lengthened, or, if there is more than one stimulus, the order of presentation of stimuli is changed. The familiar opening notes of Beethoven's *Fifth Symphony* would provoke an orienting reflex in us if their order were changed.

The idea of a photo-montage image mentioned in relation to the smiling response—a model configuration against which new stimuli are compared—crops up in a variety of fields: psychoanalysis, psychology, neurophysiology, for example. Freud proposed such an idea many years ago when he postulated that human thinking begins with the infant's formation of hallucinatory images of remembered objects which had given the baby gratification—the image of the breast, for example, against which image other new perceptual images entering the infant's gaze are compared. In 1959, Sokolov proposed the theory that sensory stimulation sets up chains of cells in the nervous system in a pattern which make a sort of model—a kind of diagram—of whatever stimulus the organism has experienced. This neuronal model preserves information about the "remembered" stimulus—its intensity, quality, duration, and order of presentation. These concepts (models, images, sets, and so on) will be brought together in Chapter 17 in the concept "Plan."

The orienting reflex is set off not by a single stimulation alone, but by impulses which arise as a result of any mismatch between the model and the new stimulus. If the new stimulus corresponds with the neuronal model of the previous stimulus, the existing model is reinforced and confirmed—as it were, "grooved in." The result is a conditioned response, not an orienting one (as one might emphasize a passage one wished to emphasize in a letter by pencilling it over more heavily). In this case, the organism has learned a rule about the world—a plan, a regularity, an expectation. Whenever this rule is *broken,* a new orienting response occurs.

Orienting Responses in Efforts To Effect Change

Patients, particularly those in long-term therapies like psychoanalysis, develop very precise plans concerning their therapist's habitual behavior. Any variation alerts them—a change in facial expression, a slightly longer pause than usual in responding. In this respect the relation between patient and therapist resembles that between partners in a marriage: After years of marriage one can sense one's partner's mood with scarcely a word being spoken.

Patients in psychotherapy make orienting responses not only to their therapists, but to minor changes in the consultation room. I had a patient who suffered elevated blood pressure, and I was interested in correlating fluctuations of his pressure with his patterns of emotional conflict from day to day. I brought my stethoscope and sphygmomanometer (blood pressure measuring instrument) into my office, and placed both in a quite inconspicuous niche in the lower corner of a bookcase covering one whole wall of the office. The next day every patient commented or inquired about these instruments. They had oriented to a minute change in the configuration of the bookcase.

The capacity to do this sort of matching, this sifting and winnowing of the new with the sieve of past experience, is impaired when the cerebral cortex is relatively inactive, as in drowsiness. One experiment will show this: Sokolov presented a tone to a man who was wide-awake. The man rapidly became used to the sound and thereafter showed no orienting responses. When the man began to drowse, the orienting reflex reappeared. Four presentations were sufficient to bleach out the orienting reflex when the man was wide-awake, whereas dozens of presentations of the tone continued to elicit the full orienting reflex when he was drowsy.

Such observations have many implications for therapy of all types. An obvious one is the use of the couch in psychoanalysis to promote increased orienting on the patient's part to wispy fragments of his own thought processes, his "free associations." When the patient is able to relax and enter a drowsy state, his cortex is relatively inactive in processing incoming stimulation. His capacity to inhibit the orienting reflex is diminished—the patient on the couch reacts more alertly to each new stimulus, whether arising from within or without. He is therefore more influenceable by the primitive reflex orienting route than he would be if therapy were conducted while the patient was sitting face to face with the analyst.

Each new perception activates a wide range of reflex body activities during states in which the cortex is not fully active. These in turn constitute special problems of integration for the nervous system. This throws light on an ever-present (but neglected) problem in general medical wards: Delirious patients do better in well-lighted, quiet rooms, accompanied by a trusted relative or friend on whose judgments of sights, sounds, vibrations, or odors the patient can rely. Research on the orienting reflex shows why this is so: The drugged or toxically infected oldster is unable to inhibit his reflex-orienting to the noises of the hospital. The feverish sleeping child is at the mercy of stimuli which he cannot sort into familiar safe packages. The sound of a dog barking outside the house can provoke nightmare panic, which subsides when the child is awakened, taken outside, and shown the dog. Various drugs like marijuana and hashish appear to produce a similar state of hypersensitivity to stimulation. This is part of their attraction, according to the accounts of their users. Rhythms become more compelling, colors more vivid; all sorts of sensual experiences are raised out of the ordinary to a level of unusual poignancy (perhaps this is why witch doctors and shamans have relied on such potions in their efforts to exert therapeutic influence since time immemorial). Freed from the inhibitory influence of the cortex, lower centers respond to sensations in a kaleidoscopic way— this is probably what is behind the slang term describing the effect of these drugs as being "turned on." These drugs take the cortex, with its inhibitory influence on the orienting reflex, out of action. The subjective experience of patients who are hovering on the borderline of many types of psychosis is similar. They describe a bewildering press of sensory experiences which cannot be sorted out into usual and appropriate categories—this "press" overwhelms their ability to make sense of the world.

Implications of Orienting

The orienting reflex, with its automatic emergence from suppression in drowsy states, provides one example of a principle of influence Freud built into his theoretical system: As a consequence of our biological equipment, we *are thought* (passive voice) a much greater proportion of our lives than we consciously think (active voice). Let the cortex drowse, and the receptors and lower brain centers reflexly take over control.

The model of the way the brain functions held by most people until recently could be compared to the situation of a scientist studying some process of interest to him in the laboratory. The brain guiding the study is in the scientist's head. He arranges for various measurements to be made at a distance from his brain—wires, tubes, thermocouples, and such run from the object studied to gauges and dials the scientist can read. Sensing devices faithfully (like dutiful serfs) bring him the information he wants concerning the object of study. He selects these devices, knowing that they report only on limited aspects of the object of study, for their accuracy and reliability. It is his, not the instrument's, problem to put together the reports of new data along with data of previous experiments, perhaps filed away. The scientist then makes adjustments of the experimental apparatus appropriate to the next step in the experiment. In the experiment the sensing devices behave like serfs, or like good runners for a field general, transmitting messages given them— adding or subtracting nothing of importance.

This model can no longer be held. Instead, our nervous systems function more like the workings of the body politic than the workings of the laboratory experiment: The higher cortical centers are in a position more analogous to the position of the President of the United States than that of the scientist in the laboratory. The sensing devices of the human organism, we know now, are more like the memoranda of Presidential advisors or newspaper editorials than the simple messages of serfs, military runners, pony express riders, or other messengers who once carried information without changing its nature. Editing and evaluating begin far away from Central Headquarters and occur to a much greater degree than in the message "The British are coming." The President (the cortex) is given edited copy. He is both *instructed* ("Take careful notice!") and *informed* by his sources of information ("This is the latest news").

It appears now that the instructional aspects of reports reaching higher centers from receptive organs (eye, ear, and so on) are much more powerful than was ever suspected before. The retina does not present to the occipital cortex an exact replica of what impinges upon it. The retina seems to have a mind of its own. It is like a good political reporter sorting and skewing the data presented for relevance, pertinence, and emphasis. An example far from everyday life or the consulting room, but ingenious in showing the precision of retinal "thinking" will make the point. The neurophysiologist David Ingle (1966) was interested in intra-retinal transfer of information: Can the eye "learn" by itself, without the help of the brain? He trained goldfish to swim forward in a tank in order to avoid an electric shock he administered. Each fish was given a signal by a vertical black line drawn on a white card, the image of which impinged upon the anterior portion of the retina. The fish learned to distinguish this line, as meaning "danger," from a line inclined at 30°, which meant "no danger." The question of relevance here is whether the eye or the brain had learned the distinction between the lines. If these line patterns were then exposed in such a way as to impinge on the posterior part of the retina, which had not previously been exposed to the lines, the fish still knew that one meant danger and the other didn't. The "reporters" in the anterior part had passed on their learning to their colleagues in the rear. But if the angle between the two lines was diminished to only 15°, so that the lines had a very similar slant, the fish rapidly learned to make the distinction with the "educated" anterior part of his retina. However, he failed to swim forward to escape painful shock when the two lines, made hard to distinguish by their minor difference in slant, were presented to his unschooled posterior retina. Yet Ingle found that the fish's heart rate changed under these conditions—as if he "knew it in his heart." Some rumor had spread among the hoi-polloi of lower centers, even though the lack of adaptive skeletal muscle response in swimming, which depended on Central Headquarter's orders, failed to save the fish from shock.

It is now clear that a complex analysis of sensory information occurs in the retina of animals. This, rather surprisingly, does not closely correspond to the position of the animal on the evolutionary ladder. Impulses in the ground squirrel's optic nerve contain discriminations for color, direction of movement, and size. But the lowly frog's retina is capable of quite a sophisticated sorting of the information coming in via light rays, and the information passing up the optic nerve in frogs is already skewed by these processing operations (called the "bug response"—fly-catching operational planning starts in the retina itself). By now it is clear that there is highly specialized tuning for differing information at various levels of the visual system. One example: In primates (and presumably man) retinal processing sorts out information about the movement of objects and shunts it to levels of the cortex lower than that connected with fine "vision," the occipital cortex. This sorting-screening process has been shown to depend on the processing capacity of individual cells, some of which are attuned to recognize one or another type of action— certain cells recognize slant, others recognize slant in the opposite direction.

The comparison of neural functioning with political reporting gains force when one considers the general principle of feedback of which the orienting reflex is an instance: The peripheral sensors (or would it be more accurate to say censors?) not only instruct the brain but are instructed by the brain in return. Sensing change, they, like reporters, alert the chief executive, who then gives orders for increased coverage of the political event, troop movement, or scientific discovery reported by his informants (via the specific components of the orienting reflex). And it is not only the special receptors, eye and ear, which participate in this mutual influence; many more general systems function in the same fashion. For example, almost a third of the nerve fibers in a nerve, thought until recently to be purely motoric in function (that is, devoted exclusively to carrying impulses from the brain to the muscle) are now known to function in sensory ways. The cortex not only sends orders to contract or relax via these nerves, it also receives constant on-the-spot reportorial coverage from muscle-spindle receptors as to the state of tension in the mob of muscle fibers. These reports are subject to variations as part of the orienting reflex. In the consulting room, when a patient sees his therapist raise an eyebrow, his muscles immediately respond via reflex, as if preparing for a punishing blow.

The analogy of brain function with the workings of the government holds even further: Officials at lower administrative levels than the President can control the access of people and information to the President. Appointment secretaries guard his time; subordinates screen reports; local military commanders have some freedom of decision within their area of command. Some decisions never come to his attention. So it is with our brains.

Because the retina itself acts like a peripheral brain, sorting and comparing events in the receptor cells (the rods and cones), impulses transmitted up the optic nerves are already edited copy, and further modification of the signals occurs at the way-stations. Impulses arising in other parts of the brain have been shown to modify the messages reaching the visual cortex. A similar situation would obtain in our government if some secretary in the White House could suppress or increase part of the President's mail on orders from the executive officers outside the White House, and not merely suppress, but make suggestions for actions about incoming mail. For example, stimulation of a part of the brain not involved directly in the visual analyzer (the inferior temporal cortex—that part of the brain which in man rests on the floor of the skull just above the inner ear), alters the information passing to the visual cortex, the White House level of perception.

Similar findings apply to the acoustic apparatus. The receptor, the cochlea, together with the auditory nerve and ascending tracts in the brain, do not form a passive transmitting system like an earhorn, but have their own variations and also are subject to influences from higher centers which modify their transmissions. It would seem that beauty is not only in the eye of the beholder but also in the ear of the listener.

The newer view of the neural apparatus has some rather chilling aspects. In the political analogy, a similar situation obtains in wartime when citizens receive only censored reports. But what if not only citizens but also the Chief Executive were to receive only highly censored information from the CIA, the FBI, and the Intelligence Services of the Armed Forces? What if the censorship of information were designed in such a way as to cover up the operations of the censors themselves? Actions and operations going on continuously could take place under these conditions without control, either public or executive. The psychotherapeutic situation, according to this new view, involves a great many automatic reflex operations occurring millisecond by millisecond. These function according to the built-in structure and function of the nervous systems of both participants, neither of whom are either aware of, nor in control of, these operations until after they have taken place, but all of them influence the data consciously available to the participants.

The day is long passed (if indeed it ever existed) that intelligent human beings held the view that conscious mental processes were the whole story of psychotherapy or any other human functioning. Freud convinced the last several generations that our egos are like riders of an unruly stallion—only partly in control (this was also not unknown to the Catholic Church Fathers some time before). Of course, it is not news that many habits, many rules of behavior, drop out of awareness and become automatized—where would one be without them? Motor skills, like playing a game or a musical instrument, depend on this capacity of the nervous system. It was bad enough to think of another kind of unconscious mental apparatus, distinct from the unconscious functioning of habit. Freud showed us there is unconscious functioning which is out of control, either because it had been at one time unacceptable and hence had been rejected when we were young and impressionable or because it had never been accessible to conscious awareness. The task of psychotherapy is to discover the unconscious impulses and thus bring them under conscious control again.

Freud was keenly aware that many biological processes are inaccessible to awareness simply because we lack perceptual apparatuses (sensory nerves), to pick up such processes (secretion of pancreatic juice, for example, as compared with the secretion of saliva), but the new knowledge of the degree to which our minds are captives of reflex processes and perceptual censoring makes a disturbing impression indeed. To discover how one can be manipulated by skillful demagogues, or skillful hypnotists, and to discover further that this manipulation uses design characteristics of one's nervous system is another matter. Knowledge of the orienting, defensive, and adaptive reflexes, with their modulating effects on the perceptual apparatus and the automatic process of conditioning through reinforcement strike yet more blows at one's illusions of personal freedom.

Summary

The orienting reflex plays a central role in any intervention to change another person. Automatic alerting and attention occur in response to any change in perception, whether an increase or a decrease. Unlike other families of reflexes, the orienting reflex fades rapidly with constant repetition of a signal. It is remarkably precise and rapid, and is set off by any mismatch of a signal with a previously established pattern or model in the nervous system. Orienting occurs in every moment of conversation, teaching, nursing, and psychotherapy, and is especially active when the cerebral cortex is relatively inactive, as in toxic deliria. Knowledge of this reflex, along with recently discovered evidence that peripheral centers generally edit information passing to higher centers in the brain, makes it clear that we must curb our childhood illusions of omnipotence ("Step on a crack, break your mother's back") even further than had been indicated earlier.

5

Uses and Abuses of Noticing and Ignoring

Science has tended to study human influence on animals first, human influence on humans later, and later still the practical application of such influence in a variety of fields—education, psychotherapy, politics, salesmanship, and so forth. Several signalling systems guide orienting: Cues may be verbal and nonverbal, external and internal, conscious and unconscious. All these systems are involved in psychotherapeutic influence. It turns out that not only does orienting occur rapidly and precisely in several sensory systems, but also within each system orienting it occurs at many different levels.

Human Influence on Animals

The famous horse Clever Hans has been the object of study in psychology courses since the turn of the century (Pfungst, 1911). It seems surprising that these influences have attracted little notice among theorists of psychotherapy, despite ample time for diffusion of knowledge. This horse could do all sorts of complicated mathematical operations including adding, subtracting, dividing, and multiplying. It could analyze musical tones and perform a variety of other astonishing operations. Hans, when given a problem of, say, addition, would signal his answer by tapping his hoof on the pavement. His expertise was so astonishing and dazzling that it attracted considerable scientific interest and study among the psychologists of the day. At last they discovered the secret: The person questioning the horse, whether it was the horse's trainer or anyone else, was signalling the answer to the horse by minute motions of his, the questioner's, head. These unconscious cues given the horse, a minute lowering, signalling "begin," and a minute raising, signalling "stop," proved almost impossible to prevent even after the secret was known. One of the group of psychologists, Oskar Pfungst, was even able to mimic the horse by mastering the system, learning to observe the cues questioners give, and mystified a fresh group of psychologists by taking the role of Clever Hans in tapping out answers to questions asked him. Twenty-three of the 25 psychologists in this new group unwittingly gave cues as to the correct answers to their own questions. Clever Hans and his trainer were engaged in mutual influence, and this influence can be explained on the model of the orienting and conditioned reflexes of both participants. All of these influences were outside the awareness of the trainer, a proper German mathematics teacher named Von Osten. According to his account, one could conclude at least that the influence he exerted did not depend upon the conscious operation of human intelligence. Equipped with knowledge of the orienting reflex and the conditioned reflex, one can make a stab at an explanation. Originally, the trainer must have evoked the horse's orienting reflex, which was signalled by a minute head raising at the point the horse reached the correct number, which startled the trainer—who wouldn't be startled at discovering a horse that could count? In turn, repetition conditioned this response of the trainer outside his awareness. The trainer's head raising ("What's going on here?") must have alerted the horse via an orienting reflex. This reflex interrupted the tapping and brought a reward from the trainer.

Since Pfungst's work in carefully recording and tracking down the cues Hans used to find the answers to the questions posed to him, considerable work has shown that similar signalling occurred in a variety of remarkable human to animal communications, all of which presumably depend upon the orienting reflex. Hans had a contemporary circus counterpart, the horse Clever Rosa, who could also apparently understand the verbal signals of her trainer, but who was shown to be responding to postural cues of the trainer. There have been reports of "learned" animals preserved for the last 1500 years—in the last half century Sir William Huggen's dog Kepler, the "reading pig of London," the "clever dog of Utrecht," and in recent years the celebrated talking horse of Virginia.

Well-nigh undetectable influence of a similar sort must go on all the time in the consulting room. It certainly does intrude in the laboratory. The experimenter's expectations come across even to white rats. Two experimenters, Rosenthal and Fode, undertook to prove this in 1963. They asked a dozen students of experimental psychology to serve as experimenters in the study of the learning of a task, discrimination between different degrees of brightness, in which some of the rats who were studied were declared by Rosenthal and Fode to have been specially bred for cleverness. Each experimenter trained five animals a day for five days. One group of the experimenters were told that their animals were from an especially intelligent strain of rats, and the remaining group were told that their animals were from an especially dull strain of rats. All the rats were in fact of the *same* strain of rats and were assigned at random to the two groups of experimenters. The task posed to the animals was a particularly tricky and difficult one, and those who were thought to be dull by the experimenters refused to try it at all about a third of the time. Those thought to be "smart" by the experimenters refused only one tenth of the time. The difference in performance must have hinged on the way the experimenters dealt with their rats (and the way the rats experienced their keepers). Those believed to be smarter were described by their experimenters as cleaner, tamer, and generally more pleasant. Those who thought of their rats as possessing such characteristics stated that they did handle these rat subjects more often and more gently than the experimenters who expected less of their subjects. In other words, they must have supplied different orienting cues to the rats, and a different emotional milieu.

The Silent Influence of Man on Man

In the case of human-to-human nonverbal transmission, years ago the American psychologist Stratton (1897) used methods similar to those of Pfungst in unravelling the way a professional performer named De Rubini was able to "read the thoughts" of others, presumably using their patterns of muscle tension as signals for his own orienting responses. De Rubini would hold one end of a watch chain while the subject whose thoughts were to be read would hold the other. The subject was asked to think of some object in the room, which De Rubini was able to point out, without verbal cues, at a level well beyond the estimate of chance. De Rubini never claimed to have occult powers or "ESP" and cooperated fully with the investigators of his talent. Stratton and several of his colleagues at Berkeley in 1921 were able to eliminate one after another type of cue-passing from the subject to De Rubini by cutting out first auditory, then visual, cues. They finally concluded that some sort of visual signals were involved, though the precise nature of the cues was never pinned down. From this vantage point in time, with the advantage of knowledge of the orienting reflex, we may guess that De Rubini was doing nothing more mysterious than budgerigars do every second of flight.

Then there was the Minnesota pastor who was a water and metal diviner, who provoked sufficient interest to lead another psychologist, W. S. Foster, in 1923, to a similar investigation of the diviner's powers. This minister had achieved quite a reputation over a 45-year period for being able to find not only water, gold, iron, and silver, but also oil and natural gas. Professional engineers had, in spite of their occupational skepticism and distrust of mystical occult powers, studied his work and come away impressed at his capacities. Foster and his colleagues put the minister to the task of finding and following the course of water mains on the campus of the University of Minnesota. He convinced Foster that he could do this well beyond what one would expect from chance alone, but Foster concluded that the old man was responding to minor cues given out by the person accompanying him, who knew the location of the mains, without intention on either participant's part. By a series of tests, Foster showed that the pastor could divine the distance beneath his feet of a box of gold and silver objects (placed at various heights on the rungs of a vertical 13-rung ladder on the next lower story of the building) with amazing accuracy.

The catch was that a group of observers stood on the landing of the stair between the two stories of the building in which the experiment was being conducted, in order to study the process. Since the pastor could see the observers and they in turn could see the ladder, Foster's interpretation was that minimal involuntary cueing might be passing from observers to the pastor without either's intention. Removing the observers did not totally destroy the pastor's divination ability; he still was able to do better than chance guessing could explain, but there was still the possibility that some cues had reached the pastor from those persons around him. The clinching test came when a divination problem was posed the old man in the absence of anyone who knew the correct answer and who could unintentionally give it away via some miniscule signals capable of activating the pastor's orienting response; under these conditions his performance fell to the level of random chance.[1] We now understand the nature of these cues better via the study of motion pictures of human interactions, examined frame by frame in minute detail. Such study opens the language of gesture and facial expression to analysis. Spoken language can be broken down to basic units of sound, called "phonemes"; similarly, nonverbal language can be analyzed into units of motion or facial expression which have been called "kinemes" (see Birdwhistell, 1970).

Noticing and Ignoring Outside Awareness

Influence by cues too subtle and too minute to reach conscious recognition seems less mysterious today than it did in Pfungst's era, for today's reader is familiar with subliminal perception from the popular press. Advertisers, writers of detective stories or science-fiction novels, and political commentators have alerted the public to the many possible uses and abuses of such stimuli in order to influence the tastes, the political opinions, and the buying habits of the mass-media consumers. Scientific journals report how subjects' conscious perceptions of the world can be altered by subliminal cues; in one such study, for example, the psychologist George Klein (1959) showed subjects a slide of a drawing of a man's face wearing an indifferent expression. Subjects saw the face as smiling or frowning depending on whether the written words "happy" or "sad" were presented subliminally alongside the drawing at the time of viewing.

There is even evidence that subliminally presented pictures cause orienting responses and registration outside awareness. Such registrations are capable of finding their way into the dreams of subjects on the night following their presentation in the laboratory. When Fisher (1960) asked subjects to draw their dreams the day after he had presented such pictures, the original subliminal images could be detected in the drawings in forms which would satisfy any but the most skeptical that the source of the dream had been at least in part the subliminally presented pictures.

No account of such subtle orienting and registering influences can match the impact of actual experience. We really are poor judges of what we note or pass by in life. If one goes to an experimenter who uses the

[1] For a summary of these studies and relevant bibliography, see Rosenthal, 1965.

equipment which presents subliminal stimuli (called a tachistoscope) and asks for a demonstration of its influence, one is in for a surprise. A tachistoscope (in spite of its unpronounceable name) is really a simple device, something like an ordinary camera, by which an image can be flashed upon a screen for longer or shorter lengths of time, or at greater or lesser intensity of the light. The experimenter might flash on a blank screen a series of numbers, say, 19674572, at a duration of exposure which is below the usual threshold, as measured over a large group of people, of conscious perception. If the experimenter then asked the observer what he saw, the observer would probably say something like "I don't know—*maybe* a line of numbers?" Pressed further to say what numbers he saw, the observer might say, "Well—I'm only guessing—but I think the first three or four might have been—maybe 1967?" If the experimenter gently insisted that the observer guess the rest of the numbers he "might have seen," in spite of his doubt that he had seen anything at all, the observer would complete the series correctly—to his subsequent amazement when the experimenter showed him the whole series of numbers on the slide he had earlier exposed for less than a blink of an eye.

This capacity for recognizing perceptions and orienting to them instantaneously (or, better, fractions-of-instantaneously) can be cultivated. While we scarcely believe its existence, it can be trained. It was used in World War II to train soldiers and sailors to recognize the silhouettes of friendly as compared with hostile aircraft at much less than a glance. The trainer presented various silhouettes, first at durations of exposure well above the threshold of perception. The trainer then reduced the length of exposure of the silhouette to durations so short that the soldier in training would swear he had not seen anything—yet would be able, when pressed to guess, to name correctly the type of aircraft he had seen. The human eye and brain seem capable of budgerigar-level performance —which a moment's reflection on Babe Ruth's batting average confirms.

Such instant recognition was an influence which had obvious survival value for both ground soldier and pilot in wartime, but the perceptual capability on which such training rested is used moment-by-moment in many interactions between people, such as those of teaching, nursing, or psychotherapy. "Good therapists" probably have trained themselves to use this capability to the full. Both patient and therapist receive, orient to, and record subliminal perceptions of each other. Only some of these perceptions achieve conscious recognition. Two investigators at the University of Wisconsin, Kepecs and Wolman[2] are currently carrying on studies of the latent perceptions patients have of their therapists—the rules concerning their expectations of the therapists based on information outside conscious awareness. When a patient in therapy is shown photographs of his therapist, exposed at subliminal levels, and is asked to describe what he saw, some interesting reactions come out: For example,

---

[2] Personal communication.

one rather paranoid patient described the photographs of this therapist as "something like a walnut" early in therapy, but later on, when feelings of a hostile flavor had developed toward his therapist, the same photograph was seen as a "toilet seat." Patients who seem to be having hard going in therapy often reveal under these conditions what they seem unable to grasp consciously. They may see the therapist's picture as a threatening monster or a policeman. A young lady who early in therapy saw her male therapist's picture (presented below threshold) as a menacing cat-like figure later saw the same picture as a photograph of a statue of Brunhild—it was as if she had successfully identified herself with him, fusing herself and her image of him into an Amazon of strength.

The Effect of Instruction

The situation with humans, who possess speech, has further complications. It is possible to influence the effect of visual orienting stimuli by simultaneous verbal instructions about those visual stimuli. Such instruction can tip the balance scale of noticing or ignoring decisively. The effect of even horrendously powerful visual influence can be molded almost at will by anyone so disposed. For example, there is a film which has been used for some years in psychophysiology laboratories to produce emotional stress in subjects, which stress was then measured in various ways. This film was made by the anthropologist-psychoanalyst Geza Roheim in the desert country of Australia. Roheim photographed a ceremony in which the native bushmen perform a pubertal initiation rite on six boys. Each male child must experience this operation to be accepted as an adult member of the tribe. This ceremony is ghastly to civilized eyes: Some of the adult males get on their hands and knees, making a sort of operating table, while other adults hold the pubescent youth immobile. Then a tribal official incises the youth's penis, opening wide the urinary tube (urethra) from the scrotum to the urethra's natural opening (the meatus) so that where, before the incision, there was a tube there is thereafter an open trough. This is done with no surgical finesse, no anesthesia, no scalpel or hemostat—just a stone knife and brute force. In addition to blood, sweat, and tears, the film confronts the viewer with mud, flies, and agony.

Viewers of this film tend to be strongly influenced by it. Males in particular seem unable, as the vernacular has it, to keep their cool. All sorts of physiological alarm-bells, orienting responses, go off in their bodies, which can be easily measured. Yet an ingenious psychophysiologist, Joseph Spiesman (1965), showed that he could modify these alarm-orienting responses markedly by devising different sound track accompaniments to the film. A description of the action which dwelt on the grisly aspects of these doings made for even greater physiological orienting responses than did the silent film. The verbal instructions tuned up the sensitivity of "notice this!" reactions. A vapid "and-now-we-leave-beautiful-Hawaii" sound track, full of nicey-nicey euphemisms describing the ceremony as if it were a Sunday-school picnic, reduced the orienting responses of subjects to levels below those they had shown when viewing the silent film. Oil was thus poured on troubled waters. A sound track that described the ceremony in a detached fashion, like a surgeon lecturing to medical students —cold, reasonable, cerebral—reduced responses even more. Spiesman showed that he could produce "instant" defenses against orienting and conditioned responses to powerful visual stimuli by his verbal influence on his experimental subjects. He proved that he could act like a Toscanini, conducting the orchestra of his subjects' responses, bringing some to high volume and others to low, altering their tempo or their rubato at his will, merely by verbal signalling.

This same verbal influence on "physiologic" processes shows up in a series of studies by Richard Sternbach (1968), conducted while he was at Harvard University. Sternbach showed that he could mold the orienting and conditioned responses of subjects to identical painful stimuli by providing them with different expectations and anticipations of the painfulness of the shocks they were to experience. He also showed that differences exist in the experience of pain in relation to a given amount of painful stimulation according to the past experience, mainly verbal, of subjects. Around hospitals there are many bits of medical folklore, passed on from one class of interns or one generation of attending men to the next class or generation. Sternbach heard these folktales and put them to the test: Yankees are supposed to be stoical, Irishmen and Italians emotional, and Jews hysterical in the face of pain. Sternbach showed that Yankees not only tolerate more pain, will submit to even greater pain with greater acquiescence when the researcher asks them to do so, but also show less *physiological* response to a given amount of shock than do the other ethnic groups.

Sternbach concluded that mothers transmit to their children the same sort of defense toward pain that Spiesman produced in his laboratory in relation to visually shocking stimuli: Mothers, by verbal and nonverbal influence, can create in their children a "set"—an expectation or predisposition, which the child builds into his view of the world—as part of his rules. For Yankees, the rule is to deal with pain by Spartan attitudes —not quite "grin and bear it" but a more stoical "tough it out." For Jews, what counts about pain is that the doctor should know the ultimate truth about what he is dealing with: Jews will often refuse pain relief, lest they confuse the doctor. Aspirin may relieve headache, but what if the doctor of the aspirin-taker misses a brain tumor he would have diagnosed properly had the headache persisted?

It appears that Pavlov was right: In humans the enormously powerful nonverbal signalling system of orienting and conditioned reflexes is supplemented by a second signalling system, that of verbal processes, which has overtones at higher levels of abstraction. There is, unmistakably, an interplay in humans between the first and the second signalling system. One modifies the other. Both are involved in the control of behavior and hence in what makes people change as a result of any type of intervention such as psychotherapy. Rules and expectations in either system are like old streetcar tracks, guiding the behavior of the individual. Exceptions, in either system, are like stones in a road which jog the wheel out of its rut: They call for immediate reorienting compensatory and adaptive behavior on the part of the driver to bring the vehicle back into the desired direction. If, in any psychotherapy, one aims to produce change in the guiding rules of behavior in a patient, one should make signals which set the patient in motion along old lines, but then pose variations which act like the stone in the road and require—even impel, via the orienting response—a new accommodation, a change in the rules. But in addition to Pavlov's division into two systems, the signals can be further divided into those which reach conscious awareness and those which don't, and those arising from within and from without the individual.

Summary

Communication between creatures, some of which seemed mysterious in the past, depends on the orienting reflex and is at present more understandable, as the nature of this reflex has been explored. Subtle human-to-animal and human-to-human signalling can occur without using the medium of speech, as shown by the famous horse Clever Hans and by several persons who seemed to observers in the past to possess almost uncanny powers. One can notice or ignore (orient or fail to orient) without conscious awareness, and either tendency can be modified by signals which also are not consciously perceived. These modifications of noticing or ignoring tendencies by subliminal signals are subject to learning and training, as shown by many examples, including the skills that underlie helping professions (such as teaching, nursing, and psychotherapy). Verbal instructions can mold subliminal noticing or ignoring, even to the extent of changing the perception of pain and the physiologic response to powerful stimuli: As Pavlov pointed out, humans possess two different signalling systems which interact at many levels.

And thus the native hue of resolution
Is sicklied o'er with the pale cast of thought,
And enterprises of great pith and moment
With this regard their currents turn awry,
And lose the name of action. . . .

Hamlet, III. i. 84–88

6

The Regulatory
Influence of
Speech

The Power of the Orienting Reflex

The orienting reflex puts a powerful tool in the hands of anyone who wants to influence another person. It took science until the twentieth century to document what has been known to good orators throughout all ages. Drone monotonously, and you lose your audience. Vary your voice and your gesture, as well as the content of your spoken thought, watch your audience carefully for signs of alerting, and you capture your audience. Audiences are, after all, partial prisoners of their own orienting reflexes. (This may be part of the secret of that elusive talent, charisma. A charismatic leader must have lively orienting responses to the orienting responses of his followers.) To be a spellbinder, one must be able to do more than tell people what they want to hear. To make people hang on your every word, you must be able to capture, moment by moment, their rapt attention. Good actors, lecturers, and teachers have always used the orienting reflexes of their audiences (without ever naming them as such): They counsel studying one's audience closely for signs of wavering attention, and advise pitching one's message at a level which "holds" the audience. These same talents have obvious value in psychotherapy. If the therapist "loses" his patient by pitching comment at a level which is discrepant with his patient's interests and understanding, he loses his influence. Skillful therapists are alert to boredom or flagging interest in their patients.

Influence through orienting responses is seen in almost pure culture in the confusion technique of hypnosis, to be described below at greater length. Expert hypnotists can induce trance behavior in subjects without the use of any spoken patter whatsoever—in the congenitally deaf, for example, or in persons whose language is unknown to the hypnotist— simply by stimulating the subject, giving rapidly alternating signals in opposing directions. If the subject will merely agree to cooperate as far as holding out his hand, the hypnotist can induce trance behavior: He grasps the hand and starts stimulating it by pressures upward with his thumb alternating with pressures downward from his forefinger, both of them mixed with less distinct pressures in other directions from the hypnotist's other fingers.

Another form of influence, the malignant variety called brainwashing, makes full use of the victim's orienting responses. The usual accounts of the technique in the newspapers tend to stress conditioning by endless monotonous repetition and by rewarding any response in a desired direction. But the victim is deprived of sleep, is questioned at all hours of the day or night, and, in most cases reported, is constantly drowsy, which maximizes the orienting response. Endless variation of question and questioner, and subtle or obvious threats, have similar effects. Eventually the victim, bombarded by incessant stimuli, gives over control to his tormentors and signs the confession they demand. The hypnotic subject orients each time there is a change, but changes come so rapidly and bewilderingly that soon the subject, like the victim of brainwashing, suspends his attempts at controlling his reactions and puts himself at the hypnotist's disposal by going into a trance. If the subject were to speak, the observer of this process would expect him to say something like, "OK—you've got me bamboozled, *you* take over!"

Confusion technique can be used to induce trance by giving confusing signals in the second system (verbal instructions) without even touching the subject. The hypnotist starts by announcing some reference scale—time, for instance—and proceeds to confuse the subject by rapidly altering the points on that reference scale with each succeeding signal. "You had orange juice for breakfast today," he begins, and goes on, "and you probably will have it next Tuesday, as you did this Tuesday, and many Tuesdays last year. You may have it the Tuesday or Wednesday just before next Christmas, as before all Christmases. Today you liked it, but next Friday and last Friday the orange juice may not be chilled enough, just as it wasn't on your birthday. . . ." No sooner has the subject oriented to one time signal than he is given another, to which he orients reflexly. To accomplish this most effectively, all the hypnotist's references to time are announced as if great meaning were attached to each succeeding one. The subject is given the impression that his life, his fortune, and his sacred honor depend on keeping track of the time he's living in at each moment.

According to Milton Erickson (1967), the originator of this technique, the idea of developing the confusion technique came to him after an incident of waggish whimsey. While still a student at the University of Wisconsin, he came around a corner of a building one blustery winter day and collided straight on with a man hurrying in the opposite direction. Erickson picked himself up, bowed gravely, looked at his watch, and said in a sonorous, serious tone, "It is exactly ten minutes of two," and walked away. (It was in fact several hours later.) He glanced back when he had walked half a block and saw the baffled recipient of his enigmatic message still standing in the same spot, gazing in wonder in his direction. The exaggerated emphasis on time in a context in which such an utterance was utterly irrelevant was such a jolt to the man that he remained nonplussed for quite a while.

Something similar occurs in the example of confusion technique described: The subject simply cannot get his bearings and maintain them. The subject is so busy responding to change he seems to lose the capacity for coherent planning, and turns over control of his thought and behavior to the hypnotist. This state of mind is understandable to anyone who has tried to drive his car, following his friend's car as a guide, through busy traffic in a strange city (especially if the friend is a fast driver). In such circumstances, one experiences a mild degree of the subjective state of utter confusion which overwhelms the hypnotic subject exposed to confusion techniques of trance induction. Such a state also overwhelms any chairman of a meeting who is a bit rusty on Robert's Rules of Order, when various protagonists of opposing groups begin to use fine details of parliamentary procedure to obstruct decision making. Points of order, motions to table, to adjourn, to amend—and controversies as to the propriety of any of these—can escalate so rapidly as to paralyze the chairman's capacity to conduct the meeting, and if the organization has an official parliamentarian, the chairman will turn to him with relief for a decision—or indeed to anyone who has clear convictions as to proper procedure.

The more conventional psychotherapies do not exploit the orienting reflex in the obvious way it is used in confusion induction of hypnosis. Classical psychoanalytic technique, for example, has the patient recumbent on a couch. The analyst sits out of the patient's view, does very little talking by the standards of ordinary conversation, and avoids any physical contact with the patient. Such a situation would seem at first glance to provide minimal occasion for orienting responses as compared with trance induction by confusion techniques. Anyone who has been an analytic patient knows, on the other hand, how potent silence is in itself —for example, when one asks one's analyst a simple question like "Have you ever ridden a horse?" and receives only stony silence. (All through the vertebrate kingdom, sudden silence is an orienting danger signal so potent that it crosses species lines of communication and alerts the rabbit when the birds fall silent.) In the analytic situation, after such a period of silence, the analyst's cough becomes pregnant with meaning. The sound of what might be the analyst squirming in his chair can be positively threatening. While seeming to be doing nothing at all, the analyst inescapably influences the patient's orienting responses. Family therapy, on the other hand, is characterized by such an overwhelming barrage of orienting cues as to bewilder the therapist, observer, or family member. In order to keep his bearings and proceed with any purpose, the therapist needs special aids. He must be temperamentally able to selectively ignore data which would confuse him. An especially helpful aid is to have a co-therapist with whom he can occasionally step aside and regain his usual orientation.

In the confusion technique, Erickson succeeded by several routes in gaining control of the behavior of his subjects. He supplied verbal and nonverbal cues. Either or both types of cues sufficed to induce trance: Signals in both the first and second systems can be used to gain control of another person's behavior. But how can we explain this extraordinary influence? A moment's reflection on emergency situations suggests the answer: When our usual capacity to integrate perceptions is overwhelmed by a barrage of stimulation—fire in a crowded theatre, kamikaze attack, riot in the convention hall—we humans regress (like true Freudians) to the tried and true patterns, the conditionings of our early years. Let one man stand up in a fiery theatre and shout "This way out for safety" in the authoritative tones one heard from one's father in years long past, and the disorganized mob of panicky theatergoers follows dutifully. At such times, it is the rare person who coolly appraises the situation, cortex fully active, to determine whether the shouted proffer of safety is in fact reliable or not. Too many corpses of too many victims of mass panic bear witness to the statement that humans have limited ability to think clearly in chaotic situations, and to control their behavior in such a way as to save their own lives. One of the reasons for this disorganization is clearer in the light of the research findings about orienting, defensive, and adaptive reflexes —all with their residues engraved on the mental apparatus as rules of behavior.

When stimuli flood in, each producing a new orienting response, some organized behavior is possible providing there is sufficient coherence in the stimuli which otherwise threaten to drown the capacities of the person stimulated. Consider a highly chaotic wartime situation like an amphibious assault on an island: If a line of fighter planes, in a clearly visible pattern, dive on a beachhead in a course parallel to the shoreline, spewing machine-gun fire along the water's edge, troops head en masse for covering palm trees nearby on the land side, as if some giant invisible windshield wiper had swept them off the beach. But let there be shelling, mortar fire, and air attack by planes coming at the beachhead from all directions, and there will be random—sometimes witless—scurryings for any cover available, even if that cover is another man's body. In such conditions, a clear order from a superior officer can galvanize the panicky troops into concerted action.

What Erickson does with the confusion technique, it seems, is to produce a miniature replica of the disorganized beachhead situation, stimulating orienting responses paradoxically until total disorder threatens. He then adroitly switches to calming commands which recall the soothing, calming parental words of our earliest years ("Mommy's here, go to sleep"). No wonder patients surrender control of their thought and behavior to his signals (playing the "hypnotic game" involves less work!). The subject approaches the hypnotic experience primed to respond in accordance with all of his past learning, whether this learning is conscious or is latent in some ancient memories laid down in early experience. Whether he is positively disposed, negatively disposed, or both, his own active coping is undercut by the confusion technique: "Is this a situation which conforms to my rules, or is it a negative case, or is it both?" Given expertise in exploiting orienting responses, the hypnotist can override the subject's reasonable assessing maneuvers, stripping the patient of his more leisurely judgments. In such a case, what is there to guide him save some ancient magic faith in the wisdom of the Mighty?

Abrogation of the Orienting Reflex's Power

There is a way out, a way for the victim of confusion to save his autonomy. This route employs another basic principle of influence. We humans are able to choose which system to attend—the first (the ringing of a bell) or the second (attention to a built-in verbal plan) at will.

Experienced hypnotists know that there is an escape route from hynotic influence which subjects can use. This route is not the route of defiant resistance: People who defy hypnotists are easy marks for the induction of hypnosis. It is the bored, the disinterested, or the indifferent person who challenges the hypnotists' expertise. This is because defiance in relation to the influence of another upon one's self is the same as compliance in its effects: In each case one is patterning one's actions in accord with another's demands, whether the pattern is positive or negative. The position of independence in dealing with another man's influence upon oneself is indifference, not rebellion. (This is a recognition which has long comforted the parents of adolescents, whose rebellious rejection of parental standards unwittingly honors these same standards in the breach.) People who attend to the hypnotist, but who react to the hypnotist 180 degrees *out* of phase can be as effectively manipulated as those who react *in* phase. But those patients who can successfully *ignore* stimuli—whether by leaving the consulting room physically, hailing the nearest taxi and heading for the airport or bus station, or by figuratively leaving by systematically treating whatever the therapist says as gibberish—can evade influence. A patient who can literally or figuratively close his eyes, clap his hands over his ears, or concentrate on thoughts of pleasurable things elsewhere, can thwart the therapist who is bent on influencing him.

The ability to influence *oneself* by imagery, conjured up voluntarily, carries with it the ability to selectively ignore some of the evidence of one's senses in favor of such imagery. Though some apparatuses of the brain censor information automatically, giving the cortex edited copy, there are other apparatuses which can be activated at will. These voluntary apparatuses can do a similar type of editing so that information coming from the peripheral sensory organs is partially screened out—they can inhibit the orienting reflex. They can, in hypnosis, edit out the pains of childbirth or of major surgery. These apparatuses depend in part on memories of all types—visual, acoustic, kinesthetic, olfactory. They also depend upon the curious combinatory capability of the human intellect which produces new fantasies. Philosophical debate concerning free will aside, it is a clinical fact that one can evade confusion or any other hypnotic technique by forcing one's attention away from external stimuli onto signals one produces within one's own mind. Almost any vivid fantasy activity will do—write a poem, recall an old nursery rhyme, walk a familiar street in fantasy while vividly recalling the visual image, work a mathematical problem, or invent a new recipe. Humans have multiple signalling systems and can elect to attend to one instead of another. When we speak of someone having extraordinary powers of concentration, or call the professor absent-minded, we are recognizing this ability.

Attention to one's own internal signals, whether memories, fantasies, faiths, or beliefs, can sometimes have extraordinary power in guiding behavior in the face of otherwise overwhelming external stimulation. The Christian martyrs in the Roman arena must have been attending to their own imagery, their own beliefs, rather than the presence of the lions when they went stoically to their deaths. So, too, with the unprotesting victims of the Nazi gas chambers. It has often been observed by those who have studied the victims of brainwashing that soldiers who hold clear and firm patriotic beliefs which they can call up at will withstand the onslaughts of their captors far better than those soldiers who lack such beliefs. The power of prayer in time of peril must lie at least in part in the ability to attend to prayer rather than to the welter of incoming stimuli. The reader can grasp such influence intuitively from his own experiences of struggling with fear or pain, yet these images are mostly beyond scientific measurement and tend to be left out of account by researchers of influence.

The influence involved in internal imagery has many varieties. It need not be verbal to be effective. Artists can visualize scenes, even ones they have never seen, with great vividness, and use this imagery to guide their brush strokes. Artists are not alone in the capacity to influence themselves and their behavior by vivid visual imagery: One need only think of the arousal produced in adolescent males by their own sexual imagery, which can be so vivid as to result in orgasm. Composers hear their compositions in their heads, without any external stimulation. They hear what their written compositions will sound like by imagery in the auditory mode and make corrections in their written compositions. The existence of internal plans that guide orienting is clear in humans, because we can tell each other what we intend to do. "I'm looking for a needle in this haystack," we can say, and what otherwise looks like pointless shuffling then makes some sense. But, though speech makes it easy for humans to reveal plans, there are other behaviors besides speech that permit the inference that organisms have plans. The Bower bird hunts not for needles in haystacks but for appropriate trinkets to decorate his bower. The salmon hunts for his native stream. The warbler navigates over thousands of miles for his native nesting ground. All migrations depend on plans, and all plans involve internal imagery, whether present in consciousness or not. Even in humans it is possible to get into such a rut that complex operations sink out of awareness. The commuter can get himself to work and back, day after day, hardly noticing what he is doing. Only when some familiar building is demolished does he notice it was there.

Thus, plans can provide resistance to confusion, and we can orient ourselves to not just one set of signals, but several. The patient and the therapist are continually deciding which signals to attend at each step of the psychotherapeutic process. The patient feels some twinge of anxiety: "He seems awfully stiff and formal . . ." or "This man is a wild man —I always thought psychiatrists were a bit daft themselves. . . ." The therapist feels on edge: "Is this patient going to be calling me at all hours of the night?" or "I doubt if I'm getting more than a fourth of the truth— he seems awfully slick. . . ." Both patient and therapist compare their experience of each other with their plans of how people work, using the full range of verbal and nonverbal signals to size up each other, and comparing the present with their accumulative knowledge from the past. This knowledge appears subjectively as complicated varieties of imagery.

The Power of Verbal Signals

The form of imagery-influence which has been most carefully worked out is the imagery involved in verbal self-instruction—internalized speech. Years ago Piaget began recording the spontaneous speech of little children (three to five years old) playing by themselves. About a third of what they say is addressed to themselves in the form of instructions, injunctions, and such: "Mommy says don't touch," or "If you eat that you'll get fat!" By the time a child is six or seven such self-instructions have ceased to be uttered to the world—the child keeps them to himself. During transitional phases such vocalizations are uttered sotto voce; in the absence of spoken speech they can be picked up by instruments which measure the activity of muscles used in vocalization.

Pavlov, as mentioned earlier, proposed the idea that humans continually condition themselves to signals in this second system in addition to signals in the first, externally arising, system. In Freudian terms, this is the commanding voice of conscience, the superego, which becomes the guardian of our integrity. We walk past a bank, and suffer no thrust of wish to rob it. The superego censors once-brute impulses until predatory wishes no longer appear at all. This idea is not Pavlov's creation de novo. It has a history. It was foreshadowed in Freud's "Project for a Scientific Psychology" (1954), dating from the turn of the century. Given some interpretive license, its history goes back at least as far as the ancient Greek stoic, Epictetus. Freud's formulations of the role of language in the control of behavior were much more specific and mechanistic than the philosophical notions of Epictetus (however profound these were), and in today's age of the computer, the 70-year-old formulations of Freud have a remarkably contemporary ring. (Pavlov was himself markedly influenced by Freud's thought: He told the distinguished neurophysiologist Ralph Gerard that the first thoughts of conditioning, whether in the first or second systems, had come to him from Freud's work.[1]) Freud was well

---

[1] Personal communication.

aware that vocalization is a powerful surrogate for action in influencing behavior. Since everyone who talks also listens to himself (except the deaf) it is as natural to be influenced by one's own words as those of others. The influence of the sound of one's words upon oneself is another of those obvious regularities which tend to escape notice—one thinks of himself as speaker, not as a hearer of his own speech. Drastic effects occur when the feedback of the sound of one's own words is by one means or another denied. Deprivation of auditory feedback, to say the least, is disorganizing. (See G. S. Klein's "On Hearing One's Own Voice," 1965, for an extended survey of the literature and a report of his own research in this area.)

Signals in the second system link signals in the first system together. Both dog and man, for example, may salivate at the sight and scent of a steak, but man can salivate at his friend's, or his own, verbal description of a steak. A vast amount of experimentation has taken place in the Soviet Union over the last 40 years testing this idea. This research explored the developmental origins in childhood of verbal self-signalling. Russian investigators studied not only normal development but also failures and the effects of injuries and diseases upon the second signalling system. (Only those aspects of this work relevant to influence in psychotherapy will be considered here, but a lucid summary of the voluminous literature of this research is available in A. R. Luria's book *The Role of Speech in the Regulation of Normal and Abnormal Behavior,* 1960.)

Consider the man with whom Erickson collided: He most probably stood speechless on the spot, thinking something like "What in heaven's name did he mean by that? Is the man mad? Or have *I* suddenly lost my mind?" What he did next hinged on his own internal dialogue, on how he answered his own questions. Adults carry on such dialogues with themselves so continuously that they take them for granted. James Thurber's delightful satire "The Secret Life of Walter Mitty" depends for its comic effect upon this human propensity. The central figure carries on elaborate daydreams involving heroic dialogue and deed, all hidden from the outside world. Only when Mitty absent-mindedly slips and speaks aloud a segment of his perpetual internal dialogue (a part of the shopping list he has been rehearsing to himself) does he give a clue to its furtive existence: As he passes a lady and her daughter in the street, the startled young girl turns to her mother and says "That man said 'puppy-biscuit'!"

Most of us have trouble recalling any period of our lives when verbal self-signalling was absent. Since it is always present, we find it almost impossible to weigh the effects it has in determining our actions. Some hint of the role of internal speech in programming adult behavior comes when one looks up a number in the phone book: He almost always says the number either silently to himself, or aloud to the world, in the moment between putting the book down and dialing the number. Just how vital is this seemingly inane announcement? How much does our speech govern our actions?

Sensorimotor Phases of Self-Regulation

Some 30 years ago the Russian psychologist Vygotskii (1934) began to explore the way children solve problems. He gave young children simple tasks such as drawing a picture or tracing a diagram. Vygotskii then added complications. The child would approach the task only to find that there was no pencil handy, or that the pencil lead was broken, or that some essential piece of equipment was missing. The youngest children Vygotskii tested were three- and four-year-olds. They responded to complications by appealing to adults for help, usually naming the missing equipment, and then waiting inactively until given the missing item. Older children, six- and seven-year-olds, coped with the difficulty in a different fashion: The problem provoked an intense burst of active speech, addressed to the world in general as well as to the adult present. This active speech was no random babbling. When Vygotskii studied it carefully, he found that it was a kind of scanning of possibilities, an intensified verbal planning and problem-solving effort on the child's part. The child was planning aloud, drawing on more and more possibilities for solution and exploring alternatives. Vygotskii recognized that this verbal planning preceded and guided what the child did next, just as adults rehearse shopping lists and telephone numbers to guide their next moves. Vygotskii and his students thereafter began an intensive exploration of the earliest beginnings of self-instruction in the second signalling system, gradually extending their studies back to the earliest origins of speech in the second year of life.

Before considering this research, a preliminary look at how language is acquired is in order, since certain early stages of language acquisition have bearing on several types of psychotherapeutic influence. At first, word signals are treated much as babies treat visual signals. When mother points to the cat and says "kitty," or to father and says "dada," she supplies the infant with what is called an "indexical" sign (using her index finger) which the child records as part of his theory of the world, just as babies combine visual signals with the idea of a peekaboo game. Soon the child begins to point to things actively, saying the name aloud, as if, again, he were an infant scientist bent on verifying his theory of the world, and replicating his experiments in order to establish his hypotheses. He does not wait for associations to be forced upon him in some simple reflex fashion—reflexly associating salivation with the sight of a bottle, on the model of Pavlov's laboratory animals. He actively reaches out, assigns labels to things, makes plans, and tries to pigeonhole the world around him to see how he can influence it.

Living with a baby is very lively—so active is their influence upon those around them that elderly adults find them hard to bear. All physicians (and parents) know that the physical examination of a baby is a lively game—babies poke in pockets, pull on stethoscopes, and grab at eyeglasses. They don't behave like docile adult patients offering up their bodies to a neurologist for examination, permitting this reflex or that to be tested. They behave in a fashion which might be analogous to having the adult patient, while having his reflexes tapped, conduct his own examination of the neurologist's body. The categorizing curiosity of babies is such an impediment to physical examinations that pediatricians usually distract them by offering them attractive baubles to play with. And babies display the same active exploration in learning to attach names to objects. One can almost hear them saying to themselves "Is this new thing a cat?" or "Is this man really the same as that man I called dada?" Their voices often lift questioningly in their early naming experiments. They look up at their parents as if they were saying "Have I got it right?"

Piaget named the early phases of this process of active search "the stage of sensorimotor intelligence." Babies cannot grasp verbal concepts like "over" and "under" until they have repeatedly performed actions which disclose the meaning of the term—for example, picked up and put down a handkerchief covering a ball. Concepts start from actions and sensations. It is as if a child literally felt his way into the use of verbal processes ("actions speak louder than words"). Nursery school children link words with actions in their definitions: Arms are "to hug with," forks are "to eat with." There is a charming collection of such early definitions, the title of which itself provides a prime example: *"A Hole Is To Dig."*[2]

Vygotskii's associate, A. R. Luria, showed this action connotation of words as far back as 1928 in studies of babies. He measured the length of their reaction times to words (how quickly they "caught on"), and the stability of these reaction times compared to words *not* involving actions. Action connections between words form early in life and remain stable ("Hole–Dig"), whereas associative connections between words which do not involve action ("Table–Stool") come much later, characteristically under the influence of schoolroom teaching.

The use of active physical action in self-influence, as seen in normal development, has its counterpart in influence by action experienced passively. If one goes to a foreign country and cannot speak the language, the natives will revert to sensorimotor levels, to guiding, and to sign language. A native may even resort to such manipulations as placing one's hand on the proper drawer, lever, or doorknob involved in some intended action.

Some Implications for Therapeutic Influence

A sort of *proto*-psychotherapy involves sensorimotor phases of influence. This has been used with patients showing behavior diagnosed as catatonic schizophrenia by the physiotherapist Paul Roland (Davis, 1957), who was able to re-educate his statue-like patients to a remarkable degree of recovery by active training of sensorimotor activities, beginning with such activities as handing a ball back and forth with staff members.

[2] Krauss & Sendak, 1952.

Roland, unencumbered by the taboos which restrict most psychotherapists from any physical contact with patients, carefully guided patients into other more complex physical activities. Roland would take hold of the patient's hands, legs, and face, assisting the performance of whatever motion he wanted the patient to carry out—waving of arms, smiling, relaxing, sweeping with a broom, playing volleyball, and so on. Roland operated on the simple theory that catatonic patients have "forgotten" how to move. He was innocent of such theoretical concepts as Piaget's sensorimotor intelligence, but many schizophrenic patients actually are functioning at this early level. This is shown by the way they use language: They often act as if they took words to be puns, with double meanings, one of which is abstract and the other a concrete sensorimotor instruction. One of my patients was walking along the hospital corridor, bumping her shoulder against the corridor wall. When I questioned her about this action, she said the voices she was hearing (hallucinatory ones) kept telling her she was to be "bumped off"—that is, murdered. Another such patient responded to my comment that she seemed "pretty high" today (she was in a happier mood than usual) by getting up out of her chair and climbing on top of the highest piece of furniture in the room. Such evidence of regression to the sensorimotor level makes influence by sensorimotor methods a reasonable approach to patients who are functioning at this level.

Other forms of sensorimotor influence were in common use before the advent of tranquilizers. Disturbed patients who were beyond the influence of the second system, soothing words, once were placed in tubs of warm water for long periods: All parents know that soothing baths can calm down overstimulated children. Cold wet packs tranquilized many a rampaging patient (sheets wrung out of ice water were wrapped around the patient, mummy-fashion). High-pressure streams of water, called "needle-showers," stimulated lethargic or apathetic patients into showing signs of life for a time. This sensorimotor influence had an antidepressant action, forgotten with the advent of the antidepressant drugs of today. It was a modern, attenuated version of the brutal types of sensorimotor influence which dot the long history of psychiatry—dunking patients into cold water while they were strapped in chairs attached to a sort of seesaw, beatings, canings, and floggings. Swaddling, a form of sensorimotor influence used with infants, has a counterpart in restraining devices like straight jackets and leather handcuffs attached to belts. These devices were often abused—even their mention strikes fear in the hearts of most people, who associate them with a snakepit type of insane asylum. When properly and gently used, however, they often influence disturbed patients in a benign and effective way. A patient who could not accept verbal statements to the effect that the psychiatric staff were "all his friends," and that he had nothing to fear, either from his own impulses or those of others, would often quiet down remarkably when these devices were applied.

One intrepid pioneer of the hospital treatment of patients diagnosed as chronic schizophrenics, George L. Harrington, achieved remarkable therapeutic results in recent years by a program depending mainly on influence by nonverbal sensorimotor techniques (see Glasser, 1965). These patients, who had been in Veterans' Hospitals an average of 14 years, were placed on arrival at Dr. Harrington's ward in belt-and-cuffs and told they had only to eat, sleep, and rest—not talk. None of the staff would respond to "crazy talk," only to sensible requests or comments. Disturbed patients quieted down, began to talk sense, and were gradually started on such projects as laying sidewalks around the hospital grounds. Harrington, a gentle Atlas of a man, would return patients to swaddling—that is, to belt-and-cuffs—at any sign of anxiety or agitation. It was not unusual for a patient, sensing some impending internal turmoil, to come up to the ward staff with extended wrists and ask to be put in belt-and-cuffs. The influence of this regime was sufficiently effective that when I visited the project in 1964 over a hundred of the original 200 chronic patients had left the hospital and were living in the community again. (Unfortunately this exploratory project ran into outside administrative opposition and had to be abandoned after only a few years of operation.)

The Change from Sensorimotor to Semantic Regulation

Sensorimotor phases of influence gradually give way in development to verbally influenced actions. Once a baby has a name for an object, he has separated the object from the rest of the world in his mind and can begin to deal with it in a much better organized fashion. (As William James commented, it is hard to focus our attention on the nameless.)

The Russian experimenter Lyublinskaya found in 1955 that babies who are at the age of learning to talk (12 to 30 months) have great trouble with what might be called the "which-hand-do-you-choose" problem. He gave them red boxes which contained sweets and green boxes identical in shape which contained none. Babies this age are a bust on such a problem (which might surprise any parent who has lived in a house full of kids and seen their fiendish ingenuity in finding cookies, descending like locusts upon them—one would swear they could find cookies from day one). When Lyublinskaya named the colors aloud as he handed the babies the different boxes they acted as if he had given them the key to a puzzle-box: Although a few precocious youngsters could make a tentative guess on their own, the addition of the spoken name "green" or "red" to the solution of the problem made it possible for the babies to find the sweets in about a third of the time it took them without the name. Without the name even precocious babies forgot where to find the cookies from one day to the next, whereas once they had heard the name they had the game beaten even after a week's vacation from the problem. The name green or red applied to a box not only engraved the right answer in the babies' minds but also helped them remember the clue when given red and green blocks or bricks to play with—they would sort them by colors as if hoping for a payoff. Naming things for a child as young as 18 months of age gives the child a roadmap of the world he can use to find his way around.

It is easy to influence a child of 18 months by verbal instruction. Easy, that is, to *initiate* an action like hand-clapping. But once an action is initiated, words won't stop it. Speech is ineffective when it conflicts with an action already underway: Try telling a two-year-old to take off his stockings while he is pulling them on and you will find you merely intensify the child's struggle. At this age the adult's instructions can start an action but can't stop it: Verbal instruction is quite ineffective in switching the child from one activity to another. If a child this age is asked to squeeze a rubber balloon he will nearly always comply. He keeps on squeezing, once he starts, as if the continuous tactile stimulation of his palm by the bulb took control of his behavior. Luria reports that verbal attempts to stop him by saying "That's enough" or "Don't squeeze" are more apt to intensify than diminish the baby's repetitive squeezing. This has its parallels in the influence of one adult upon another: The demagogue bent on influencing a mob to lynch a man or to pillage an embassy knows, somewhere in his being, that action once started tends to carry humans along even in adulthood.

In their extensive studies of verbal influence on behavior, Russian investigators used a piece of equipment which has been rather standard in Soviet laboratories since the late 1920s (see Luria, 1960). A brief description may help the reader understand subsequent references to experiments employing this apparatus. The child (or adult subject) is placed before a display panel on which various visual signals can be presented by remote control by the experimenter, who is in another room. The child is given a rubber bulb to squeeze, on instruction, which is connected to a recording device that makes a permanent record of the child's responses to various signals—visual signals, bells, buzzers, and so on. The barrier between the experimenter and the subject in Luria's laboratory (the walls of the room) prevents the type of orienting, subliminal influence which Pfungst had shown was operating in the case of the horse Clever Hans.

A two-year-old child has trouble following any complicated verbal influence. Instructions given in advance of a signal, such as "When you see the light go on, squeeze the balloon," are too much for him to handle; he responds immediately to the word "squeeze." With expert training, however, even an 18-month-old baby eventually learns to respond correctly.

The next step in the verbal regulation of behavior comes when the child's own speech develops to the point that he can give himself signals —influence himself verbally—to start or stop his behavior. This occurs at about three to four years of age. By this time, a child can do what was impossible earlier: He can link the preliminary verbal instruction to the subsequent action to which it refers. He can absorb the request "Now, when the light goes on, squeeze the bulb" without stumbling over the immediate instructional import of the word "squeeze" as he would have done a year or two before. All attempts to teach the child to supply his own verbal signals at the age of two to three years fail—and in fact make things so complicated for the child that the additional task compromises whatever ability he has to respond to the light signal by squeezing.

Children only a year older show different behavior. At three to four years children will continue to press the bulb after a light signal is shown, continuing the repetitive response pattern of the two-year-old (called "perseveration" in scientific lingo), but if they are told to say aloud the word "go" with each light signal, their performance shows a dramatic improvement. They respond only to the light signal, and to *every* light signal: The records of their performance show none of the "noise" found in records of experiments in which this self-signalling was absent. The regulatory influence of the child's verbalization upon the child's behavior at three to four years of age is nonspecific. It is tied to the nonsignificatory aspects of speech (in other words, to the motor behavior involved in speaking) rather than to the meaning of the words the child is saying.

This situation changes as the child grows older. At 4½ to 5½ years the child becomes able to grasp complex verbal instructions, such as "Press when a red light shows and don't press when a white light shows." Two important developments occur: The regulatory influence of the child's own speech begins to become internalized; and, second, this influence becomes more and more detached from the motoric muscular signals, coming to depend on the semantic—the meaningful—aspects of speech. With regard to the first of these two, Luria's group recorded electrical potentials from the muscles used in speaking and showed that the three-year-old's spoken "go–go" becomes a whispered "go–go" in the four-year-old. At about five years self-instruction is inaudible but still recordable, as mentioned before, via electrodes placed on the child's throat, which pick up the electrical impulses going to the muscles used in speech.

Such recordable motor impulses gradually disappear in the next few years of growth, as internal speech becomes intrapsychic. By early adolescence the second change is evident: Children have the capability to respond to the sense of the meaning of an instruction—the semantic aspect of its message—and even to transpose the exact words of the instruction into their own preferred form, no longer being tied to the motoric aspects of speech.[3]

Luria and his colleagues have brought forth another line of evidence disclosing not only the important influence of speech in the regulation of behavior but also the devastating effect of interference with this influence. This evidence comes from patients who suffer various types of brain lesions—such as defects in development, degenerations, and tumors. Generalized defects or degenerations of the cerebral cortex lead to general

[3] For a clear explication of semantic and other intricate variations of Pavlovian conditioning, see Razran, 1961.

impairment of the second signalling system, and if these occur in childhood, the result is an inability to progress through the normal stages of
verbal self-regulation. On the other hand, localized defects of lower brain
centers which tend to impair motor performance can be remedied by
retraining methods which exploit *verbal* regulatory processes. The disease
called Parkinsonism, which involves the degeneration of centers deep in
the brain, called the basal ganglia (which have a function something like
the power-steering apparatus of automobiles), has as one of its characteristic features an inability to perform repetitive motions. Patients suffering
this disease find it very difficult to squeeze repetitively the bulb in the
standard Soviet apparatus. After eight, ten, or fifteen squeezes, victims
of Parkinsonism progressively lose the ability to squeeze with each new
attempt. The end result of continued effort is total inability to squeeze at
all. If, at this point, they are instructed to accompany each squeeze with a
verbal signal to themselves—not even aloud—consisting of merely counting each squeeze ("one, two, three") they regain the capacity to squeeze
over and over again, almost to normal levels. What was lost at the pure
motor level can be restored by resorting to verbal programming, just as
babies who say "go" when the light goes on can master the bulb-
squeezing problem.

Workers in Lurla's lab have also shown that lesions of the part of the
brain most directly involved in speech, the temporal lobe, disturb the
ability to comprehend spoken speech but do not interfere appreciably
with its regulatory function: Patients continue to use their garbled, acous-
tically defective speech successfully to regulate their behavior. It appears
that "go" or "one, two, three" can regulate, even if slurred. By contrast,
frontal lobe lesions, which have no effect on the ability to process and
comprehend auditory signals, lead to a pronounced derangement of the
regulatory function of speech. Such patients hear perfectly well and can
repeat clearly in rote fashion the instructions people tell them, but they
have lost the ability to create their own self-instructions. Frontal lobe
lesions also impair the second development of self-influence seen in
normal maturation, the shift from the motoric to the semantic aspects of
speech.

The process of internalization of speech in development is reversible—
one only has to give the child instructions which are more complex than
he can easily handle at any given age to produce a reversion to vocalized
self-instruction and a reversion to motoric rather than semantic influence.
This process of reversion happens in everyday life among adults when
one person gives another complex directions about almost any procedure, such as street directions or safe combinations. The recipient
adult is likely to say "Now let me see, have I got you right? Go three
blocks and turn right, two more until I get to a white church and then turn
left. . . ." This double checking obviously serves the purpose of assuring
accuracy of transmission, but if accuracy alone were involved, a simple
request to have the instructions repeated several times might serve. The

importance of saying aloud the self-instruction, which will silently guide later behavior, goes mostly unrecognized in the maneuver, although teachers have always used it in saying "Now repeat after me . . . ." Responsive prayers and religious services take account of the force of vocal influence by drawing the congregation into the service and mobilizing participants into active verbal self-influence.

These sequences of normal development have been documented not only by Luria's group and other Russian investigators but also, as mentioned, by Piaget, in his records of the spontaneous talk of children when they were playing away from grownups. The re-emergence of active vocal self-instruction is an everyday event in adult life: Unless a person is in good practice, as by doing a good deal of simple arithmetic in his occupation, he is apt to find himself solving arithmetical problems by repeating the multiplication tables under his breath—or even aloud. Most people use verbalization to help their adding and subtracting, even if only sotto voce. One often reverts to vocalization to aid memory. If one gets bogged down recalling an old song or poem, it helps to say aloud the part one recalls: Subjectively it feels as though the spoken words give a running start, a momentum of movement which has its own railroad tracks, and the missing word or phrase reappears. To count seven cups of sugar in making jam, a motoric operation, is far easier if done aloud than if done silently (especially if the process is subject to interruption). The age-old wisdom of the Catholic Church recognized and ritualized vocal self-instruction—a reversion to externalized self-influence—not only in the confessional but also in the acts of penance, the rosary ritual of vocal prayer. The Pledge of Allegiance to the Flag, the marriage vows, the communal singing of the National Anthem, the swearing-in oaths of soldiers, public officials, and witnesses in court, all implicitly make use of the power of vocal self-influence—else why not simply read and sign a document containing the same statements for everyone to witness?

Piaget pointed out an important concomitant of the process of internalization of self-instructions. This concomitant has a profound effect on psychopathology in later life. Piaget was impressed by children's tendency to establish internalized rules and also by their lack of critical thinking regarding the premises upon which such rules were based. A five-year-old, walking along a street, observes that the image of the moon behind a line of trees seems to follow his progress along the street. This, for the child, becomes a rule for him which he almost never subjects to critical examination. Parents hardly ever examine the premises their children adopt—they fail to ask what their children are saying to themselves about the nature of the world. It was by the logic of this age that the majority of mankind once believed the world to be flat, and, by the process of internalization, continued this belief unchallenged into their adult years. Children invent their own magic, their own talion rules (an eye for an eye), but they get powerful assistance in this process by whatever cultural magic is provided them. Once implanted in the form of verbal self-instruction, these formulations act as silent conditioning signals in the second system—warning the child of dire consequences should he do this or that forbidden act, threatening him with evil presences and magic personages whose power he dares not question. As the child matures, these self-instructions tend to drop out of awareness, to be replaced by an automatic response in the place of conscious reasoning.

As Freud pointed out long ago, the injunctions of parents, internalized as verbal instructions, reappear in deliria and psychoses as auditory hallucinations. "Voices" bombard such patients with archaic threats and commands, echoes of the past. And in most psychotherapies, such childhood rules are excavated, bit by bit, and brought into consonance with adult reality and rationality. These operations change the plans which either confuse or permit resistance to influence. In the Salem of Pilgrim times, the accusation that one was a witch had devastating consequences. The label alone was sufficient to activate old plans in those so labelled, starting with fear and ending in total demoralization and panic. The accused embraced any escape. But in Rome, to declare one's affiliation as a "Christian" was to activate other plans and to armor oneself against horrendous torture. Therapists cannot avoid tinkering with both negative and positive plans in aiming for therapeutic change in their patients.

Summary

Several lines of evidence show the power of the orienting reflex in guiding and changing the behavior of human beings. Though orators have long used orienting to sway their audiences, systematic study of the reflex has only occurred in recent years. It plays an important role in such interpersonal relations as psychotherapy and hypnosis and in malignant operations such as brainwashing.

There are ways of minimizing the power of the orienting reflex. These hinge on the intentional attending to internal imagery of a variety of types, which humans can at will summon to awareness.

Chief among these internal images are silent verbal self-instructions, which Pavlov called "the second signalling system." These internal signals are referred to as beliefs, faiths, convictions, prejudices, in ordinary parlance. The power such signals possess in regulating behavior has long been known, but the steps by which these regulating influences form, and the ways in which they can be changed, have only recently been studied. Freud's insights, derived from clinical cases, concerning internal regulation (ego and superego) have been bolstered by several lines of research (Piaget, Luria, and others) which demonstrate that what we tell ourselves at five years of age becomes a silent regulator at seven, and continues to guide our behavior long after.

Each phase of language acquisition affords a model for therapeutic intervention. Early phases (called by Piaget "sensorimotor") have been used in such techniques of therapy as those of Paul Roland and G. L.

Harrington, which stress nonverbal communication. In later phases of language acquisition, sensorimotor orienting responses give way to semantic orienting: Sensation gives way to meaning in the guidance of behavior. Lesions of the brain demonstrate in a variety of ways what effects follow from a deprivation of portions of the first and second signalling systems in the regulation of behavior.

*When all things began, the Word already was. The
Word dwelt with God, and what God was, the Word was.*
John 1:1–3

7

The Influence
of Language:

walls or wings?

Development of the Second Signalling System

Originally, in childhood, a word is not the signal-of-signals it later becomes. The preschool or school-age child only gradually grasps the concepts of classes, categories, and names for the operations of his own thought processes. At five or six months of age certain words produce an orienting response (involving head turning, eye fixation, smiling). Such responses are at first tied to specific intonations and gestures on the part of the speaker—even to the presence of a specific person in a specific situation. They are concrete as distinguished from abstract. A sitting child, for example, at six months can learn to give an observer a hand in response to a verbal request and accompanying gestures, but the same child will fail to respond if the same request and gestures are made to him while he is recumbent. Only in the second half of the first year does the child acquire the ability to respond to the more general case of handshaking, irrespective of the social occasion.

Kol'tsova (1949), a colleague of Luria, showed that a child has to learn approximately 20 to 30 connections between a word and the objective occasion to which the word refers before the meaning of the word acquires a stable and generalized character. Before this happens, a word is tied to its context of use. At about the time the child has formed this number of connections, the word takes wings: Thereafter it refers to a class of objects unlimited in number, but Luria showed that even with children as old as 16 to 20 months it was easily possible to confuse the child again by introducing what would seem to an adult to be a relatively inconsequential complication. At this age, a change in the position of an object a child is learning to name from the child's right side to his left disrupts his naming experiments. Once a word has become detached from concrete contexts, it becomes part of the independent second signalling system, able to evoke its own orienting and conditioned responses.

The second signalling system keeps cropping up in our subjective lives in an impelling way. Our beliefs, our prejudices, our values—our definitions to ourselves of things as "good" or "bad"—involve such signals. One man's meat is another man's poison—Thailanders disdain what they define as rotten milk, our cheese, but esteem what nauseates us, what we define as rotten-fish sauce. One man's sublime is another man's sin: Temple statues in India—even in the Vatican—exalt sexual acts which are believed to be, and are defined as, crimes in most of the

United States. When the majority of mankind believed the world to be flat, their second signalling system warned them to stay far from the "edge" of the ocean. In Pilgrim Salem, the designation "witch" led to stoning. Even a casual look at one's own subjective life, searching for habitual statements one makes to oneself about Reds, Blacks, Whites, or Yellows, shows the second system (the belief structures one carries about and keeps reiterating nonverbally to oneself) to be a powerful influence in human affairs.

Change in behavior generally requires change in the second system. It is deeply involved in all psychotherapies except those conducted entirely without words, such as some nonverbal conditioning methods—after all, psychotherapy is not just aimed at momentary encounter, but at lasting change. Any psychotherapy sets about to modify the second signalling system, willy-nilly. The interpretations of analysts, the clarifications of Rogerians, the desensitizations of behavior therapists—all hinge on getting new messages implanted into that self-signalling system in a reliable way.

Changing the Second System: The Limits of Language

The next question is whether verbal regulations supply something unique to human affairs which makes psychotherapy different in kind from other types of influence applicable with subhuman animals, for example, Pavlovian conditioning. If so, then the proponents of any school of therapy could reasonably object to applying inferences about the behavior of lower animals (like Clever Hans) to the processes of therapy. Since only humans possess a language, this argument runs, they are set apart at a higher level from the other animals—just as birds, possessing flight, are set apart from crawling lizards. What limits lizards cannot confine birds; an influence such as a wall will define a lizard's behavior but is irrelevant to the flying bird. How much is human behavior defined by the walls of the linguistic processes?

This is a hoary philosophical question which has engaged the minds of men for thousands of years. Can one really think without words? Can one think *beyond* words? Or do words supply the essential categories and relationships upon which conscious human thought depends? Parrots and myna birds have words—but do they think like humans? Philosophers are still differing in our times. Ernst Cassirer, in *The Philosophy of Symbolic Forms* (1953), argued that words supply categorizations that give a new element to thought and free thought from the immediate concrete details of whatever situation surrounds man. The function of education, it is said, is to free us from the accidents of our individual histories; education lifts us from our home provinces into the Great World. So also with language: The acquisition of language is, for Cassirer, something akin to the invention of an airplane that frees us from gravity—a sort of helicopter which raises our mobility to the level of the bird, immune to pedestrian limitations. With language, we are no longer confined to counting real fingers or oranges: By severing the ties of symbol to object, by sensing the possibility of classes of objects which once had individual names but were recognized at last as having properties which permitted class names, we are free to understand the general case of $2 \times 2 = 4$, whether two fingers, two oranges, or two people. Cassirer's view gains support from Piaget's demonstration that we start language use with operations of our bodies ("arms are to hug with") and only gradually come to detach words from things as we learn more and more abstract linguistic categorizations. But is this only a new cage we have entered, just as airplanes escape the ground only to be caged by the atmosphere?

This is a question which eventually separated two of the best minds of the twentieth century, the philosophers Bertrand Russell and his student Ludwig Wittgenstein, and led to differences in philosophy which had far-reaching consequences for the thought of the Western world, extending into many different fields of inquiry and scientific research. Is it true, as the youthful Wittgenstein once argued, that of what we cannot speak we must be silent? Is the Wittgenstein of his stunning early work, the poetic *Tractatus Logico-Philosophicus* (1951), who so argued, right? Or is the view he held toward the end of his life (which Russell did not accept) correct—that language is not mere naming but rather is the assigning of things to contexts and to purposes and even to such ephemeral abstractions as hopes?[1]

Relevance to Psychotherapies

The question of the limits of language is not one irrelevant to workaday psychotherapy. Schools of therapy are built around one or the other view of language function; that is, whether language is the smaller or the larger circle, whether language is the agent that frees or the cage that confines. Several examples of therapies and other types of behavior in which language function is paramount may help show the relevance of what might otherwise seem abstruse. One is the school called by its originator, Albert Ellis, "Rational Emotive Therapy." It is built around the assumption that it is the sentences we say to ourselves in unspoken words, like the self-instructions Piaget recorded in the spontaneous talk of five-year-old children, which cause psychopathology. These sentences, together with their faulty childhood logic, must be examined and modified if therapy is to be maximally effective. This school will come up for separate discussion later, but for the moment it serves as a prime example of emphasis on the verbal regulation of behavior, and the limits language imposes upon us, as the keystone of therapeutic intervention.

There are many other examples. Wherever one looks in the psycho-

---

[1] For an extended discussion of these issues, see Ogden & Richards, 1926; Korzybski, 1941; Hayakawa, 1949; and Chase, 1954.

therapeutic world the link between words and behavior lies just under one's nose. Behavior therapists expect confidently that their verbal instructions will modify the physiological processes involved in their patient's symptoms, in phobic or other anxious responses. Psychoanalysis implicitly involves the translation of vague, cloudy, preverbal or non-verbal processes into the manipulable and controllable processes of conscious language—as, for example, the patient's translation of a re-membered dream into verbal symbols, which can be communicated, discussed, and recalibrated in their meaning, with the analyst's help. Simply telling one's analyst a dream involves translating mostly non-verbal imagery into words.

To be sure, a therapist can practice one or another form of therapy without bothering his head about the abstruse questions Wittgenstein struggled with, but influence in psychotherapy involves nonverbal and also verbal channels: How the two relate and interweave determines the practical tactics and strategy of any therapy. Mr. Van Osten influenced Clever Hans by nonverbal cues—the meaning of what he was saying in words to the horse was lost to the horse. Bower influenced babies with-out words. But when the psychoanalyst asks a patient for his associations to a slip of the tongue, he is searching for the context in which a par-ticular word was used, assuming (with the Wittgenstein of his later writing, *Philosophical Investigations* (1958), that language is *not* a static code, such as a Morse message, whose function is revealed by its gram-matical, syntactical, logical form.

Language and Thought: Which Includes Which?

If one visualizes two circles, one much larger, enclosing the smaller other, the question philosophers have pondered is which of the circles, the larger or the smaller, would represent language capability and which circle would represent man's capacity to think—to conceptualize, cate-gorize, abstract, combine. Cassirer's view would be that language pro-vides the larger circle and expands man's thought by providing him with categories unavailable to one denied language—a deaf mute, for ex-ample. At first, Wittgenstein thought similarly: that language recorded what was (or what might be) the case. These records, he argued, were inescapable walls for thought: Words contain the facts of the world, as corrals contain horses. Without these corrals and their relations with each other, the facts of the world would roam free like wild horses. As the anthropologists have shown,[2] the names we have for things differ so much from language to language that one is often hard put to translate. It is not just that Eskimos name many kinds of snow we never notice, nor that Bedouins name and think about varieties of camel unknown to cattle-raisers—it is that names of *processes* in different languages vary so much as to, in many cases, make translation almost impossible (for ex-

[2] See Boas, 1966; Sapir, 1956; Kluckhohn, 1967.

ample, translating the Hopi Indian language into English). Benjamin Whorf (1956) proposed the theory of linguistic relativity—namely, that our thought processes are determined in large part by the language we speak. We are, so to speak, corralled by our own corrals.

Russell's collaborator in the *Principia Mathematica,* Alfred North Whitehead (1910) (who distrusted linguistic corrals as only catching the smallest fraction of immediate experience), once commented that every great truth is necessarily only a half-truth—every truth can only set a corral fence between what is included and what is excluded—and the greatest truth of all could be no broader in its scope than a straight fence dividing the world into "inside" and "outside." Freud's findings challenged the static view of language as code, showing that the totality of man's thought is by far the larger of the circles. What he called the "primary process" is the larger circle, which encloses that portion of thought mediated by language and formal logical processes. This is the form of thought we use in dreams, fantasies, preverbal thought, and symptom formation—it is intertwined with body feelings and closely tied to their perception. The form of thought that is used in conventional discourse, and in the schoolroom, Freud named the "secondary process." Late in his life, Wittgenstein came to agree, reversing himself almost completely. Both Russell's and Wittgenstein's views of language have relevance for interpersonal influence.

Russell's theory of logical types, to be described shortly, led to the development of, for example, the psychiatric theory of the "double bind" (see Chapter 15), which is vital to many contemporary types of therapy, particularly transactional and family therapy. This theory points out the walls language gives to thought. On the other hand, the later Wittgenstein (and the largely neglected Whitehead) supplied a solid intellectual and philosophical basis for reopening language study to a wider view, incorporating Freud's findings, and exerting powerful influence on researchers in many directions. This latter view of the symbolic function lies beneath many current attempts to escape static language and to embrace nonverbal communication via many unconventional therapeutic techniques (encounter groups, Zen, nude therapy, and so on).

Two slips of the tongue show the issue:

1. A young girl, daughter of a pianist and piano teacher, was asked to play the piano at a party. The hostess expressed surprise when the girl said she could not oblige: "Didn't your father give you lessons?" The girl, meaning to demur gracefully, set out to remark that shoemaker's children never have shoes. She said instead, "Shoemaker's shoes *never* have children."
2. A young man escorted his fiancée to a cocktail party given by socialite parents of the young lady friend of his fiancée. The latter's grandmother, a brilliant regal dowager, was in the habit of holding musical soirées, inviting the soloists of the concerts of the local symphony orchestra to play the piano at her salons. Often she would join with these artists in four-hand, or two-piano, performances of piano works. The hostess brought the grandmother up to the young man, himself a pianist, saying, "And this is Grandmother Smith—you've never heard her play the piano, have you?" The

> young man, wishing to say something courtly for the occasion expressing his feelings of deprivation and his hunger for an entrancing experience which had been denied him, said instead, "No, I've been *spared* that. . . ."

Both of these sentences are linguistically and logically impeccable. No contradiction or confusion clouds their verbal form. The sentences spoken do not mix logically separated levels of abstraction—an error Russell (see below) was able to show at the bottom of the ancient paradoxes like "all Thebans are liars, I am a Theban." The sentences do not attempt to climb beyond the limits of words—of definable things—a limit which Wittgenstein had at first believed to be impassible. The slips confirm the thoughts Wittgenstein finally endorsed: The emotional impact of the slips (and in the case of both the young man and the young woman the impact on their audiences was visible in uncontrollable blushes) is only understandable in the context in which they were used, and from the feelings which slipped out and guided the grammatically correct (but unintentionally revealing) use of language. Freud would probably have said that, in the first instance, one need only recall the way little girls say, "When I grow up I'm going to marry daddy," to understand how the slip expressed the young lady's wry and bitter disappointment in her wish to marry and have a family with her beloved father. In the second instance, one need only think of the way boys bridle at being taught manners and niceties by their mothers to understand the disparagement of refined social convention the young man expressed in his remark.

Changes in Categorizations via Psychotherapy

A look at various schools of psychotherapy reveals that many of the operations involved consist of translations, supplying new verbal categories for old ones. Therapists speak of "differentiating fine shades of feeling from one another," and "improving communication." A patient's initial statement, "I'm afraid of heights," may become translated in the course of therapy into various other statements depending upon which conceptual framework the therapist holds and transmits to the patient. If the therapist is a psychoanalyst, the patient might say much later, "I'm not really afraid of physical heights—I know this now—it is rather that as a child I feared another type of physical fall—that is, sexual surrender. I was afraid of a symbol—being on a cliff no longer seems so scary." If the therapist is a behaviorist, the translation proceeds along a different path: The patient may say, "I now realize that I am lumping all heights together, and that I can train myself to relax in a situation of slight elevation, so that I am finding that I feel more and more relaxed in higher and yet higher ones." An existential translation might be "I realize that I have been deceiving myself with this symptom—that I never before could tolerate the idea of nothingness—of nonexistence. But, sharing this basic fear with my therapist has diminished my misguided fear of heights."

Psychotherapy not only supplies new categorizations but also attacks errors and confusion in categorization. A common error is overgeneralization from the child's category "caretaking people" into the patient's later overreaction to the therapist. Therapists clarify and interpret overgeneralizations ("all doctors are not necessarily like your father"). The opposite error, overrestriction, meets a similar fate in most therapies. Therapists, having won some trust from the patient, are at pains to see that the patient begins to trust others in similar fashion (it is only the rankest beginner who values such a bridgehead in itself). Therapists also address themselves to breaking up intrinsically paradoxical categorizations and instructions ("My wife always says 'Don't do as other people tell you—be spontaneous!' "—which contradiction the therapist helps the patient unravel). Language structure, then, is for psychotherapy something like the carrier wave for radio transmission. In the latter context the radio wave has a basic frequency, upon which are impressed the superordinate variations which give rise to the music or voice sounds at the speaker end of the whole apparatus. In psychotherapy the "carrier wave," language, is not only used to convey messages about persons and things; the very structure of language is examined and altered as categorization systems are changed. This might be compared to altering a broadcasting station's frequency or mode (AM to FM, for example).

Categorizations at Various Levels of Abstraction

A matter which could otherwise be left to the philosophers, then, intrudes into the moment-by-moment exchanges of interpersonal relations of all varieties. The world of allusion, double-entendres, fine shades of meaning and emphasis, and the vital effect of context must be accounted for in viewing any therapeutic process. There is plenty of trouble in everyday life in coding the larger area of thought into language, and then decoding it correctly. Errors in the coding process are legion, but this is only part of the problem of what specific contribution verbal processes make to the process of psychotherapy. Are they so crucial as to make therapy qualitatively different from conditioning or not? Can an existential therapist or psychoanalyst, or any other type of therapist say with justification that what he is doing is of a different order of operation from Erickson's nonverbal confusion techniques or other types of nonverbal influence—or is there in fact a continuum from nonverbal to verbal techniques of influence which puts all avenues of influence under a general paradigm? Do humans have a special and unique talent which comes with their genes, like the navigational ability of warblers who can fly from Germany to North Africa depending only upon signs given by the night sky, or is this ability conferred and transferred from one generation to another by language? Or is it both, so that evolution is not only genetically conferred via mutations but is also passed on culturally as each generation refines the work of the preceding, changing language as it does other tools, moving from abacus to computer?

The point of development at which Kol'tsova (1949) showed the child able to make stable word classes is the point at which the human child comes into his own. Animals categorize; they form for themselves classes of perceived objects according to similarity and difference—the prey from the predator, the group member from the outsider, the potential mate from some member of a distant species which superficially resembles his own. The categorizing ability of an animal is species-specific —a biological "given" with inherent limits: Some sharks look a good deal like porpoises to us at first glance but neither sharks nor porpoises have any trouble in distinguishing each other. No doubt there are fine shades of coloration, configuration, or plumage which elude the human eye but are obvious to birds. Eagles are equipped to spot from the heights the waving grass caused by a mouse as being in a different category from that waving which a small brown ball, rolling down a hill, would make.

What we humans have is the ability to abstract—and to abstract at several levels above, so far as anyone can tell, the classifying capacity of other creatures. This sorting-classifying capacity helps the experienced therapist make rapid evaluations. His ability to recognize themes and variations of the human condition parallels the expertise of automobile salesmen, who have an astonishing ability to recognize a late spring 1968 model of a particular car and distinguish it from a late fall version of the same, or some other, make of car.

Mammals living with humans show clear signs of recognizing several levels of abstraction beyond the simple recognition of a class of objects. The dog can easily classify the world into family members and outsiders. He also shows signs of higher abstracting capacities: He not only sees his owner, but sees his owner's expression and hears his tone. He can distinguish whether the owner's words to him—perhaps the dog's name —belong in an affectionate or a dipleased emotional context (category), even though the word spoken is the same. He can go further. Perhaps, on entering his house, the dog owner recognizes that the animal has an expression and bearing which can only be called guilty, suggesting from past experience with his pet that the owner's housebreaking training has yielded to biological urges. Those who know dogs well can see the dog's response to hearing his spoken name, and recognize the rudiments of guilt in the placating maneuvers shown by the dog. The owner then sees the dog responding at the next level—the dog sees the owner seeing the dog seeing the owner—a sort of third level of reflection in a mirror-in-a-mirror—and, depending on what the dog sees he will approach, tail awag, or sink into surrender before punishment. When we housebreak a dog (condition him), we *change* his categorizing system regarding his bodily functions.

Humans can go further yet: They can say "I see you, seeing me, seeing you, seeing me." This is dizzying, but if this is transposed into "I, the doctor, see you, the patient, viewing me as scrutinizing you in the way you expect a psychiatrist to see you," the first three levels are easy sailing. The fourth level can be added without *too* much trouble: "I, the patient, see you, the doctor, expecting me to see you the way patients generally do—that is, as using a gimlet-eyed detective's scrutiny, seeing me shrivelling before the expected examination." Compare: "I see you, seeing me, seeing you, seeing me." Why is one form easy to comprehend and the other difficult? Is it because the expanded version is couched in different words that, as it were, supply implicit subscripts for each level of abstraction so that it is easier to keep them straight? This appears to be the case, for "I see you, seeing me, seeing you, seeing me, seeing you" is virtually incomprehensible—whereas "I, the psychiatrist see you expecting me to have the standard view psychiatrists have, to the effect that all patients anticipate the psychiatrist will see patients as expecting parental-type scrutiny" is manageable (with effort). The addition of more verbal subscripts—that is, different ways of saying things which make clear that they refer to a new level—makes keeping the levels straight even easier: "I, the psychiatrist, want to be rid of the stereotypes of Hollywood or of fiction—I expect you, the patient, to see me as not relating to you as a real person but rather in the fashion of Lillian Ross's fictional character Dr. Blauberman, the horrible example of the condescending analyst, anticipating every one of his patient's real reactions as a transference distortion."

Distinguishing Levels of Abstraction

Can one make such wheels-within-wheels distinctions without the help of language? The importance of the help which language gives is shown in that even *with* language, careless use of terms which are *not* subscripted leads to logical disaster. This was Bertrand Russell's great breakthrough. Just after the turn of the century, he had come close to total demoralization over a problem in this area. For months he had sat, he says in his autobiography, staring at a blank sheet of paper, unable to find a way out of a problem which threatened the whole structure of the mathematics and the logic of the time. This was the problem of the ancient paradoxes alluded to before. The simplest form of these paradoxes is the statement, "I am a liar"; if the statement is true, it apparently must be false. Russell recognized that a concept at one level, like the psychiatrist-seeing-the-patient, is one thing and the psychiatrist-seeing-the-patient-seeing-the-psychiatrist is at a quite different level. Statements at the psychiatrist-seeing-the-patient level might be couched in terms of height, weight, hair color, time of day, and so on. Statements about the next level, the psychiatrist's awareness of the patient's reaction *to him* are not binding on one's statement about patient's height, hair color, or the time of day—the statements of the first level.

The importance of words in helping (or hindering) the classifying problem (the thinking process) can be made clearer by re-treading the path Russell took to his problem and its solution. Such classifying problems occur moment to moment in any interpersonal relation as the participants size up each other; so an excursion into rather dizzying realms of logic may clarify problems which are otherwise insoluble. This excursion involves a greatly simplified version of Russell's theory of logical types.

There is a class of people. This class can be subdivided into a class of helpers and a class of those who want help: for example, nurses and patients, lawyers and clients. There is also a subdivision of the class of those who need help into the class of people who admit they need help and the class of people who do not so admit. None of these subdivisions, these classes, is a single person—the class "psychiatrist," "nurse," or "lawyer" is a word, not itself a flesh and blood psychiatrist, nurse, or lawyer. But the word "word" names a class of recognizable phenomena which apparently *is* a member of itself. Russell identified two big subdivisions of classes: those classes which seem to be members of themselves, like the class "words" (the class is itself a word) and a class of phenomena which are *not* members of themselves, like the class "nurses" (a word is not a person). Russell foundered on the problem of how to think about the collection of all those classes which do not seem to be members of themselves—such as the classes of "nurses," "lawyers," or "psychiatrists." If all these are collected at a higher level of abstraction into a class of all-classes-that-are-not-members-of-themselves, what about this superclass? Is this class a member of itself or not? Russell reasoned at first that if it is, it is not, and if it is not, it is.

This is one of those problems which are so obvious that they escape notice—but this one baffled the sages several thousand years ago. The solution is so obvious that, once having seen it, one can hardly understand how one failed to notice the problem.

Russell finally realized that our language traps us, in that we loosely treat the name of an object or of an idea at one level of reference or abstraction as if it had the same reference when used at another level of abstraction. We almost never specify the subscripts naming the reference level, and hence we confuse ourselves. Russell showed that this confusion of levels was behind the paradoxes. A class *cannot* be a member of itself. A "word" is not the same as the class "word." Psychiatrist (sub-one, a particular Dr. Jones) is not the same as psychiatrist, (sub-two, the class of physicians practicing psychiatry). Statements about Dr. Jones are perfectly proper, sensible, and logical so long as they are subscripted: One can say validly that one found Dr. Jones, the psychiatrist, to be an ignorant blockhead. When enlarged to include the class of psychiatrists, meaning all psychiatrists, such statements court at least error, if not confusion, and in the extreme case disaster when a psychiatrist other than Dr. Jones has the tools to cure a particular illness—say, a suicidal depression. The hot line from Moscow to Washington is designed to provide a way to resolve confusions about the levels to which a particular action on either part, Russian or American, is to be understood—is it a local police action or a global commitment to war? We already have had serious confusions over linguistic usages (Khruschev's "We will bury you") which make the point vividly: Language possession, language classification, is not a matter of esthetics but touches the questions of survival (sometimes) and sanity (frequently).

Summary

As the second signalling system develops in childhood, categorizing (by naming) moves from the concrete sensorimotor level to the abstract semantic level. Thereafter, the second signalling system functions powerfully, independent of external objects.

One can change some human behaviors by conditioning methods similar to those applicable to animals, but generally lasting change requires alteration of the second system—alteration of the guiding definitions and beliefs which control a person's behavior. The interventions of all psychotherapies aim at such alterations, whatever the name given to the type of intervention. Since the second signalling system rests on linguistic categories, the way names are given to classes of objects has an important relation to thought, to behavior, and to efforts to change people. This raises the question of whether language limits or expands thought, a philosophical question that, however, is revelant to practical interpersonal affairs, as exemplified by several types of psychotherapy.

Anthropologists have studied the effect of language on thought, and Whorf's theory of linguistic relativity proposed the idea that language determines thought to a great extent. However, phenomena scrutinized by psychoanalysts indicate that language only captures a portion of thought, as exemplified in slips of the tongue. Psychotherapies supply new categorizations and improved categorizations: Language structure is for psychotherapy as the carrier wave is for radio transmission. Animals can categorize at several levels of abstraction, and conditioning changes categorizing, but humans have the ability to categorize at far higher levels of abstraction. This ability to abstract and to think at such levels is assisted by language, and by implicit and explicit subscripts for words, specifying the level at which the word is being used. Failure to specify the level of abstraction at which a word is being used can lead to serious —even lethal—consequences. These consequences involve behavior, emotion, and thinking.

8

Thoughts without Words

Suppose one has no way to make subscripts—no verbal corrals to contain collections of facts, no verbal subscripts (or different ways of saying things which implicitly specify different levels) to designate corral number one from corral number two: What are the consequences?

Since language guides behavior, what happens to the human being who lacks speech? Does deprivation of speech devastate behavior? Are those who lack speech beyond psychotherapeutic influence? One wonders if the behavior of those who have no verbal capacity is confined to a level equivalent to that of lower primates since they lack the human capacity to create language. If so, we might conclude that our view of the world and ourselves is inaccessible to other creatures in this world. Philosophers and those faced with clinical problems, like Freud, tried to answer these questions in their different ways. As is often the case, additional scientific observations help clarify the problem. There is the evidence referred to before that inability to hear oneself tends to disorganize thought and behavior for those who are used to hearing their own voices—but is this catastrophic? Perhaps it is the sort of temporary disorientation Stratton (1897) demonstrated years ago, by fitting people with glasses which turn the world upside down (they learn to adjust to the topsy-turvy world they see quite rapidly, and soon get about quite well). There are people who grow up with one or another defect of the linguistic process—the congenitally deaf, those unable to speak because of defects of the motor apparatus involved in signal sending, and those generally retarded in their capacity to receive or send verbal messages (for example, Mongolian idiots). The data on child development help. How is it that children are able to learn language at all—and with equal ease languages of enormously divergent varieties? Lesions of the brain which destroy language-using and language-learning ability, whatever the language involved, give yet another perspective on the problem.

Categorizing by the Congenitally Deaf

The congenitally deaf lack verbal corrals. They have had no help in the process of categorizing from hearing words, such as Luria gave to the four-year-olds in the bulb-squeezing situation.

Those who are on the clinical battle-line—those who have to confront the effects of congenital deafness upon children—have formidable problems in evaluating just what crippling consequences this defect produces.

Congenital deafness so modifies the child's relation with his world that it is hard to be sure whether one is measuring the effects of the symptom itself (deafness) or the effects of the symptom on the whole complex of the child's relations with speaking persons. Is the child able to think as well as his compatriots who have the help of language? Does he suffer a deprivation of his ability to compare, ignore, calibrate, and contrast, lacking the categories other children use to corral the world via discussion? One wonders if this is a deprivation which is lethal to thought. The evidence is something like the evidence about other complicated matters —like political movements, or the stock market. It depends on what information you're interested in, and whom you trust.[1]

Since one can't test a deaf child in the way one can test a child who has hearing, some measure of categorizing ability other than a verbal one is necessary. Lenneberg (1967) and others devised ingenious methods of testing a deaf child's sorting capacity—or, for that matter, the sorting capacity of any person whose language is not one's own. In this effort, research must rely on the translation of verbal coding into the coding system of other sensory analyzers—visual, tactile, and so forth, in a way similar to the way visual signals are translated into tactile signals in order to enable the blind to read via the Braille alphabet. The categorizing capacity given by words is not the only possible means of categorizing. Lenneberg, and many others, set about to test whether deaf children are really crippled in their capacity to sort out objects perceived in other perceptual systems than the auditory one—in other words, whether Luria's work shows that verbal regulation is definitive and decisive for thought and behavior or not. Can the deaf categorize and function at various levels without the help of verbal subscripts?

This is a knotty problem and the answers are not yet decisive. Deaf children are not a homogenous population—some, for example, suffer from diffuse brain damage, and others have merely a peripheral sensory loss. When extraneous defects are ruled out by careful study, it has been found that healthy deaf children, up to the age of six years, show no defect in sorting objects as compared with their unimpaired schoolmates. They do not have any greater trouble in recognizing and sorting colors than do those who can hear. The *Leiter International Performance Scale* (Leiter, 1937–1965) is a test of concept formation which is largely language-free, in which pictures have to be sorted into classes—toys with toys, symbols with symbols—at various levels of abstraction. Both concept formation and reasoning are required for the adequate solution of problems raised in this test. Thus far, studies of deaf children with this test show no defect in their ability to characterize, differentiate, and interrelate objects—in short, to perform the basic operations of thought.

Preschool deaf children play spontaneously in a most imaginative and intelligent way: They build intricate box or block castles and manipulate toy trains through complicated switches and track circuits, and their

---

[1] Much of the evidence, for those interested, is admirably summarized by Lenneberg, 1967.

drawings are as complex and skillful as those of children who can hear. They recognize the drawings of others and love to look at pictures. They are not confused by caricaturization or stylization in the drawings of others. By contrast, mentally defective children who can hear show severely impaired patterns of play, even though their language development is far ahead of the deaf child's. This would argue that the categorizing ability of thought, cognitive processes, must have some independence from language possession.

Categorization Transcends Language

As Lenneberg (1967) points out, many of our human cognitive activities transcend the boundaries of our native languages—mathematics, music, and scientific activities in general are examples. The pantomimist Marcel Marceau can convey elaborate cognitive schemes to his audience without a single spoken word (as did Charlie Chaplin, as does Red Skelton—see Birdwhistell, 1970). Russian, Chinese, and American scientists understand each other's abstract concepts with an ease which contrasts sharply with the way diplomatic negotiations (depending heavily on verbal exchanges) bog down. When a native from New Guinea confronts American technology for the first time, he has no words in his own language to describe bulldozers or fork-lifts. He solves this conceptual crisis by simply inserting our names for those objects into his language, or by combining old names in an inventive way to handle the concepts involved. Naming, it appears, is a creative process, not a static convention—Plains Indians called locomotives "iron horses."

Babies experiment with various ways of categorizing objects, as Bower (1966) and others showed for the visual realm. The same processes and experimentations seen in the peekaboo game occur in the formation of concepts which later are given name-labels. The thought precedes the name, and private naming precedes public communication. As in the peekaboo game, babies entertain alternative ways of conceptualizing and categorizing the world: They express the same thing in different words. At first, "Daddy" is used in a general way, as if it meant "people" or "anyone-who-takes-care-of-me." Babies often call their fathers "Mama" for quite a while (this is no reflection on the father's masculinity, but stems from the infant's general classification of "caretakers"). Luria's group (Luria, 1969) showed this to be the general mode of classifying. The two-year-old child collects and applies the same label to all soft things, all sharp objects that scratch, and in one grand sweep may include under the same rubric his furry and scratching kitty. Here again the baby behaves like an infant scientist, trying actively to test hypotheses about the nature of the world, betting on what seems to work and discarding what doesn't, looking for relational *rules* rather than simple labels for single objects. This lifelong process has its peak long before the school years, but it never ceases, and it extends into all human activity including the processes of psychotherapy.

The child's tendency to lump things together in ways which adults consider "loose" is actually a great human strength. Natural languages have different ways of labelling objects and processes. At two years of age these different classifying methods pose no problem to the baby. It appears that children can as easily accept the Hopi method of classifying as the English one, and can acquire both languages simultaneously with ease. A child is constantly trying a wide variety of classifications anyway, and if one or another happens to click with the classifying system of adults around him, he acquires a communicational rule. His many experiments in naming for himself may never become rules of communication. They may remain unuttered in his mind. They may appear in later years in the form of obscure poetry no one understands, or as neologisms—those idiosyncratic labels created by poets, mystics, and persons sometimes called schizophrenics. The richness of babies' experimenting with categorization methods makes language acquisition easy, no matter how differently structured the two (or more) languages he learns—an achievement every adult who struggles to learn another language finds chastening by comparison. To hear a five-year-old child speak four languages fluently is impressive, but not unusual: Any single language coincides with only a small segment of the categorizing experiments children naturally make.

New Categorizations in Psychotherapies

The combinatory virtuosity babies show is a talent which is not lost entirely in maturation. It provides in later life the creative wellspring of arts, music, science, poetry, and all other innovative endeavors, including psychotherapy. It provides the capacity for seeing things a new way, as in dreams. This is one reason why dreams are used in therapy: They offer a glimpse of the way babies combine or dissect events to construct a world view. The therapist's view of the dream provides another additional frame of reference to find yet another working plan for the patient. Therapist and patient together can create new "languages," new ways of categorizing, with the help of dreams. Dreams often take the conceptual process back down to its roots, out of the use of the conventional signs of language, to the early visual and sensorimotor combinatory level. What had been lost in the symbolizing process of language becomes once more available as data for a new hypothesis—a new "feel"—concerning oneself in the world. One world view taps only a fragment of the world views possible to us, just as our mother tongue provides one of a limitless number of languages we once could have learned with ease.

One single example of sensorimotor stages as expressed in dreams will help the reader grasp the point. A patient, a man in his thirties, woke with a sudden start and an abrupt brushing-off arm motion. He realized he had dreamt that he had been smoking in bed and had dropped the cigarette on the bedding between his wife Jane and himself. Relieved to recognize that this accident had been "only a dream," he relaxed, and as he was slipping off to sleep again he caught a fleeting memory of a dream just preceding the one which awoke him. In reality he had broken off a romance which had developed through a business relation with a beautiful young woman. This romance had threatened to disrupt his otherwise excellent and loving marriage, but the renunciation had cost him considerable suffering. The dream fragment which preceded the cigarette-smoking dream had depicted his office. He was standing in this room when the woman he had renounced came in and started toward him with open arms. His sleeping thought processes abruptly switched to imagery which expressed in sensorimotor terms (pushing away, brushing aside, an intruder) what he might have expressed in waking life in the words "This will get us both burned—Jane and me."

This dream made no use of words. In thinking aloud—associating to its elements—the patient came upon aspects of his relation to his wife which needed further understanding and improvement. Cigarettes led him to think of early dissatisfactions with his relations with his mother—his dependent oral impulses—and the rage at the frustration of these which he had experienced in early days. This reference to angry passion reminded him of the threat of fire in the dream, which in turn led him to recognize that he had been less than forthright at times in his sexual longings toward his wife. After a period of silence he mused "I guess I was thinking angrily that I'd like to heat up our marriage bed with a hot cylindrical object." Learning to use the language of psychoanalysis, he then turned toward exploring ways of clarifying and changing things for the better between himself and his wife.

The language rules babies learn apply not just to the labelling of objects. The meanings of words one can obtain from study of the dictionary have relatively little to do with the way words are actually used. Records of conversations between adults show clearly that adult humans are not restricted to the nominative, designating use of their words—instead, spoken speech is allusive, reflective, elliptical, metaphorical, and surprisingly incomplete. A single word can, between persons possessing associations and relations connected with the word, speak an entire sentence, paragraph, or volume. In William Gibson's play, *The Miracle Worker,* a single word has brought a gasp of wonder and a rush of tears to many an audience. The play depicts the indomitable struggle of Helen Keller's nurse-companion, Annie Sullivan, to reach the blind and deaf child. At the play's poignant climax the child at last grasps the connection of object and name. Following a knock-down drag-out brawl with her teacher over who is the boss, the child goes to the well for a drink, and in a moment of stunning beauty, to the hushed audience, whispers haltingly "W-A-T-E-R." This haunting, single, even banal word captures the action of the whole play.

Idiosyncratic Categorizations

The capacity of children to categorize in almost infinitely numerous ways shows up vividly in occasional natural experiments. In 1956, Luria and his colleague Yudovich studied (Luria, 1960) a pair of twins who showed retarded speech but were otherwise normal. (Children distribute themselves according to the usual bell-shaped curve in respect to the age at which they begin to talk, irrespective of any mental impairment—some are just "late talkers.") These twins had worked out a language of their own with each other, and they got along quite well in communicating, as though they had invented a tribe of two, complete with tribal dialect. The investigators were even able to find enough ties between the twins' language and the concrete situations in which the twins conversed to be able to begin to learn some of it, much as one can learn a foreign language through simple experience in the absence of instruction—from context, that is. When the twins were separated at the age of five about 80 percent of their speech was unintelligible gibberish. Within a few months after separation the gibberish diminished, and a short time later, with the aid of intensive speech therapy, they were both speaking correctly formed sentences all the time. Luria reported that the play-patterning of these twins had been very primitive—no castle-building, drawing, or complicated games—but when their language patterns changed to normal over a period of several months, their activities were strikingly reorganized. They began to be able to role-play and to use objects in complex ways not previously shown. They began to draw, to sculpt, and to show intellectual manipulations they had never achieved before, all within a short time corresponding with their acquisition of conventional language.

Similar distortions of linguistic usage occur in families who have members diagnosed as schizophrenic. Two American investigators, Wynne and Singer (1969), have made recordings of family conversations, which were then evaluated by one of the researchers (who had no other information about the family) for the formal qualities of the communicational style the family used. This researcher, Singer, was able to detect the disorganization and confusion at levels well above chance. The discourse which goes on in these homes has a weird quality—family members appear to fail to hear each other, respond at confusing levels of meaning, and fail to make sensible closure with each other. How much such idiosyncratic categorizations are influenced by socioeconomic and educational factors is not presently known but Haley (1963, 1965) has published beautiful examples of such discourse, and described the nonverbal as well as the verbal confusions loading the communications of those labelled schizophrenic—much of their dialogue with the world mixes in liberal doses of sensorimotor (preverbal) language.

Simply removing the sick member from the type of idiosyncratic tribal discourse shown in such families has been shown to exert an effect similar to that achieved by separating the twins Luria studied. This was an accepted rationale for hospitalization among psychiatrists for many years. Currently this is unfashionable, and major interest is devoted to attempts to change the type of discourse, verbal and nonverbal, of the whole family of which one member is diagnosed as schizophrenic. Dr.

Harrington's steadfast effort to effect, with his staff's help, the separation of his patients from their deviant private languages (p. 67), which Luria and Yudovich achieved by separating the twins, has also been effective. Other therapeutic attempts with schizophrenics, such as the large project Carl Rogers organized at the University of Wisconsin to apply client-centered techniques of psychotherapy with hospitalized schizophrenics (Rogers et al., 1967), also have automatic operations hidden within the techniques used that recalibrate the patient's categorizing habits—his attempts to acquire language usage. The nondirective therapists in this study stayed very close, in their responses, to the words their patients used—as if constantly seeking to make sure they, the therapists, had correctly gotten the message. Close study of tape records of their exchanges with patients (which was the present writer's privilege) showed that a kind of continuous translating effort was going on in which the therapist implicitly crossed-checked his understanding of the patient's nonverbal and verbal messages, as one would check one's grasp of street directions. "Is my classifying system the same as yours?" was an implied message—even though the therapist was consciously attempting to reach other goals—such as "accurate empathy," "congruence," and "unconditional positive regard" (to use Rogers' terminology). This effort could not fail to be noted by some of the patients, nor could it fail to have some effect upon the patient's language system in producing a recalibration of his classifying categories, whether this was a goal held consciously by the therapist or not. Though overall results of this effort were disappointing, the principle remains: Thoughts without words were gently guided into thoughts with words which others could understand.

Summary

Study of individuals lacking the help to the categorizing process which language provides has clarified the relation of thought to speech, and hence to the process of interpersonal influence. Congenital deafness does *not* destroy classifying and categorizing. These are talents which transcend language. This is also shown by pantomimists and gifted comedians. Children experiment with many different categorizing schemes and can learn several languages simultaneously. Adults continue such experiments, as shown in the creative arts, in dreams, and in the conversational use of words (in contrast to dictionary definitions). Experiments in categorizing can sometimes go astray, as shown by a pair of twins Luria studied who developed their own private language, which appeared to stunt their categorizing abilities even in nonverbal areas; when they learned conventional language, their intellectual manipulations returned to normal levels. There is evidence of idiosyncratic categorizing in families in which psychiatrists have diagnosed one member as schizophrenic, and some treatment methods can be thought of as repairing these idiosyncratic uses of the categorizing talent.

9

The Talent
for Language
Acquisition

Contexts and Creative Categorizing

Categorizing systems in actual use, in spoken (or written) language, are creative, innovative, and subject to being bent, stretched, and changed almost without limit. The naming function of words is almost an afterthought to the underlying classifying effort which places a word in a context. Every exchange between humans involves such cross-calibration. Occasionally newspaper article headings, in their terse, telegraphic condensation of conversational patterns, show this legerdemain-with-words in stark relief. Consider the heading "Brat Fed to Lions on Birthday." A foreigner whose school English was impeccable, whose dictionary knowledge was nigh perfect (or a patient greeted by his therapist one day by such a pronouncement) would puzzle over whether some zoo-keeper had decided that lions had a special yen for bratwurst and were being indulged with a birthday treat, or perhaps that the keeper (or was it his parents?) had run out of patience with a fractious brat and had, on his birthday, tossed him to the lions in their cages. It would scarcely occur to this scholarly foreigner (or baffled patient) that the "brat" referred to was a famous football player, Zeke Bratkowsky, nor that his team, the Green Bay Packers, had elected to have him lead their assault on another team, the Detroit Lions, on his, Bratkowsky's, birthday.

Such playful, creative punning with words goes on all the time and is hardly compatible with a theory of word usage as a static, fixed function —it depends on context, not dictionary definition. That master verbal artist, Oscar Wilde, once said he could create a pun on any subject: When challenged to pun on the subject "Queen Victoria" he replied, "But she is not a subject." Children grasp puns and context changes of all sorts easily. Even young children can handle the following with ease: (at dessert time) "All *that* for daddy?" "No—that's for you." "That *little* bit?"—or, "I understand cracked eggs are cheaper." "Yes, that's right." "Well, crack me a dozen."

Children have no trouble comprehending classifications of objects which do not exist in external reality (poltergeists, leprechauns, or those delightful creatures of the cartoonist Al Capp's imagination of yesteryear, Schmoos). Nor are children as limited by the walls of words as philosophers have sometimes assumed. A nine-year-old boy asked his father what "sophisticated" meant. The father launched into a rather too lengthy description of the ordinary use of the word—the jet-set reference—and

96

the more precise use, referring to the acquisition of a critical faculty. Midway, as the child's interest flagged, the father asked "But I guess I lost you with too many words. What did I say it meant?" The boy casually replied, "Oh, it means you know what you're doing." Children of school age use words to name their own thought processes and other functions at a level well above the object level of naming, but are not limited to these middle-level abstractions. All children, for instance, use the "magic word"—"please." Nuances of context surrounding the word come across to children: A 16-year-old boy became embroiled in an argument with a nine-year-old brother about the possession of a toy, a marble—both claimed it. "All you have to do is to say 'please' and I'll give it to you," said the 16-year-old. The nine-year-old, aware of the abject surrender involved in the use of the word in this context, tearfully but obstinately refused to do homage. A seven-year-old brother, standing by, said to the older boy, "Will you give it to me if *I* say please?" "Of course," said the 16-year-old and handed the marble to the seven-year-old, who delivered it to the nine-year-old, and all three departed the field of battle with honor and dignity.

These examples point to the amazing capacity children possess to get behind the actual words spoken and to recognize contexts. If an unknown word occurs in a context which the child grasps as being a correct sentence, he knows how to deal with it. "The fuddles are coming tonight" brings a question from the child—"What are fuddles?" or "Who are the Fuddles?" The Massachusetts Institute of Technology psycholinguist, Noam Chomsky (1957), has pointed out that a now-famous sentence he concocted, "Colorless green ideas sleep furiously," is immediately recognizable as a complete correct sentence by anybody who speaks English, whereas "Furiously sleep ideas green colorless" is suspect—it "sounds" wrong, as if it were not likely to be a sentence. Children pick up such patterns and assemble them in a reliable way out of the fragments and semi-sentences they hear in the spoken speech of their parents—a task much harder than learning to comprehend complete sentences, as adults attest who go to another country and try to learn the language from conversation.

The Remarkable Process of Language Acquisition

Very young children first start to babble sounds, then use a series of single words, and then speak in strings and partial sentences. They develop what Chomsky calls generative grammar, and he has worked out the structure-generating rules which guide speech. These lie behind the conventional left-to-right sequences of written language. It is now apparent that sentence making starts with that remarkable "intention to say something," the faculty which so impressed and puzzled William James (1890, p. 253). It is now apparent that it is quite impossible to understand speech as being like a chain, the links of which are determined by simple rules pertaining to the individual words used in the sentence. Sentence generation would be far beyond the realm of the possible for humans if sentence formation depended on rules like "Having said these words so far into the sentence, you have only the choices given by all the ways you have heard the words used before to tell you whether the next word is according to Hoyle." That is, if the child were restricted to his learned experience, he could not complete a sentence. It has been calculated that a child would have had to have 100 years of 24-hour-a-day perfect listening and perfect attention in order to store the information necessary to produce a correct sentence according to the simple left-to-right, word-to-word rule of sentence formation.

This left-to-right guessing from the past usage of a word assumes a situation in which the child would have to behave like an infantile statistician or horse-race bettor. It clearly cannot explain the way a five-year-old child can form new sentences, which he has never heard before, with ease. (The reader who is intrigued with these problems and processes, called in mathematical circles "stochastic chains" and, when applied to language and grammar, "Markov processes," may wish to refer to *Plans and the Structure of Behavior* (Miller et al., 1960, pp. 145–158).

Sentence generation cannot depend upon the immediate links of a simple chain learned in the past. Instead, sentence generation starts like the trunk of a tree and branches out as the speaker forms the idea he wished to convey. The words used in a sentence require a kind of master plan at a higher level. In the case of the slips mentioned above (pp. 80–81), there were two conflicting master plans for generating the sentence, selecting and ordering the words that come out, with an end-result of humorous confluence and incongruity. Therapists watch for evidence of such plans in the speech of their patients, since slips of the tongue reveal deeper motivational plans, often in conflict with each other, than can be found in the concrete meaning of a sentence. But even the young sentence-maker, the baby at four, is experimenting in sentence production: He behaves like the babies Bower studied. A higher-order hypothesis than the simple concrete experience of one-word-related-to-another seems to guide the process of language production.

Let the reader think of the nursery rhyme "The house that Jack built," which children learn easily. "The cat ate the rat" can be transformed into "The rat was eaten by the cat" and also, "Was the rat not eaten by the cat?" with great ease. The meanings of the individual words give us no clue as to the meaning of the sentences. Likewise, the slips reveal plans for sentence generation which are independent of individual words. It is these structure-generating rules and transformational rules which the normal child somehow grasps within the first two or three years of language acquisition. This astonishing capacity is done "by ear" so to speak, as some people learn to play the piano, since it occurs without instruction in formal rules, but merely by example. The capacity is not lost in maturation: It operates in the process of psychotherapy, as both patient and therapist learn each other's characteristic individual style of expression—assembled out of words, sentence fragments, pauses, uhs, and various embellishments, called "word whiskers" by students of speech, which give clues to each participant's personal language.

Most people are hardly aware of the sort of generating rules Chomsky and others have brought to light and analyzed, and even if parents knew the rules, the child has grasped them by himself by the time he could receive verbal instruction about them, just as the babies Bower studied had grasped the spatial relations of the cubes and bar-triangles long before anyone could have conveyed those relations to them in language. Children achieve virtually complete mastery and understanding of the entire grammatical structure of their native tongue in this short period. There are minor changes and corrections up to the age of five or six, but it is not, the linguist Martin Joos asserts (1964), *normal* to learn *any* grammar after the age of eight—one can of course learn "school grammar" rules, which one either forgets or ignores, but the child masters the working language with all its hidden generative rules before he goes to school.

Inherent Limits of Language Acquisition and Use

There are limits imposed on this sentence-generating capacity which come from the limits of the human memory and information-processing capacities. The Harvard information expert George A. Miller wrote an amusing paper in 1956, in which he said he had been persecuted by an integer. Miller pointed out that seven is a number which crops up repeatedly in laboratory experiments testing the limits of human memory spans and judgments of various sorts (such as tones, colors, tastes) as well as in ordinary life—the seven seas, seven wonders of the world, seven ages of man, seven deadly sins, seven days of the week. Most of us have trouble in remembering lists of things; various tests show that the maximum number we can recall is just about seven. Miller spoofed the idea of magic in relation to this number, but pointed out that, whatever the limits to our information processing, these limits can be transcended by what is called "recoding." When we listen to someone talking we don't listen to the bits of information contained in each phoneme individually— we recode these into larger chunks, the individual words, or even into phrases. Musicians, practiced in sight reading, recognize whole passages at a glance, not each individual note.

So, too, with experienced therapists. They often astound their patients with what is for them an incredible recollection of the events of the patients' lives, including the details of their fantasies and dreams of former years that had become blurred for the patients. Therapists develop a recoding ability over the years by which whole passages ("chunks") make sense as a unit; the patient himself is too close to the data of his own experience to be able to collect them in larger packages.

If seven items is somewhere near the limit of immediate recall for numbers, it is possible to extend that limit by a process similar to that of recognizing words. One can handle a number expressed in binary notation, 010011010, with difficulty. If one practices packaging methods, organizing various patterns into chunks like the words of language, one can train himself to listen to 40 such digits and repeat them back without error.

Another limit was described in Chapter 7. Rules of grammar allow constructions which we are unable to use, such as the reflexive "I-see-you-seeing-me" sentences, which tend to become incomprehensible after the fourth or fifth level.

Still another limit is shown by what are called "nested dependencies." "The cat ate the rat" is clear. "The cat ate the rat who ate the food" offers no difficulty. "The cat ate the rat who ate the food the farmer ate" is still clear sailing, but nest the dependencies—those relations covered by "who" in these sentences—and you get "this is the cat that the rat that the food that the farmer ate ate ate," and you have near gibberish (see Yngve, 1961).

A child's virtuoso performance in language learning comes home when an adult tests his own limits of language comprehension—when the adult comes out into the same sort of arena that faces the learning child. The following is not an excerpt from the record of a psychotherapeutic hour, it is from the Milwaukee *Journal* column "Open House" by Charlie House, but it will serve to illustrate some of the pitfalls of nested dependencies (which occur also in the speech of patients):

> I fear that the growing custom may afflict us, as it does the Germans, with interminable words made from short ones all glued together. German people are well aware that their own language has a penchant for frighteningly long compounds. And literate Germans tell an amusing story designed to make fun of their confounded compounding. It goes something like this:
>
> Once upon a time in a certain village of Hotentots (Hottentotten) a new company was formed for the manufacture of cages (Kotter) with bars (gitter) in which to keep small pouched animals like opossums (beutelratte).
>
> These special cages were equipped with covers (latten) to protect the animals from the weather (wetter). The covered cages were called lattengitterwetterkotter.
>
> When an animal was in such a cage he was naturally called a lattengitterwetterkotterbeutelratte.
>
> One day a hottentot mother (hottentotenmutter) from the village of Straterstrottel wandered into town. But, alas, she was murdered by an assassin (attentäter).
>
> The attentäter who killed the hottentottenstraterstrottelmutter was soon captured by a local citizen. He was thrown into a covered beutelratte cage. The citizen then hurried to the police and reported that he had captured the attentäter.
>
> "Which attentäter?" asked the policeman.
>
> "Why," said the citizen, "The hottentottenstraterstrottelmutterattentätergitterwetterkotterbeutelratte!"[1]

1 Reprinted by permission of the Milwaukee *Journal*.

(If the reader found himself lost in this linguistic monstrosity he is no worse off than the columnist, who got himself lost in his own rules: This 100-car freight train of a word would have made sense if the middle section of it, the word attentäter, were transposed to the end of the sentence. As it is, the columnist has recounted the anecdote in such a way as to tangle himself up in a web of nested dependencies. The monster word is a meaningless hodgepodge, even by Teutonic rules.)

The Effect of Various Deprivations

But what if the process of distilling generative grammar is interfered with in various ways? What if an inborn inability to speak (a neurological defect which results in an inability to coordinate the muscles of the vocal tract) interferes with a child's babbling experiments in practicing language generation—does this destroy his classifying talent? For five years Lenneberg (1967) studied a child who had this problem, compiling observations of great range and detail. At the age of nine, after intensive therapy, there was no question that he had complete understanding of English, including an ability to read and write. Lenneberg managed to accomplish this latter tutorial feat of influence by having the child match pictures to words and to simple sentences. Lenneberg was alert to the Clever Hans problem, and although everyone who knew the child was convinced that the child understood all spoken communication, Lenneberg tested the child even further: The child was able to comprehend and follow complex instructions given to him by a tape recorder and could follow complex sentences like "Was the black cat fed by the nice lady?" when the person questioning him was out of the child's sight. This is a rare condition, this inability to speak at all, but this case is not unique. As Lenneberg concludes, since knowledge of a language may be established in the absence of speaking skills, the former must be prior and, in a sense, simpler than the latter.

Retarded children provide a chance to study language acquisition and the limits of classifying talents in yet another way. Each type of retardation, produced by different types of neurological and metabolic deficiencies, has somewhat different manifestations. The process of language acquisition in general is, however, not different in nature from the unfolding of language in healthy children. The whole process is stretched out, and detailed study of retarded children gives an opportunity to observe the process of language acquisition and the influence of the categorizing talent, as it were, in "slow motion." This is a process which unfolds all through childhood in the intellectually retarded, until it freezes in the early teens at whatever level it had attained prior to that point. Adolescence marks the close of the period in which one can any longer influence the patterns of speech of retarded children.

Of the types of mental retardation caused by various lesions, the one most convenient for study is Mongolian idiocy. Identifiable at birth, the victims have a good chance for reaching adulthood, even middle age. The condition is common. A large number of those suffering it are taken care of at home and grow up in a normal social environment. A team of investigators (Lenneberg, Nichols, & Rosenburger, 1964) have studied for a three-year period 61 Mongoloid children, all raised by their parents in their homes. The team examined them periodically and intensively with a wide variety of sophisticated measurements.

Mongoloid children show remarkable similarity of personality—they are affectionate, pleasant, and eager to please. They are natural clowns and natural mimics. Their babbling-speech phase is prolonged as compared with normal children, as is their dependency on adults—factors which, one might think, should work in their favor if these were the crucial variables of influence in language development. Their parents often give them special attention, hoping by special educational efforts to bring their development up to normal levels. These special attentions include the same type of rewards given to those chimpanzees which have been raised by human parents—that is, the reinforcement of nonverbal communicational gestures—by which adults attempt to influence their offspring very early (and by which psychotherapists like Roland (Davis, 1957) or Wilhelm Reich (1948) try to break through the disorders of more abstract languages). One might expect to see that Mongoloid children use strategies of language acquisition that differ from child to child. Because of the slowed time-sequence of their approach to language, one might expect to see some variation in the way they tackle the problem (which might shed light on general problems of influence). One child might stress vocal virtuosity, one might play verbal chopsticks (primitive babblings as substitutes for words) before trying the well-tempered clavichord of language, or a third might decide on a sort of spectator-sports route (similar to that used by the child in Lenneberg's study who was unable to vocalize) contenting himself with understanding language without trying to use it.

Nothing of the sort happens. All the patients studied followed the same sequence of language development found in normal children. Even seen in slow motion, and with all sorts of special attempts to influence these Mongoloid children, the development of language follows what seems to be an inexorable course.[2] The one exception is the children's articulation, which lags in spite of their penchant for imitation, their mother's special efforts with them, and their own normal muscular equipment. Parrots and myna birds can articulate sentences without benefit of human mentality, and one might expect mental defectives to be able to learn language by a similar route, especially with intensive coaching. Mongoloids do not take this route—what parroting strategies (rote miming without comprehension of meaning) they do show are strikingly similar in quantity and quality to those normal children show sporadically. The intellectual defect

2 This refers to the *pattern,* not the content nor the timing of language acquisition. Environmental influences obviously alter the rate and quality of language acquisition: for example, the effect of the ghetto.

does not produce bizarre language behavior—it only slows or arrests the Mongoloid's language development, and to levels closely comparable to those of normal children.

All this points to a characterizing and abstracting capacity in human beings which is not *given* by language, but is instead responsible for the capacity to *learn* language and many other communicational techniques (subject to all sorts of environmental interactions). Lenneberg (1967) compares the operation of this talent with the processes of digestion and assimilation of food substances into body structures. The meat we eat must be taken apart and recombined in innumerable ways corresponding with the needs of the moment if it is to be sustenance for us and to be made part of our structure. So it is with language: A child has the ability to assemble from his own babblings (which at first are very unlike adult speech) and from the incomplete sentences, the short word-strings and phrases adults utter to him, a complete knowledge of the rules of his native language that allows him to construct an infinity of new sentences. No one yet knows exactly how a child develops a natural language-learning strategy, but there is ample evidence of such talent in humans. It cannot be altered by any training program yet known, and its impairment in the mentally retarded only slows the lawful unfolding of stages of language learning.

This talent is independent of the child's capacity to speak, and appears well-nigh independent of any teaching of grammatical rules. It appears at an age at which about 60 percent of mature cerebral development has occurred. It can be lost temporarily through brain lesions in childhood—abscess, injury, vascular accidents—but the defect which results, called in medical terms an aphasia, is temporary. Most children who suffer total loss of the ability to speak simply go through another normal language-learning sequence just like the first one, and within two or three years have full use of the language again. The younger the child, the more likely this is to occur without any evidence of impairment of language use. After the brain has reached full maturity, in the early teens, this recovery ability is largely lost—adults who suffer injury to the brain resulting in aphasia may partially improve in the first five or six months after the onset of the aphasia, but symptoms which have not cleared by this length of time are, as a rule, irreversible. On the other hand, children have even regained full language use after the removal of the entire dominant cerebral hemisphere—a loss which in adults results in total, permanent inability to use language. Age changes in the effect of neuro-logical insults to the classifying talent have less starkly obvious parallels in the effects of age on psychotherapeutic influence. We humans get more rigid and less malleable with every year of age—but while there is life there is hope, and even the aged sometimes show a remarkable ability to make use of psychotherapy.

The classifying talent survives in the face of deprivations one might assume to be crippling to language development. The children of totally deaf parents (who talk far less than hearing persons, and who cannot even tell when their child is talking—hence cannot respond to his vocalizations) show not the slightest deficit in their language development, either in the age of onset or in the degree of proficiency reached as compared with children who hear their parents talking all the time. All evidence suggests that babies begin to talk, and go through the same stages in language learning, at almost the same age in every culture.

There are other evidences of a biological basis for the classifying talent and for language learning: There are families in which there is a deficit in some aspect of language use or acquisition in the presence of normal intelligence. In these families, the transmission of this language impairment, whether it is of one type or the other, follows the usual patterns of heredity. It is also known that identical twins show much more similar patterns of language acquisition, or defects thereof, than do fraternal twins. It is now additionally clear that rates of language acquisition follow the stages of physical maturation much more closely for a given child than they relate to any other index, as if learning to talk were hardly different from learning to walk. Lenneberg (1967) has made observations which indicate that the press of language development is almost as insistent as that of the press toward walking. Children who live in badly staffed institutions during the period of language acquisition and suffer severe general effects of a lack of mothering still manage to acquire language. Even though they grow up in large bare rooms with but one person in attendance, herself often a retardate without full command of the language, there are always a few who manage to pick up an amazing degree of language skill—apparently from listening to their only entertainment, a television set.

Summary

Further study of the process of language acquisition and its defects confirms the idea that the categorizing talent is a larger faculty and that it makes the learning of language possible, rather than the reverse (that language provides the categorizing capacity). The importance of context in altering language use, seen even in young children, points to a categorizing faculty larger than language. The change children accomplish in acquiring language is a model for later efforts to change oneself and others. There is a native talent for making hypotheses and testing them which children show as they learn languages. This talent has inherent limitations, such as those imposed by memory, reflexive constructions, and nested dependencies in language, but it also has remarkable facility and resilience in the face of deprivations one would expect to be devastating, such as the inability to practice speaking because of neurologic deficits in vocalizing. Mental retardation of the Mongoloid type, most carefully studied, merely slows and limits speech acquisition, but the same sequences occur as are seen in normal children. Even destruction of an entire dominant cerebral hemisphere with its speech center in childhood after language has been learned fails to compromise language acquisition; the child simply learns to speak in the original way, all over again. Language acquisition occurs inexorably in spite of severe social deprivations (such as being raised by deaf parents, or by mentally retarded caretakers). The thrust to categorize, to make guesses about the nature of the world, and to engage with other humans is powerful. As we shall see, all efforts to work change in people depend upon this talent. Interpersonal relations of all sorts use it, whether so stated or not.

Speak of the Devil; the Devil appears!
Folklore.

10

Feelings, Words, and How They Connect

People seek help because they suffer. A man does not come to therapy because he wants to acquire an intellectual skill, such as mastery of trigonometry or French. He comes because he hurts, and he wants relief from pain. The suffering can have many names—anxiety, depression, panic—but whatever labels we attach to them, it is feelings that drive patients toward therapy, and it is feelings that make patients work in therapy (the very words "drive" and "work" imply the force which feelings supply). The relation of feelings to their modes of communication between people, in or out of the psychotherapeutic scene, is vital to a theory of influence.

Two Classes of Feelings: Why They Differ

We arrive in the world equipped within hours to feel pain when pinched or poked, hunger and thirst when our internal environment—a watery solution—changes its composition past narrowly defined limits, and fear within the first weeks or months of life when our distance receptors, the sense organs, tell us of threatening events in our surroundings. As we develop and mature, these primitive emotions, which are somewhat like primary colors, expand and refine into a full palette, capable of expressing all the shades of feeling of adult life.

Feelings are of two main types, immediate and prolonged. Some feelings come to us immediately from altered bodily states. If a man comes up to another man and kicks him in the rump, we consider it natural that the second man's altered bodily state (arising from compression of the rump muscle, the gluteus maximus, and the skin overlying the muscle) should give rise to anger. So also with many another emotion closely tied to provocative circumstance.

People vary with regard to just how closely their emotions reflect the circumstances of the moment. We call some "phlegmatic," "stoic," or "schizoid" if they are relatively immune to momentary events, and we call them "volatile," "ebullient," or perhaps "childish" if they are highly reactive relative to the average expectable human response to a particular event. Some humans seem insulated against stimuli which most of us find irresistible—let us say, a savory steak placed before us when we have tramped outdoors all day. We call them "ascetics." Other humans react to the immediate presence of any pleasing food by eating as if they were ravenous walkers: They gain weight because of this propensity, and earn the pejorative label "obese."

Immediate reactions differ from sustained emotions—those lasting decades or lifetimes. The latter require an internal plan, a line of thought usually keyed to an internalized verbal statement. One cannot continue to hate another man for days, months, or years after one has been kicked by him unless the fires of emotion are continually fed, day after day, by signals in the second system. All prejudices have this human propensity as their wellspring. Call a blond Swede "nigger," and he will laugh at you: Not so the late Ali Khan, who delighted in retaliating against the snobbish Englishmen who applied this label to him by taking their wives to bed. Mankind's hatred has always been intimately tied to labels and shibboleths usually expressed in some string of defining sentences: "circumcised dog of an infidel," "dirty hippie Communist," "pig capitalist tool of the Establishment." So also with other enduring emotions. Love, patriotism, religious faith—all are carried along via words. And Mr. Nixon is physically the same man but somehow a very different man since he became President: It is not just that "the job makes the man," it is also "the title makes the man," as anyone who has ever held high office in an organization knows.

Categories of Feelings Given by One's Culture

Words for *feelings* are far less well understood than words for objects. One can, as Lenneberg and others have, test the categorizing habits and abilities of persons whose language is unknown to oneself. The categories tested which have thus far been described were classifications of objects and activities, not feelings. The names we give bodily sensations and emotions in general are hard to communicate to one who doesn't already know the name. When one's language does not supply labels for particular shades of feeling, one finds oneself curiously inarticulate.

The Tahitian language has over 40 words to express varieties of anger (for example, like our "irritation," "rage," "pique," "fury"). But the Tahitian language does not contain even one word for emotions of the type we call "sadness," "loneliness," "depression," "nostalgia," "homesickness," "grief," and so on. The anthropologist-psychoanalyst Dr. Robert Levy after a prolonged stay in Tahiti, reported[1] that he interviewed many Tahitians suffering classical depressions—say, following the death of a near relative. The Tahitians could not say what was the matter with them beyond saying that they were "sick." When Dr. Levy pressed them further he obtained only such comments as "I feel out-of-sorts" or "I don't feel good."

Dr. Levy pointed out that this behavior and the striking lack of linguistic labels makes sense in the light of Tahitian child-rearing practices. Children are booted out of the family nest quite abruptly after an initial four or so years of tender loving care. Thereafter, their "family" is the entire village. Tahitian children go through depressions at this age and, after a time of suffering, recover. Any behavior suggestive of homesickness or

---

[1] Personal communication.

grief on the part of the child is grounds for shame and ridicule by the group. As adults, Tahitians appear to live for the moment—to be happy, fun-loving children (the embodiment of the fabled happy savage) to our eyes. They think *we* are children. All our emphasis on romantic ideals of love, loyalty to the country, devotion to principle, and such seems to them a childish thing, put away long ago by them. A word for depression or grief seems for them as useless and passé as is babytalk to us.

How We Forge Links between Feelings and Words

The literature of psychotherapy contains a great many references to the process of naming (or *re*naming) feelings. Therapists devote much time and thought to helping patients discover that they are really feeling guilty when they think they are merely feeling angry, or that behind the facade of indifference the patient presents lies a quaking terrified child. By now we know an immense amount about the development of children's reasoning powers and language manipulation at various stages, but very little about the realm of the language of feelings. How and when does a child learn to name a feeling like happiness?

Recent studies provide some clues. In one such study, two colleagues, Dr. Richard Wolman and Dr. Muriel King, with the present writer (Lewis et al., 1970), asked children of nursery and elementary school ages a series of standard questions about words which name feelings—happy, sad, nervous, angry, scared, sleepy, hungry, and thirsty. We asked the children if they had ever felt happy; under what circumstances; how they knew they were happy; where they felt it; and what they wanted to do when they felt happy. We asked the same questions for all the words. The youngest children knew words like hungry—those simplest in the sense of having a simple cause and cure—but could not recognize words labelling more complex states. Happiness and sadness have many causes and many solutions, most of which require for description a grasp of vocabulary and concepts five- and six-year-olds don't seem to possess.

Though Piaget assumed emotional and rational processes to be really inseparable, his studies concentrated on rational processes. Modifications of the naming of feelings occur, similar to those Piaget observed in intellectual developments. At first, children connect the feeling of hunger not with an internal state but with classes of activity, often the activity of other people ("I get hungry when my mommy puts food on the table"). From the first they know that "hungry" implies a clear intention to act—even five-year-olds can say, "I want to eat." As they mature, they begin to locate a feeling in their own bodily sensations, paralleling the internalization of speech Piaget (1951) and Luria (1969) observed. At age seven some of these can be highly individual—one little girl insisted that she knew she was hungry whenever she had a certain feeling in a particular tooth. As the locus and focus of feelings move inside his body, the child is less tied to concrete external classes of actions in his categorizing, and this appears to free him to recognize the states which have fuzzier meanings and many precipitants, like anger or sadness. Even adults have a surprisingly hard time telling just how they *know* they are angry or sad—let the reader try to identify the signals that come from within that specify these states.

It takes years for the child to establish links between the names of feelings and his own bodily sensations. Our schools give our children little help in this process. Of the thousands of words elementary school children are taught to spell, less than 2 percent relate to feelings (even broadly defined)—a fact recently turned up by Wolman (1969).

Once formed, the links have great strength. A simple proof: Let the reader tell, or have a friend tell *him,* an account of the saddest event of his life. As the verbal account proceeds, the tear glands respond. Or, recount the most infuriating, humiliating, and demeaning moment of one's life, while counting pulse rates and assessing palmar wetness: The heart's beat and the palm's glands "remember" the link forged years ago, and respond as if the verbal description were the actual event. It is as if telling of an event charged with strong feelings were the equivalent of plugging in a program from the memory bank of a computer—a program containing subprograms for visual, auditory, and visceral recollections that can be stated at will, and that result in automatic involuntary bodily responses.

The symbolic process is a road that runs both ways. We are accustomed to think of abstraction and symbolization in the conventional signs of language as if they were processes something like the distillation of whiskey. This model is fallacious. Whatever else it does, whiskey doesn't recall with hallucinatory vividness the glory of the sunbaked wheat field. The raw material, the wheat, is lost in the distillation process. (The symbolic process is *sometimes* used this way, as in the dry ruminations of obsessional neurotics, who take out of the stuff of life all but a tasteless— and poisonous—extract.) The symbolic process follows a different model: It is more like the kind of distillation involved in perfume production. A whiff of verbena or gardenia takes one back to the scented night, the real flower, and the lady. Verbal distillations can lead one back down the road of symbolization from abstractions to real events, especially in the words of poets, and re-create via these words almost the full glory of a moment of experience. Other words produce bodily reactions whenever they are recalled vividly. Think hard on the word "vomitus," its sight and smell, and who is there who does not feel queasy?

The mass media and much of the literature regarding human functioning support the view that influences linked to biological processes are usually "deep"; that is, they are apt to be layered-over by various defensive psychic operations. The unpleasant quality of the feeling we label "anxiety," for example, leads us to avoid situations which arouse this feeling, and to repress thoughts which lead to this variety of pain. These defenses become so habitual that they seem "built in" through constant

practice, so that the material of a one-hour initial interview would be un-
likely to reveal (except via sophisticated inference) linkages of words
with the unpleasant bodily processes of psychosomatic illnesses in un-
disguised form. People generally take time (and work on the part of the
analyst) to get through habitual tactics of avoiding pain, before they talk
about their innermost conflicts—those which they hide from everyone
(even from themselves), those conflicts closely tied to their hearts and
viscera. In casual parlance we hear, "Let's get down to the guts of
the matter": This recognizes the layering of discourse, thought, and
feeling.

The distinguished expert in psychosomatic medicine David Graham and
a colleague, William Grace, noticed that patients suffering from a number
of psychosomatic illnesses showed a tendency to make comments in
initial interviews that fell into regular patterns, specific for their illnesses
(Grace & Graham, 1952). If one asked patients what was going on in their
lives just prior to the onset of a flareup of symptoms (for example, ulcer,
hives, ulcerative colitis, or asthma), they tended to make very much the
same sort of statement about disturbing events. Suppose the event had
been the loss of a job: The ulcer patient in this situation would say he
"had been deprived and would like to chew the boss out." The asthma
patient in this same situation would say he "had been shut out in the cold
and would be glad if the company ceased to exist." They linked their
feeling-words to external events and to the actions they intended. Similar
characteristic statements, different and specific for each illness, can be
identified in interviews with those who suffer migraine, ulcerative colitis,
acne, eczema, and a number of other diseases.

The writer was privileged to share in a research project designed
and carried out to test this hypothesis. It was what is called a natural experiment; observations are made about natural events after
the fact, rather than arranging events to observe. All precautions in
this study ensured that those who knew the hypothesis could not bias the
results. The interviewer of patients suffering various illnesses knew nothing of psychosomatic disease, much less of the specific hypothesis. Interviews were edited to remove any cues in the interview's transcript which
had reference to symptoms or the disease process. The task set for the
judges of this study was to answer a simple question: If an interviewer
merely tries to get a patient to say what events were important to him,
just preceding a flareup of his illness, and then asks him how he felt about
those events and what he wanted to do about them—can a judge spot
what illness the patient suffers by matching the "specific attitude statement," supposedly characteristic of his illness, with the patient's statements? The reader may find this idea preposterously simplistic, as did the
present writer at one time.

Graham was right (Graham et al., 1962b). The "naïve" interviewer who
knows nothing of the theory can obtain interview data which a "naïve"
judge can match with attitude statements characteristic for a given illness,
with the result that the patient's actual illness can be predicted on the

data of the interview at levels well above chance probability. The linkages that establish whether the words assigned to a life-event are of one sort or another and that tie these words to blood vessel, gland, or heart-rate responses, are remarkably stable.

We recognize that grief is tied to lacrimal gland responses for most grievers. We speak of being "white with rage," and we recognize that words that bring embarrassment are handcuffed to blushing dilations of facial blood vessels. The slip of the tongue, "I've been spared that" (pp. 80–81) was tied to a fiery red facial reaction. The other linkages involved in the illnesses studied have thus far escaped common knowledge.

Experimental Demonstration of Links

In another series of studies (1962), Graham was able to show that normal subjects (when their attention has been focused on verbal signals through light hypnosis) showed the physiological reactions known to underlie the pathological disturbances characteristic of some psychosomatic illness when they were asked to feel vividly the attitude statements given by patients actually suffering those diseases (Graham et al., 1962a). Raynaud's disease involves a pathological constriction of blood vessels, usually those supplying the hands. Under stress of a specific type, the patient's hands blanch and may show a blotchy, dead whiteness. The stress involves feelings whch are verbalized in the "attitude statements" characteristic of sufferers of this disease: "I wanted to hit back." "I could have strangled him." Hives, on the other hand, involves localized dilation of blood vessels. Fluid leaks out of the blood vessels and produces the welts of hives, which, like mosquito bites, itch. The specific stress (whatever allergic sensitivities the hive sufferer possesses) to which hive sufferers are prone is a feeling of "taking a beating," an attitude subjects expressed verbally about events just prior to an attack of hives. Graham and his collaborators were able to show that the hypnotic suggestion of the attitude characteristic of Raynaud's disease produced measurable change from baseline records of normal subjects in the direction of the Raynaud-type pathology—blood vessel constriction—whereas the suggestion of the hives attitude to these same normal subjects produced the opposite effect—dilation of skin blood vessels.

The symbolic process goes from concrete data to abstract concept. It also goes backwards from abstract concept to bodily ("gutsy") response. The specificity of linkage between attitude and bodily response has further support from the work of Lorna Benjamin (Benjamin & Graham, 1962), which showed that stick-figure drawings depicting attitude statements could be used to establish specific linkages between diseases and attitudes. When patients suffering from one or another psychosomatic illness were given a series of such drawings and were asked to select the one most characteristic of their own attitudes just prior to the flareup of their illness, they selected the drawing designed to depict the verbal attitude statement thought to be characteristic for their illness, at levels well beyond chance. The hives attitude drawing, for example, shows a stick figure wielding a whip on an abject stick-figure victim—hives sufferers picked this as expressing their feelings more often than other drawings. Benjamin's work confirms both the attitude hypothesis (the words-to-feeling link) and the view that categorizing transcends language; the visual, nonverbal, attitude presentation linked up with the patient's feelings as did the verbal statement of the attitudes. Benjamin's work shows that while verbal processes are important rule-making influences, they are not the *only* influence, since visual symbols are also tied close to bodily experiences.

Implications for Efforts to Change People

All this argues for the vital role of the symbolic processes of language and the corrections thereof in psychotherapy. It supports the idea that symbolic references of the five-year-old level ("I will fall off the edge of the earth" or "The moon is following me") tend to remain unexamined once they are internalized, but remain sufficiently powerful to mobilize bodily reactions appropriate to them. Currently, researchers are testing whether direct intervention with attitude statements (perhaps they could be characterized better here as "unwarranted assertions") will provide an effective way of reversing old linkages and their consequences.

Psychotherapy is often effective in psychosomatic illness (see Strupp & Bergin, 1969; Alexander, 1953; Nodine & Moyer, 1962; and especially Kellner, 1967). Only the personal experience of treating a number of patients suffering severe illnesses such as ulcerative colitis, peptic ulcer, and asthma, resulting in marked and prolonged relief from symptoms previously incapacitating (in spite of excellent prior medical management) brings conviction, however. This clinical experience of shared victory has been the writer's good fortune. The specific linkages of verbal self-instruction with disease processes shown thus far offer a chance for much more effective and faster therapy.

Attitude statements may prove to be deeply rooted beliefs, such as the belief in witches in the Salem of Pilgrim days. However, psychotherapy has shown that attitudes and the illnesses associated with them are amenable to influence even though they have not as yet been attacked explicitly, except for the systematic bleaching of anxiety by behavior therapies. Instead, psychotherapeutic influence has been directed toward achieving a general increase in maturity, reality, and freedom on the patient's part, leaving attitudes implicit. To treat someone in Pilgrim Salem who suffered anxiety attacks, connected with the unspoken thought "perhaps I am a witch," might have proved most difficult via a direct assault on the concept of witches, since everyone the patient knew also held to the real existence of such fictions. The psychotherapist might have been able to relieve the patient's anxiety attacks by indirect interventions aimed at helping the patient face reality in many areas other than witchery.

Eventually, the patient might come to admit a private doubt regarding the delusion held by all the members of his community.

Indirect psychotherapeutic influence on psychosomatic illness can produce improvement: A *direct* change in an ulcer patient's way of defining deprivations or an asthmatic's way of defining rejections will require a change in the patient's beliefs that may be almost as difficult as the witch problem, since many unreasonable responses receive public support and reinforcement. It is "natural" to feel gypped when one loses a job, and "natural" to want to "chew out the boss." Sweet reason comes hard, but the stakes are high: If a patient with an ulcer can come to regard job losses as unfortunate, just as bad weather, rather than as personal persecutions, like being sent to bed without one's supper, and if with such a change his body no longer destroys itself, much will have been gained.

Summary

Feelings are of two sorts: immediate responses to events such as a slap in the face, and long-term feelings lasting long after the pain of a slap has subsided. The latter require a line of thought (usually verbal) that recurrently generates the feeling via links between thoughts (usually verbal) and feelings. Some categories of feelings depend on the culture, especially the language, one is given: Without words to express a shade of feeling, one is scarcely able to recognize it, as Tahitians cannot recognize "grief." The process of acquiring the language of emotion has been given little study, as compared with studies devoted to children's thinking processes. Children's schools neglect the links between words and feelings.

Once the links between feelings and words have been forged, they remain remarkably stable. David Graham and his colleagues have shown that there are specific links between the words used to describe disturbing life events and pathologic physical changes in those suffering a number of psychosomatic illnesses. These links can be demonstrated in laboratory experiments, and efforts to change them hold the promise of improving psychotherapeutic effectiveness in psychosomatic conditions.

11

The Scoreboard So Far

An interim recapitulation: Interpersonal influence of any type hinges on the capacity to gain access to the rules which govern an individual's behavior and to change those rules. The individual must attend to therapeutic influence in order for that influence to have any effect. His attending is governed by "givens" of perception and perception processing, only some of which are under voluntary control. Once he attends, several elements of influence can be identified. The element of suggestion was scrutinized. Influence is always mutual in therapy—a rubber-band phenomenon which cannot be stretched except from both ends. Signals pass back and forth, from influencer to influenced and are processed at many levels of experience, from crude physical intervention through more complex nonverbal signalling. Nonverbal signalling may reach high levels of abstraction, and when language signals enter the picture there is no theoretical limit to the levels of abstraction, and to the interaction of these levels, which are fixed only by the design characteristics of the human nervous system.

The multileveled transmission shown by humans exceeds in complexity any other communication yet known. Rule formation depends on the categorizing function, which can be studied with profit from a variety of angles, some of which have been touched upon. Studies of normal babies have shown how they arrive at the rules, how they classify, and what some limits of their classifying processes are. Babies who have been deprived or injured in various ways—genetically, developmentally, socially, or biologically—show by the effects of these deprivations or injuries what capacities normal children possess (the exception proves the rule).

Studies of rule formation in animals lower than man on the evolutionary ladder permit greater manipulation of the nonverbal types of influence than is permissable in humans (on ethical and humanitarian grounds). Occasionally, however, natural experiments occurring with human babies spotlight the way influence develops or fails to develop. Studies of the unfolding process of nonverbal and verbal self-influencing systems in children illuminate some of the tools available for use in any psychotherapy. Discussion of these studies raised the question of the role of language, as distinct from a more general categorizing capacity, in developing the rules that psychotherapy aims to change. It now looks as if linguistic links to bodily processes in health and disease are much more specific than had been thought. Present knowledge indicates that, while powerful, language is only one expression of the sifting, winnowing, and theorizing ability of humans. Present knowledge shows that very young babies scheme and guess, in more sophisticated ways than was formerly known, about the regularities, the rules, the predictable patterns of the world, and that they are constantly testing the world in a creative way. Far from being made of impressionable sealing wax, sensitive only to temperature and external impressions, they ask themselves complicated nonverbal questions and give nonverbal answers in the early weeks of life. They seem fully capable of asking themselves, with Alice's walrus, why the sea is boiling hot and whether pigs have wings. Any culture taps only a tiny pie-segment of the baby's total capacity for being-in-the-world or creating a world of its own. No wonder interpersonal influence has so many forms!

MAN BITES DOG

The obvious is nigh obscure
The sour note is loud
Who attends to gravity?
Identifies a cloud?
What good wife sees her stirring spoon
'till someone moves its home?
We only note discrepancy—
The tooth lost from the comb.
Faceless, the subway crowd suggests
indifference is the rule
But demagogues rely upon
the orienting tool:
Difference rivets the glancing eye
(Albino from his brother):
Godivas catch attention more
than Poe's purloinéd letter.
Such a thing is influence—
how *one* can move *another.*

12

Categorizing Schemes in Psychotherapies

Several types of psychotherapeutic influences consist of new categorizing schemes. Thus far, this inquiry into why people change has concentrated mainly on the underpinnings of one element of influence, the element of suggestion, defined as influence achieved by means outside the subject's knowledge of his wishes and intentions. Suggestion turned out to be a complex operation indeed. The elements of influence called reflection, clarification, and interpretation in various schools of psychotherapy ride on the functions that make suggestion possible. These are: the ceaseless search for new categorizing possibilities seen in babies; the nature of the symbolic process, with its creative advance into novel forms and connections; the orienting response to novelty; and the anticipatory rule formation shown in sentence generating and language learning. The power of speech in the regulation of behavior supplies a basis for the patient's ability to assimilate an intervention and accommodate his behavior to a new rule revealed in interpretation, reflection, or clarification.

The differences in the meaning of these three terms lie mainly in the quantity of information and the size of classifications they designate.

Reflections

What the followers of Carl Rogers ("Rogerian therapists") call reflections consist of statements by therapists which make only slight recategorizing changes and stay very close to the signals patients give the therapist (Rogers, 1951). The patient's words are changed very little, and the therapist tries to make sure of the accuracy of transmission. The therapist sometimes risks sounding as if he merely repeats what the patient said. (One hoary joke has a patient talking to a Rogerian. He says "I feel lower than a snake's belly." The therapist says "I guess you feel really down, really low." The patient goes on, "Yeah, I ain't worth a nickel," and the therapist reflects, "You feel you aren't worth much." After a number of such exchanges the patient shows annoyance and blurts out, "What's the matter with the way *I* say it?") Of course, the patient's words, coming back to him from the therapist, are in a different context than the original message, and in addition to the nonverbal cues supplied by the therapist, the reflection is at least one level of abstraction above the original and is hence a new categorization. There are elements of "I see you seeing me" (and often of higher levels) in reflections. The term itself suggests a mirror.

In recent years, audio and videotape recordings have come into use for therapeutic influence. When patients hear their own soliloquies, their own verbal responses in therapy recorded on tape, they experience their own prior verbal behavior almost like a Rogerian reflection, at a different level of the "I see you seeing me" ladder. As mentioned before, George Klein (1965) and others have shown that deprivation of the auditory feedback of one's own voice can have marked influence in disintegrating one's thought and behavior. Since each of us when he speaks is his own listener, we instruct and reflect upon ourselves continually.

Clarifications

The term "clarification" is used to describe efforts to collect and classify larger chunks of signals than the information contained in reflections. The therapist will collect quite a few samples of past or present verbal and nonverbal behavior, sort them into patterns, and call attention to the rules he has observed. These are behavior patterns the patient may never have noticed, although the therapist's recategorizations are based on data the patient gave the therapist freely and openly and the therapist stays with this shared information—the cards are all on the table, face up, for both patient and therapist to see. The patient's response is one of pleasure —"How about that, I never noticed that before!"

Interpretations

Interpretation, as used most characteristically by Freudians (most psychoanalytic theorists—for example Freud, 1949; Menninger, 1958; Greenson, 1967—consider it the major tool), is yet more inclusive, striving to sort, classify, and find regularities of large segments of the patient's signalling and behaving, including messages he avoided sending, ignored, or in some way defended himself against (for example, yearnings he considers infantile, or that are forbidden in the culture in which he lives). If one compares the structures of the therapeutic dialogue, especially what patients convey to their therapists, to the structure of a tree, a therapeutic discourse is a very large banyan tree compared to a sentence. The operations called reflection, clarification, and interpretation concern themselves respectively with leaves of the tree (reflections), twigs and small branches of the tree (clarifications), and main branches (interpretations). Interpretation, unlike clarification, often involves data the therapist has collected which may lie outside the patient's awareness. The patient is too close to the data—his own thoughts and feelings—to observe that every time he speaks of his mother he whines and cringes. Even if he did so observe, he might choose to ignore this behavior. The analyst has a somewhat Olympian view of things, being free to sit back and sort out observations into various categories and patterns as from a hilltop, while his poor patient sniffs and slogs through the jungle trails of his own thoughts.

Great tact is needed. Interpretation often jolts a patient unpleasantly, and can leave him feeling foolish, humiliated, and frightened.

Ernest Hemingway, once interviewed about writing, commented that if a writer knows the subject he is writing about thoroughly via his finger-tips—inside out as it were—he can pare down his writing to the lean bones with the result that the writing only gets stronger. If the writer doesn't know what he is writing about in the most intimate way, he can write in great detail and at great length, but his lack of familiarity with his subject matter will show up as holes in the writing. This applies mainly to interpretation, although also to other therapeutic interventions: When an interpretation is made, it may well refer to holes in what the patient has been communicating, verbally and nonverbally. These holes are areas he has avoided, slips he has made suggesting that the tree of his com-munications had been drastically pruned and that discrepancies exist be-tween the main branch structures, as disclosed by nonverbal clues, and the surface appearance of the top foliage of the tree.

Interpretations are something like literary criticisms: Every author offers his latest creation for comment, claiming to want helpful advice but secretly hoping only for praise. The patient's reaction to interpretation is not unlike the reaction an author might have to Hemingway as a critic. Being told there are holes in one's writing (or relating) is an experience that has distinctly unpleasant qualities—the author or the patient feels an abrupt jolt. Defensive reactions abound in both situations, and the out-come for author and patient depends on many intangibles we lump under such headings as tact, trust, integrity, and strength.

Tact and Judgment in Choosing Recategorizations

Interpretation strikes for the long-range leitmotivs of the patient's life, and for explanation of gaps, those missing elements Hemingway called "holes in the writing," which the analyst has noted in the patient's be-havior in the consulting room. At this point the behavior shown by Kagan in babies' responses to distorted masks (p. 32) becomes relevant. The babies responded to minor changes in the visual pattern, assimilating these to the schema of a face they had already formed. The babies ac-commodated the old schema into a more inclusive one but were not able to respond in this fashion to markedly changed facial masks. So it is with interpretations: The rule of thumb given in psychoanalytic training insti-tutes is that one should wait to give an interpretation until the patient is almost ready to see the pattern interpreted for himself—in other words, until the patient's schemas (categorizations) of his own behavior are sufficiently advanced so that the new information coming to him in the interpretation is not so strange as to be unassimilable. To give a pre-mature interpretation is rather like Kagan's presenting a grossly distorted mask to the babies he studies—it fails to influence them.

The therapist presents new elements of understanding to his patient which supply new categorizations. But this is not enough. These elements must be noticed to produce an effect. An interpretation uttered in Swahili to an English-speaking person on the couch might well produce an orienting response and a curious searching for some category or other, some schema, to which the Swahili words might be assimilated. Most young American males would react to an interpretation, early in therapy, that certain elements of aggressive masculinity they had been showing toward the therapist covered a homosexual defense against fear of murderous conflict with their fathers would react as if the therapist were speaking Swahili—even if there were some truth in the therapist's assertion. Given time to explore the therapeutic situation and their own inner reactions, along the path trod by the babies Bowers and Kagan studied, most patients can accept such an interpretation, consider it with interest, and weld it to their inner views of themselves. They can learn to discriminate their relation to *this* man, the therapist, from that Giant of yesteryear, their father. New categorizations can form—new rules, new self-instructions and emotional reactions which fit the world of today better than those formed in the world of childhood.

Interpretive influence is not without hazards. Most people discriminate between a thought and a spoken thought. The former can be fleeting, tentative, wispy—"just a thought." Even for oneself, to speak a thought aloud, to hear oneself announce it to the world, is a commitment to action (the act of speaking) that surpasses the commitment involved in silent thought. Rogerian reflections go another step—even though what is said in the reflection very much resembles what one has said to one's therapist, one's own words in another's mouth are more a part of the world, less one's own possession, than is one's own speech. "It sounds different when you say it," says the patient. To make allegations such as those in the example above to an American male on the street is to risk a punch in the nose.

Even in the consulting room, the therapist had best know his patient quite well, know how such an interpretation will come across, before giving it. Without knowledge of the context into which the patient will fit the interpretation, the therapist risks setting off profound emotions—fear, panic, rage, depression—in his patient. The precise words used make a big difference, as they did in Luria's studies with children (Chapter 6). In the example above an interpretation like "Perhaps the assertiveness you show covers a wish to seduce me into homosexual relations, in order to avoid the fear that I would try to kill you, as retaliation for your wish to kill me, a father-figure" is a far cry from the chuckled comment of a therapist like Carl Whitaker (a lanterned-jawed, gentle Lincolnesque man) saying "Aw, quit putting me on with your shadow boxing—what are you scared of? Us queers have all the fun. You make me think of a kid like I was—where I came from a boy takes on his dad when he comes 18. If the old man wins, the kid stays home to farm. If *he* wins, he gets to go off on his own . . . ."

Summary

Several techniques of interpersonal influence involve new categorizations of a patient's behavior, feeling, and thought. These are called reflections, clarifications, and interpretations. All involve recoding the information that patients supply to the therapist, but they differ in the span and the amount of information they include: least for reflection, more for clarification, and most for interpretation. The last is the most chancy and upsetting, since it is apt to include information that the patient has excluded from clear awareness, consciously or unconsciously. The words in which all three types of recategorizations are couched are of considerable importance, but especially so for interpretations.

13

"Monkey See, Monkey Do"

the invisible influence of copying

Other processes of therapy do not so easily fit the model supplied by suggestion. Identification, abreaction, encounter, all need further explication. The latter two are intertwined, and will be discussed together. But identification is an inescapable element in any psychotherapy, and the drive humans have to copy other humans seems to be taken for granted in the same way we ignore other pervasive influences.

What is called "identification" means the tendency one has to pattern oneself after someone else.[1] Usually the object chosen for identification has the power to evoke admiration, affection, or sometimes fear and hatred. It is as if, in order to figure out some pattern shown by some human who (for whatever reason) is important to oneself, one must make the pattern in question part of oneself—"try it on for size," as it were—or, if it is felt as alien, "cast it off."

The Primitive Roots of "Trying On" or "Casting Off"

Identification (or its more infantile prototype, the kind of copying implying a sort of digestion and assimilation, "introjection") appears to rest on biological givens that we share with other mammals who branched off the evolutionary tree at about the same time our ancestors left the basic trunk. "Monkey see, monkey do" is part of everyone's childhood folklore. Harlow (1963) and others have clearly shown that monkeys copy other monkeys. This copying has been observed in bands of monkeys in the wild state, as for example when one member of a group discovers some new way to manipulate food—the other members of the group soon adapt imitatively the behavior of the first.

Freud traced introjection to behavior he observed in his own children. A basic decision-making process of early months follows the "given" pattern all babies show, which is to see, touch, and grasp. The next step for the baby is to put the object grasped into his mouth. If it tastes good, Freud noted, the baby swallows the object; if it tastes bad, it is spit out into the world. This customs-official type of sorting, Freud suggested, forms the pattern of the defense mechanism called projection—seen in its attenuated psychological derivative, whereby unpleasant perceptions of self are spit out onto the psychological sidewalk, assigned to the outer

[1] For an excellent review of theory and research relating to this concept, see Mussen, 1967.

world. When this becomes the major method of categorizing the world, the violence done to more flexible sorting systems leads psychiatrists to regard people as seriously disturbed who "spit out" everything they dislike in themselves. They are recognizably different from the rest of us. They are called paranoiacs, and their hypertrophied spitting-out apparatuses are considered an important part of their deviant behavior. One can make a good case for the idea that projections and introjection are basic, primitive, biological operations that are detectable in an attenuated form in later relations with the world. Amoebae can ingest or extrude. Such defenses as repression involve a certain mobility, an ability at least symbolically to run away. Babies spit out or swallow long before they can physically or psychologically run away from unpleasantness: Shadows of infantile defenses can be seen in the vomiting responses of adults toward aversive stimuli, such as the sight of a gory car crash.

Projection sometimes reaches grotesque proportions in paranoiacs, and becomes so blatantly obvious as to make what might otherwise seem abtruse theory an obvious fact. An internist once sent me a patient for psychosomatic consultation because the patient had a peculiar habit of belching. He punctuated his conversation as a smoker puffs a cigarette— every sentence or two he emitted a resounding belch. The patient also complained of distention and discomfort in the region of his stomach. His general demeanor passed for normal in the town in which he lived. Though in the midwestern part of the U.S., this town tolerated a range of behavior almost approaching the English tolerance of eccentrics. When I asked him about his belching, he explained in conspiratorial tones that the radio station in his home town sent messages to him controlling his digestive tract. Radio waves constantly forced an invisible penis into his mouth which ejaculated semen into his throat. All this hanky-panky belonged to a plot constructed by his enemies, the Rotary Club, and he had had to resort to last-ditch measures to combat the plot: "I find, doctor, that if I take it in (that horrible *stuff*) and then belch it out I'm just fine . . ." (all whispered to me past raised hand, shielding our discourse from imagined listeners). He had not read Freud, but he had made ingenious use of projection in dealing with impulses which he had learned were unacceptable in his world.

Introjection and Projection in Later Life

Introjection, the other solution to the infant's tactical problem of dealing with external objects, appears in adults in such comments as an adoring mother's remark as she plays with her baby, "You're so darling I could just eat you up!" The tendency to make what we love, or what we need, a part of our physical selves by ingesting it reappears in severely anxious patients—not just in alcoholics, who come to love the bottle, or in pill-taking addicts. A young girl, in therapy for a phobia which was so severe that her mother or her father had to accompany her everywhere (else she would refuse to leave the house), always carried a thermos, clutched to her bosom. When asked what it was for, she said that she had discovered that she could quell her panic by taking a sip of milk—the taste of milk somehow calmed her. Introjection not only involves desired objects and loving emotions but also destructive emotions—humans, in moments of frustrated fury have been known to ingest not only poison, or handfuls of sleeping pills, but also all manner of other objects—nuts, bolts, broken light bulbs, chains, tweezers. I once was responsible for the hospital treatment of a lady of uncommon determination and uncommon elemental passionate fury (perhaps related to her heritage, which mixed Cherokee with Irish traditions!). Twice she required abdominal surgery for the removal of assorted hardware she had "introjected" in moments of rage[2] (she finally improved and has lived outside hospitals for many years, no worse the wear for her strange diet).

The tendency to imitate, to build what one sees into a pattern of one's own behavior, certainly is not a late evolutionary achievement. Though monkeys show it, and show it to have critical periods of development (monkeys isolated from other monkeys from birth on never do learn patterns, such as sexual mounting, if they are isolated past the critical learning phase), the tendency to copy the behavior of others of the same species is at least as ancient as the fish. Schools of fish are so inclined to imitate the behavior of their schoolmates, that a fish whose brain has been tampered with in such a way as to make him immune to the school's behavior so that he swims about independently becomes, paradoxically, a charismatic fish-demagogue. His unconventional course puts him at the head of the school, and his random darts and runs dominate his conformist brothers and cousins.

Introjection, identification, and imitation look mysterious in their most advanced expression in humans. Middle-aged parents who have not seen old friends since the friend's children were babies are apt to be astonished when a child of the old friend pays a call. There, embodied in a new human being, are the voice tones, the tiny mannerisms, the minutest gesture of one's old friend. This can be embarrassing: My patients are apt to confide their intimate concerns on the telephone to one of my sons who happens to answer the phone, on the basis of the remarkable similarity of our voices.

In the light of the work of Lenneberg (1967) and others, this is not so mysterious. Identification is really no more mysterious than language acquisition. The child is constantly categorizing the world in all ways possible to him. These experiments far exceed the forms designated as culturally acceptable and culturally endorsed. Categorizing efforts show up dramatically in language acquisition, since the five-year-old can easily speak four languages fluently. But categorizing is not limited to oral, glottal movements, or the symbolic processes which take wing from these

---

[2] Of course, she had learned that such behavior was a powerful tool to get her way with the hospital staff!

viscero-motor behaviors: Nonverbal experimenting in gesture and panto-mime lead to the same sort of locking-on to the milieu (that which is the *custom* in a family) necessary for language proficiencies in the child. Language learning is a consequence of identification, or, perhaps, iden-tification is a consequence of (nonverbal) language learning. In any event, both language and nonlanguage behaviors form patterns children absorb, as if they were sponges, and build into their own rules as if they were the Japanese of yesteryear, copying all of the inventions and conventions of the Western industrial world.

One need only witness the expertise of the seven-year-old son of a ski instructor, whose proficiency puts to shame the skiing of a 20-year-old expert, to see that the same active categorizing and creative practising that leads to language acquisition also leads to acquisition of complex motor skills that are not ordinarily considered communicational (but which speak volumes to the envious observer). The children of expert swimmers learn to swim as they learn to walk, without any instruction, and their swimming styles come to resemble their parents' style, recog-nizable to an observer—just as their language use has a characteristic stamp, the local dialect.

Children and Patients: Their Sponge-like Characteristics

Watch children play. They observe other children, they imitate. Bernard Shaw once commented that when it comes to child rearing it is not that example is an important influence—it is the *only* influence. Children, sponges that they are, not only ape the behavior of humans around and about them, they also copy other creatures. What little boy has not tried to fly by running as fast as he can while flapping his jacket skirts as a bird flaps its wings? Mankind copies mankind and other envied creatures all his life long. Styles of all sorts, from hair dress to cookery (think of the smog from suburban cookouts!) bear witness. Fads can be powerful in-fluences ranging from innocent play (the hula hoop, goldfish eating, or phonebooth-cramming fads) through humor ("knock-knock" jokes or the crueler Polish jokes) to those threatening life (Russian roulette, the game hot rodders play called "chicken") or, at the extreme, to extinguishing life (the rash of over a hundred suicides in 1941 connected with the song "Gloomy Sunday," the self-immolations with gasoline in Vietnam and Czechoslovakia).

Imitation is so omnipresent one would think theorists would have ex-plored its effect in psychotherapeutic influence exhaustively. Not so. Yet again, it is one of the invisibles we take for granted. Any group of students from any school of psychotherapy give prime examples: They adopt the manners of their mentors. Just after World War II the Menninger Foundation in Topeka, Kansas established a large school for the training of psychiatrists, most of whom were doctors returning from long years of military service, not youths barely out of adolescence. Karl Menninger is a most charismatic figure, and at the time he smoked cigarettes in a long holder (he has since abstained). Not many weeks passed before the residents began appearing at social gatherings using long cigarette holders— these appeared as suddenly as asparagus sprouts in the spring. All trainees tend to copy their tutors, overtly or covertly (witness the clever imitations of their teachers in the skits which students put on everywhere there are training centers). Tapes of psychotherapy made by students of Carl Rogers sound like Carl Rogers, students of Karl Menninger, Karl Menninger. One picks up the mannerisms and expressions of any close friend. When one has been an analytic patient, as in a psychoanalytic training institute, one finds to one's surprise that for a long time one makes responses to patients, seeming to appear out of the air, which are those one experienced from one's analyst. Most parents have, at one time or another, made the awesome discovery that they behave to their children *exactly* the way their parents behaved to them, even though this behavior was, and still is, repugnant. One copies power and strength, seeking to master it: "If you can't lick 'em, join 'em" is a rule built into the species, as shown by the many patients who use the defense against fear named by Anna Freud (1936) "identification with the aggressor." This defensive identification was seen most powerfully in concentration camps (as vividly reported by Bettelheim, 1943), in which some of the victims went over to the other side, cooperating with camp guards and aping the guards' behavior toward fellow inmates. In more benign expressions of this aspiration to incorporate power and glory, children often confuse themselves with their heroes. A little boy of five may be heard to utter (following a Roy Rogers TV program) a serene and confident comment like "I sure fixed them robbers, didn't I?"

Therapeutic Implications

We take imitation and identification for granted, and so do most theorists of psychotherapy (with a few exceptions, notably Gerhart and Maria Piers, 1957, whose writings on this subject have been unaccountably neglected). Identification, introjection, and imitation are unacceptable names for influence in most schools of psychotherapy. While analysts may say that when a terrified patient seeks a therapist for help, it is a good idea that one of the two involved in this encounter not be anxious, this is not called identification. The patient, however, is presumably identifying himself with the calm of the therapist, just as the soldiers of King Leopold of Belgium in World War I were said to have been calmed by the King's behavior, leaping out of the trench, shouting "Follow me." In Freudian literature identification is apt to be called "mere identification." Existentialists, transactionalists, and psychoanalysts talk in general as if identification were not worth mentioning. Behavior therapists of recent years, on the other hand, have studied "modeling of behavior"—another way of describing identification (see Mussen, 1967).

Therapists hope to help patients grow in their own right. What they wish differs from what is given them to accomplish: Every moment of therapy contains unavoidable elements of the "I-sure-fixed-them-robbers" variety of identification. The longer and more frequently the patient sees his therapist the more likely it is that the patient will pick up and build in the patterns of his therapist. No child learns a language on a once-a-week interview basis, but the Japanese violinist Suzuki has shown that even three- or four-year-olds can learn a skill as complicated as violin playing at incredibly proficient levels, provided that they are immersed in violin music by teacher and parents, allowed to imitate their elders, and are not distracted by interfering rules or musical scores (such as schoolroom grammar in language learning). Freudians tend to dismiss identification as if it were a momentary mimicking, and distinguish identification as a different order of behavior from introjection, that early-rule-of-absorption carried on by babies.

Theorists of therapy speak of identification as different also from a relation with another person in which that person is not assimilated or copied, but rather appreciated and loved in his or her own right. In this instance, they are partly right: Much of the skill of a psychotherapist consists in fighting these built-in tendencies people have to make their existences contingent upon the existence and behavior of others—cap-suled in Martin Buber's formulation: "If I am I because you are you, and you are you because I am I, then I am not I and you are not you: but if I am I because I am I, and you are you because you are you, then we can talk." An old friend, Dr. Paul Bergman, who devoted his professional life to research in psychotherapy, remarked in a letter to me that one of the chief tools of the trade is to establish with the patient that the therapist doesn't run the patient, and the patient doesn't run the therapist, and that this is no small job. Therapy is one of the few current enterprises that devotes considerable effort to combating the tendency to conformity and survival-by-adapting, a tendency which Robert Maynard Hutchins called "the last sad message of the twentieth century."

One runs counter to biology in fighting the tendency to assimilate and to accommodate—or, called other names, to imitate and identify. Practice any activity long enough, and it becomes part of oneself, as all intricate motor skills clearly show. Blind pianists have developed an inner mental model of the piano, which becomes part of their own structure. This frees them from worrying about where a particular piano key is located. When one learns to drive a car, the first drives one takes involve thinking about the car's dimensions. After a while the car becomes so much an extension of one's own body-image, that a snarling, snapping dog, defending his territory by attacking one's right front tire as it passes his yard, can lead one reflexly to retract one's right foot. Until one has "felt into" the opera-tion of an intricate mechanism like a car or an airplane, made it part of oneself, identified it with oneself, one remains an inept tyro. Anyone old enough to have had parents who grew up in the horse-and-buggy days who later tried to learn to drive automobiles will remember how those parents continued to deal with a car as if it were an insane, fractious, unpredictable horse drawing a buggy, to be guided uncertainly by long loose reins, instead of being an extension of themselves. Riding with them showed up a generation gap: Having grown up with cars, one could hardly understand the alienation between car and driver one could feel in the disjointed and clumsy relation one's parents displayed toward what one knew to be a loyal and pliant servant, the car.

"Casting Off" Guides Behavior as Much as "Trying On"

Therapists may ignore identification, but they influence their patients via its force. Therapists have only limited power to change the old rule their patients follow: When in Rome, do as the Romans do. The point made concerning suggestion applies here also—negative identification (leaning over backwards to avoid identification) is just as much a controlling influence as is positive copying. To emphasize the *content* of imitative influence is to be misled: The response to a model or to a suggestion is the point, not the particular form of the response. During World War II sailors in the Pacific theater developed eccentricities of attitude and manner which they dubbed "going Asiatic"—a kind of "cabin fever" or attitude called in prisons "stir-crazy"—one manifestation of which involved bizarre haircuts. One haircut seen commonly was "the Mohawk" —they shaved off the hair on both sides of the head, leaving a center ridge over the crest of the skull, fore and aft, producing an effect resembling the helmets Roman soldiers wore. This zany coiffure had a vogue, imitated by other sailors, who proceeded to grow beards and long hair, and then shave their hair off in a pattern oriented 90 degrees from the Mohawk vogue. They shaved the front portion and back portion of their scalps along with most of the beard they had grown. This resulted in an effect which a totally bald man might achieve if he thrust his face through a narrow fur muff in such a fashion that the muff ringed his chin, jaws, and the middle of his skull. The direction of the furry crest told nothing concerning the imitation process. Imitation *is* the sincerest form of flattery, but one must not be misled into looking for mere photocopies in deciding whether imitation and identification goes on. Go on it does, in every hour of therapy as in every day of the child's life at home.

Summary

We know too little concerning factors governing the degree to which identification influences behavior change, especially in processes such as psychotherapy. Folklore connects identification with powerful emotion toward the person imitated, be it love or hate—it is said that old married couples come to resemble each other more and more with the passing of the years. Folklore leaves unspecified whether this rests on the model of the concentration-camp inmate (identification with the aggressor) or upon the opposite loving and admiring motive (the Roy Rogers model). The car-driving model, the blind-pianist model, even the patient-therapist model, suggest that what you desire to master you must build into yourself in a facsimile that can guide your efforts at mastery. A considerable body of research confirms this (Mussen, 1967). The blind pianist's internal piano-model remains invisible to others, unlike imitative behaviors such as the use of long cigarette holders, but visible or not, the theory-building, schema-building tendency that Bower, Kagan, and Piaget demonstrated in babies continues into adult life. Introject a rule, make it part of yourself, play with variations actively—this seems the dominant pattern.

Imitation and identification, then, turn out also to be rooted in the schema, and to take place by assimilation and accommodation. These processes seem to be sensitive to the orienting reflex, and to the categorizing talent of humans—the native curiosity and creative advance which underlie suggestions, interpretations, clarifications, manipulations, and other such therapeutic interventions.

DOG BITES MAN

Gadgets work predictably—
Man hates to conform.
Underground with Dostoievsky
men rebel and reform.
We soar past the holding circles
assigned by airport towers.
Moonfliers pierce the layer cake
—this atmosphere of ours.
Computers dwarf our abacus
and crush omniscience.
Freud and Buber handed us
autonomy's prescience.
Contingent life denies its life—
encounter gives it back—
separate, loving man and wife
confront and fill the lack.
Ants build castles intricate,
chained by instinct's skill.
Man's free-form castles indicate
creative novel will.

14

Encounter in Psychotherapeutic Influence

The Search for Encounter: The Barrier of Ambiguity

If someone were to approach the reader and say in stentorian tones, "ORANGE!"—the reader would feel nonplussed. The word-symbol could refer to any number of contexts—it could signal an air-raid alert, the name of a winning political movement, the ruling house in the Netherlands, a mispronounced command to "arrange," a fruit, a password. Such an announcement from one who shares elliptical communication with another might well be a missing word, the solution to a crossword puzzle that has baffled two communicants, say, husband and wife, for days. The word might be taken at a higher level of abstraction, as a cryptic Zen-type answer to a searching question about the meaning of life. What one ordinarily does to reduce confusion is to try to pin down which of the many possible contexts is appropriate. We do this by collateral searchings —verbal and nonverbal—and this searching occurs every second in all situations of interpersonal influence.

This endeavor is as rapid as the flight of budgerigars, and its success or failure depends on our possession of free access to all channels of information. Consider the type of information processing that goes on in a jam session or in a basketball game. The rapidity and precision of a human's data gathering and processing outstrips the best computers: The moon landing depended in its final phase on the live astronauts' ability to override the computers. But when there is interference with any one channel of information, the extraordinary ability of the human mind to orient correctly is impaired. The improvisation of the musician in a jam session would be seriously compromised by ear plugs; The basketball player wearing blinders would be incapacitated. In the example cited above, the attempt to calibrate what "ORANGE" means, it is essential that all signalling channels be open.

When all channels are open—not just the receptors-at-a-distance, such as eyes and ears, but also those signals coming from the life of feeling and emotion—the calibration of the message proceeds unimpeded. Subjectively one feels in this calibration effort a confirmation that the other person is "on the same wave length" and that free allusive discourse is possible. The heady sense of being, as it were, "skinless" with another person is what encounter involves.

The negative case occurs in situations in which confirmatory data which would peg "ORANGE" as referring to one or another context is not clear but is confusing, or, more importantly, is subject to a taboo—one must accept "ORANGE" as if one knew what it meant, for to ask what it meant would risk subjecting oneself to censure. Tact and social manners impose limits, in or out of the consultation room. Anyone who stands up in the midst of a solemn ceremony, like High Mass or Bar Mitzvah or the installation of a high public official, and says even quietly and diffidently, "May I ask what's going on here?" will bring down upon himself sanctions of disapproval, at the least—if he is not ejected from the proceedings.

Should a question of this sort be allowable in context, it is likely to bring answers which specify the level at which "ORANGE" is to be understood. The informant might say, in words, some framing comment at a level of abstraction *higher* than the one in which "ORANGE" was given—"I mean I have just remembered the name of the Dutch royal families." If the fruit was what was meant, the informant might look about the kitchen, dig into the lower compartment of the refrigerator and present a single orange, sans words. This would be a resort to a *lower* level of abstraction. The object symbolized by the word "orange" is stripped by this nonverbal communication of its representation in the conventional symbols of language. Either route works to get one out of ambiguity and into encounter —the route upward, toward a more general explanation of the context one intended for the word, or the more direct appeal to sensorimotor underpinnings, which tell without words (handing the orange to the listener) what one means. Therapists use both routes, whatever the school they adhere to.

The Delight Successful Search Brings

Such millisecond calibrations and adjustments fail in their endeavor for many human contacts, more is the pity, but in almost everyone's life there have been haunting moments—or a few hours, or a day—in which quite without prior intention, one stumbles into a depth of intimacy which transcends and confounds ordinary human behavior. It is astounding and awe-inspiring to find one's discourse with a near-stranger more profoundly personal than with those one has known all one's life. The sparrings and the conventional gavottes of manners may fall away like shed clothing. The man or woman who has not suddenly charged through open doors and found himself off balance, stripped of his bearings in meeting another, has been deprived of one of the most moving experiences of life. Encounter brings a sense of union and an awareness of "attraction toward" one another which transcends the scars of life's maiming injuries to one's capacities to *feel,* allowing one to reach to the ultimate presence of the other. Tears of joy in such moments show the close relation of this primal sense to the processes beyond our control by which we pull and are pulled by the real world surrounding us.

Moments of rapture, occasioned by the primal perception of relatedness, are all too rare in anyone's life. They presuppose the absence of fences between oneself and the other—or at least no fences which cannot be easily circumvented or demolished. Achieving encounter is a hidden and mostly unannounced endeavor in psychotherapy. If one can perceive another at the first, second, third, fourth, and "nth" levels without a jarring contradiction, one experiences what has become by now a perception almost denigrated by the overused word, "love."

The Art of Removing Barriers to Encounter

Encounter in psychotherapy becomes a craftsman's job, just as the interpretation of an unusual noise in the transmission of one's car calls for an expert—a job of discovering the *barriers* to encounter. When a patient comes for therapy, invariably his capacities for reaching fourth- and fifth-level encounters have been compromised by past experience, and it is the therapist's craft to be able to spot such barriers. Paradoxically, the patient's abilities to communicate at levels one, two, or three (sensorimotor object levels, first classifications, and second-order ones) may be *more* intact than his abilities at higher levels of abstraction. Many a psychotic patient has astounded therapists—who expect to find the usual screening of the data of immediate experience one finds in "normals." The psychotic has often overthrown higher-level categorizations and has developed a finely tuned radar for the raw data of sensorimotor communication. Severely disturbed patients often confound their therapists with comments based on perceptions about the therapist and his feelings (which the therapist then realizes he had been at considerable pains to conceal). An objective hidden in most therapies (individual, couples, or group) is to remove the impediments to the rapid escalation of encounters between the participants to the point that all feel free—free of fear, or defense against fear.

The usual "defenses" described in any textbook on psychiatry or psychopathology (and, by now, in cocktail-party chatter) form barriers to encounter that appear often enough to have merited naming. Let the reader recall the most pedantic lecturer or tiresome orator he has ever heard, droning on interminably: Such extreme flatness seldom appears in the consulting room, but subtler versions are common. The practiced observer can spot defects in the patient's discourse at various levels. This is the mechanism of defense labelled "isolation," and it shows up in a lifeless empty phrase—mere words. We all resort to isolation when we must function in an emergency in spite of feelings which would disrupt our coping capacities. Some people habitually isolate their feelings in order to defend themselves against unwelcome fears, guilts, sadnesses (psychiatrists label them "obsessional neurotics"). This is the defense Spiesman created in his subjects (p. 51) by describing the gory pubertal rite in detached, surgical terms. Isolation can make formidable barriers to encounter.

"Denial," another standard defense mechanism, gives the listener the impression that some of the facts are either being left out intentionally, ignored perceptually, or countered by overpowering statements that the facts are different. To return to an example mentioned above (p. 19), when the pastor wrote me, "I want my son to get every possible ~~hell~~ help . . . ," he had denied the evidence of his own senses. He must have had a blind spot for the information his eyes brought him, although enough seeped through to cause him to strike out the original message. Everyone tends to deny intolerable facts: "Oh no! It isn't true!" is a natural human reaction to the news of the death of a loved one. But frequent use of this mechanism risks madness, and effectively blocks encounter.

Patients don't often parade their denials the way the letter-writing father did (to do so courts being labelled psychotic), but such elisions and avoidances are orienting signals to most adults, who use them all the time in conversations with friends. Gossip feeds on such gaps in encounter—"Did you notice how she skipped over what John did last Saturday at the party?"

When, in therapeutic discourse, the therapist hears the patient say, "Don't worry doctor, I will pay your bill," he wonders who raised the question and what tendency is being restrained. In the writer's experience this comment is a sure sign that the therapist is about to be bilked. These are the patients who use "reaction formation" as a major mechanism of defense: They have built into their own rule-structures the struts and stays given them by parents, but the original intention is still there, and the patient's words reveal the internal "bending over backward" he employs in an effort to control one element of encounter (his wish to get therapy without having to pay for it) that might otherwise emerge. The discourse of an overly polite and compliant child will alert the listener to the child's internal struggle, his reaction formation against permitting entrance into the encounter of certain of the child's impulses. The observer will expect that if a permissive and relaxed atmosphere is provided the goody-goody child, the restrained tendencies will spring back. They do: Many a parent has had the experience of providing a haven to the cowed playmate of his own child, only to encounter some token of the back-spring of the cowed child's tendencies (a strangled cat, or a small fecal donation in the basement). Age saps resilience. The 50-year-old miser retains, in spite of an invitation to full encounter in therapy, his learned restraint; he remains a miser. The miser, or the philanthropist, cannot spring back toward full encounter though both might have been a cowed child once and both might realize that their behavior was originally based on a reaction against cat-strangling or feces-donating tendencies—an overreaction no longer urgently necessary.

One notices the defense called "repression" in therapeutic discourse somewhat in the same way one notices denial. The difference is that, though some essential elements of what the patient is trying to communicate seem to be missing, there are clues coming from nonverbal sources —such as tension, bristling, or cringing—pointing to the repressed thought or feeling. (One of the most subjectively convincing experiences of repression, for readers who need convincing, occurs when one tries to remember a dream on awakening: The dream escapes, almost like water going down a drain.) Listeners of the "shoemaker's children" and "I have been spared" slips (p. 80) recognized the presence of a structure of discourse not belonging to the manifest content of the discourse, and the listeners' suspicions that a double-entendre had been uttered in each case were confirmed by obvious autonomic responses on the utterer's part.

The discourse of a patient who uses the defense called "projection" is filled with references to the nature of his surroundings and intentions toward and effects upon himself rather than his own feelings and motives. The projective defense intrudes into encounter subtly or obviously (as in the aerophagic patient mentioned on p. 129) but one need not be an experienced therapist to detect its presence, as in talking with bigots of various types—or, more endearingly, with children called to explain a mishap or quarrel ("Johnny did it—he pushed me"). Instead of hearing what the patient feels, one hears how *other* people feel or behave.[1]

Limited Encounter via Emotional Catharsis

The term "encounter" refers to a global, total freedom of communication, a freedom from defensive distortions of the familiar types just mentioned. The term "catharsis" or its synonym, "abreaction," is much more limited in scope, referring to an outpouring about a particular matter or area of feeling—a "getting it off one's chest," as one might react from (abreact) a painful event. Psychotherapists have offered this experience since time immemorial, as have priests, parents, close friends, or sometimes total strangers—especially in time-limited encounters such as airplane trips or the encounters that train club-cars afford. Anyone possessing an intuitive grasp of the influence that makes catharsis easy for other people becomes an amateur therapist and could, had he the necessary titles and licenses, probably build himself a fair-sized professional practice.

We now understand the mechanisms involved in catharsis as an influence better than before. We can spell out how it works, with the help of the work of Gregory Bateson and his students, Jackson and Weakland (Bateson et al., 1956), on the problem of the double bind in human communication. The person who abreacts in the presence of a sympathetic listener has experienced in the past the elements of the double bind in regard to the matter he abreacts. These elements are first, the presence

---

[1] As the reader may know, people tend to favor one or another type of defense, which is part of what gives individual personalities their unique stamp. Habitual use of a particular defense provides a way of categorizing personality types; psychiatrists call people who habitually use reaction formation "obsessive-compulsive characters," and those who mainly rely on repression "hysterical characters." People who project a great deal win the label "paranoids."

of someone important to the person involved, someone so important or powerful that simple escape is impossible—such as parents or military superiors. The second element is a strong feeling—say, rage—which would, if unimpeded, be expressed in an angry statement. Third, there is a message shared by the two (or more) participants that, at another level of abstraction, goes counter to the first message ("If you express anger at me, I will leave you"). The next element is an injunction against discussing the conflicting statements in any way. The final ingredient is an inability to escape the situation—whether the constraint is physical, as in prisons, or emotional, as in the case of dependent children. Abreaction takes place when the injunctional element is removed—either by the person who originally imposed the injunction or by someone else who makes clear that he does not honor the same injunctional rule. The parent who can convince his troubled child that it really *is* safe, in spite of what the child imagines, for the child to say anything whatsoever that troubles him, will influence the child to abreact his hurt feelings. The psychotherapist can do the same.

Much of the therapist's expertise lies in rapidly detecting evidence of such injunctional rules, and in explicitly demolishing them. An example which medical students often experience when they first go on the wards is to encounter a patient who resists the student's history taking. The patient may give laconic replies, inadequate for the student's purposes. The beginner tends to retire in confusion, blaming his failure on his own ineptness, or on what he imagines is the patient's psychopathology. Older hands encourage the student to return to the patient and tell him that he senses his reluctance and would like to hear whatever the patient can tell him as to its source: "Maybe something unpleasant happened to you in the hospital today—I am interested in how the hospital comes across to you—what it evokes in you, just as much as I am interested in whether you had measles or not." Most patients, under such blandishments, are apt to blurt out, to abreact, about how they had been wakened the night before to take a sleeping pill, wakened at dawn for some seemingly senseless purpose, shipped around the hospital to be poked, punched, and injected all the day long, and finally to disclose that the student is the fifth person to extract the history that day. After blowing off steam a bit, such a patient tends to calm down and cooperate. The student has removed the injunction many patients feel concerning those exalted persons on whom they must depend for medical care: By saying in effect, "You are free to criticize in safety," the student removed the bind the patient felt.

There was a day when about all a therapist needed to stay in practice was to offer his patients emotional abreaction, a chance to unburden without penalty. Most people carry around guilty burdens of a private sort. They believe disclosure of these guilt-ridden burdens would lead to dire penalties, should their private Pandora's boxes be opened for inspection. The patient will disclose his most heinous secrets only after many tests of the therapist's tolerance. The essential problem here is conflict between the patient's wish for candid closeness with other people, no holds barred, on the one hand, and on the other hand, a fear of punishment in some form or other because of some habitually hidden aspect of himself. The rule brought to therapy by the patient is, if I tell, I will be hurt. Therapy for this problem can be quite simple: Having by one means or another divested himself of whatever prejudice or judgment of a pejorative type that is responsible for the patient's internal conflict, and having conveyed his freedom from prejudice to the patient, the therapist need only function as a benevolent confessor. This means that he behaves in a fashion different from what the patient expects. The therapist doesn't fall out of his chair in shock when the cat is let out of the bag. He does not scold. He does not send the patient packing. He does not even raise an eyebrow, except humorously. He may even go further than failing to respond in the expected way (along the lines laid down by parents, teachers, et al.) and offer a new way of looking at the facts in question.

Discovering Injunctive Barriers

Therapists arrive at a judgment that an injunction exists through their own orienting responses to any new cues patients supply—signs of tension and anxiety, the lowered eyelids of the embarrassed state, the beginnings of the welling-up of tears, or perhaps muscular stiffness, a catch in the voice. Experienced therapists have an advantage over the beginner in possessing some yardstick of the average expectable response to themselves and to their professional offices. Verbal and nonverbal patient reactions have settled down, for these experienced therapists, to something equivalent to responses to a Rorschach card, the office supplying the counterpart of the ink-blot. One patient waits to be summoned; another barges in without so much as a "by-your-leave." The experienced therapist notices whatever deviation (from his prior experience of such patterns) his patient shows, and also notes his own reactions to the unfolding process. For the experienced therapist, these reactions often come to him as physical responses—tension, hair raising, sweating. Over the years one develops a high-level calmness in spite of such evidences of anxiety, secure in the recognition that such consequences of orienting are *not* evidence of one's own neurosis. These data keep one in touch with areas in which patients have been bruised and caged.

When there is a block to the smooth development of communication, the therapist, like a good obstetrician observing the progress and duress of childbirth, goes into action and acts to deal with that block—to explore it, understand it, and if possible, to remove or overcome it. Inexperienced therapists are hampered by the lack of this personal Rorschach test, depending as it does upon an office and a therapeutic personality which have reasonable stability. Since beginners tend to move from office to office, and from therapeutic style to therapeutic style, they are continually off-balance, as it were. Nor do they have the sure confidence that the therapeutic process is natural, that people basically want to communicate sensibly, whether verbally or nonverbally, with another human. Lacking this assurance they cannot sit back calmly like the good obstetrician waiting for natural developments they know will occur, barring interferences.

If one has practiced in the same office for some years, the Rorschach effect of that office becomes somewhat painfully obvious when one moves to another office. Patient and therapist alike are off-balance for a while. The therapist feels vaguely unsettled in evaluating new patients in initial interviews. Long-term therapy patients re-experience symptoms of tension and fearfulness that had long since bleached out of awareness in the other office. Such patients orient to minor changes in one's old office—a new vase, a chair out of place, even a change in the usual position of an ashtray. And an entirely new office sets off a barrage of reorientations which can seize the center of the therapeutic stage for quite a time from the longer-term patterns with which the patient had been struggling.

Varied Levels of Barriers

There are many varieties of injunctions, of inhibitory rules. Much of what goes on in supervision of psychotherapy concentrates on helping the student recognize the garden and hot-house varieties of blocks that one can expect in the patient's efforts to communicate. One learns to recognize barriers close to awareness and to explore these first: Does the patient feel what he says will get him in hot water outside the consulting room? Who will share what the therapist, however tolerant the therapist himself is, learns about the patient? The therapist may convince the patient that no penalties attach to the disclosure of some behavior, feeling, or thought the patient utters, but can the patient trust that everyone else who might learn of what he tells the therapist will grant him the same immunity? Confidentiality supplies a chance to test safely the disclosure of things one fears might wreck one's marriage or one's children or one's job—even put one in jail.

Psychoanalysts call the process of detection and resolution of these roadblocks "resistance analysis." All that one knows about the patient (and all other patients studied to date) helps one to figure out what might be putting up a roadblock in the patient's effort to disclose himself. Once more, the tree of communication analogy applies: Patients slow down (resist) for all sorts of reasons, which conform to the leaf-twig-branch-trunk figure. Experience has counseled dealing first with the leaves (the barriers any sensible person might throw up in dealing with with a psychiatrist—such as newness or painful experience with other doctors) and only later with the twigs (past patterns of unpleasant feelings with powerful authorities) and still later with the main branches (the slow-burning smoldering gripes or fears that pervade large segments of the patient's life).

Life Experience: A School for Therapeutic Tact (and Tactics)

Removing barriers is not as mysterious a process as the literature of psychotherapy often suggests. The people who do psychotherapy have had many years to develop tact (the word is derived from a root meaning "touch"). They cannot, these therapists, reach graduate school in whatever field they study (medicine, psychology, social work, theology) without experiencing enormous numbers of human encounters that leave an impact on their rules of tactful human communications. Medical students seem to have a particularly hard time remembering this: Apparently, for most people, to present oneself as "Dr. So-and-So" carries with it quite an awesome assumption of responsibility, which, for a while, overrides social tact and makes for stilted stiffness in first encounters with patients. (This seems less of a problem to women in medical school—the title "doctor" seems to throw them less.) A medical student may begin by asking a patient, "What is your chief complaint?" This can put the *coup de grâce* to the possibility of encounter.

Tact acquired in social life forms the baseline for therapeutic encounter. The ancient tea ceremony of those most civilized people, the Chinese, was developed to take account of the need for people to share pleasure and safety before confronting potentially divisive issues. Having shared a common experience at the "twig" level of experience (one that all humans value) and having begun an encounter in the enjoyment of the tea, one feels affirmed and confirmed by oneself and the person sharing such an experience. If the reader has ever had the experience of being in company that considers him a representative of an unwanted minority—subject to hostile prejudice—the importance of "twig" amenities has been made vivid to him. One puts aside race relations, political views, one's sexual preferences, and all similarly highly charged matters for discussion, until a safe baseline has been established with another person. If one is white, one need only go to a country like Trinidad and swim at a beach where one is the only person with white skin to feel strange and unwanted. If a young black man approaches a white woman swimming in such waters, the woman feels apprehension. Should the young man say, "Get lost, whitey!" she would feel yet more apprehension, and if a nonverbal approach at somatic levels were to result, she would feel sheer terror. But if the black man says to the woman with a grin, "Man, you sure swim good!" fear departs.

Experience as a Patient

Therapists try to establish encounter, remove barriers to encounter, and achieve abreaction whatever their therapeutic affiliation, their experience or lack of it, or their familiarity with the culture or social class of their patients. Therapists who merit being called a "good therapist" by patients and colleagues usually have especial talent in discovering these barriers and dissolving them. In becoming a therapist one comes up against the limits imposed by one's own inhibitions and injunctional rules: It is well for the therapist to have been a patient himself—a patient of a therapist whose freedom in encounter was sufficiently greater than those of the beginning therapist—to help him dissolve his own prejudices. This is one of the reasons for the requirement that one undergo a training analysis to become a psychoanalyst. Other schools do not have this requirement, but some experience as a patient is encouraged by many. In becoming a therapist it is hard to raise oneself by one's bootstraps. It is hard to discover barriers to encounter when one shares them with a patient: A belief in witchcraft shared jointly with one's patient narrows the field of discussion.

Summary

People seek encounter, despite many barriers. The first, ambiguity of communication, can be resolved by collateral searching for information at various levels of the symbolic process. Provided this is permissible, encounter proceeds and brings experiences treasured by mankind. When barriers exist in a relationship, changing them requires art. People who come for psychotherapy bring many barriers, and the craftsmanship of psychotherapy consists in part in the rapid, skillful discovery and removal of barriers. Some frequently seen barriers are those related to the mechanisms of defense against anxiety (which are listed in many texts of psychology and psychiatry). Removal of injunctions against free discourse results in emotional catharsis ("abreaction"). Such a change breaks up double binds—those pervasive "damned if you do, damned if you don't" human dilemmas. The discovery of barriers to encounter occurs more easily with the aid of a constant setting against which to compare one person's reaction with another's. Barriers have different levels of meaning and importance. The tactics and strategy of changing barriers requires decision concerning which barriers ought to be challenged first. Experience argues that therapists should address themselves to sensible commonplace blocks first, and only later to those barriers further removed from awareness. Life experience and experience as a psychotherapeutic patient both assist mightily in developing psychotherapeutic tact and in achieving encounter.

This chapter has dealt with relatively uncomplicated barriers and their resolution. More intricate blockages of the internal and external dialogues humans carry on continuously will be described subsequently.

15

Beliefs, Paradoxical Plans, and Their Therapeutic Use

Pervasiveness of Paradoxical Messages

The photographer Baron Wolman, driving along a Los Angeles freeway, glanced upward when crossing under one of the overhead trestles which usually carry such messages as "Sun Valley Turnoff One-Quarter Mile." He saw an apparently authentic sign which said:

```
IGNORE THIS SIGN
```

In noticing it (he was so startled that he was a mile past it before it sank into his consciousness), he was disobeying its instruction. He was influenced by the sign enough to drive some ten miles out of his way to go back in order to get a snapshot of it (which the reader may have seen in *Life Magazine's* "Miscellany" section). If he had driven along, saying to himself something like, "OK, some wise-guy has finally made fun of the gestapo rules of freeway travel," he would have obeyed the sign at least at one level, while simultaneously disobeying it at another. "I know you expect to be directed," said the sign. "This one time forget what you expected to be here on a sign." This is a sensible message at one level. The direction to ignore, taken literally, however, defeats itself, for to obey it, one must disobey it.

Those who study children's attempts to make sense of the world—like Bower, Kagan, Piaget, and Lenneberg, cited earlier—risk falling into the easy assumption that "Ignore This Sign" messages in one's internal plans are the exception, not the rule. Psychiatrists have long known that such paradoxical instructions are more the rule than the exception in the internal lives of many patients who seek a psychiatrist's help. (Dan Greenberg's *How To Be A Jewish Mother* or Phillip Roth's *Portnoy's Complaint* give poignant examples of this type of bollixed-up message sending and its consequences when internalized—but, as Greenberg writes, one need not be a mother, nor Jewish, to inflict similar confusions.) One can easily inflict paradoxes on one's children, spouse, friends, or, if one is a psychotherapist, one's patients. In the latter case, paradoxes can be used in the service of therapy.

The breaking up of injunctions so that abreactions can take place when the inhibitory rules are broken, and so that encounter can proceed, is only the beginning of psychotherapy. The dead hand of the past lays its hand on the living creative present in many subtle fashions. One of these has been explored at some length above—the confusion of classifying levels involved in the "I am a liar" problem. Our internal rule-making and rule-following operations are compounded by the errors and the confusions of these same operations. Classifying experiments of the sort babies make can come a cropper, because there is nothing in the nature of the categorizing process itself which guarantees successful, relevant, workable classifications.

Once recognized, double binds and paradoxical messages can be seen in most human encounters, producing damned-if-you-do-and-damned-if-you-don't dilemmas. Jay Haley, in *Strategies of Psychotherapy* (1963), has brilliantly shown how these pervade the psychotherapeutic scene. For example, the cornerstone of psychoanalytic technique is free association, which means simply encouraging the patient to say whatever comes to his mind without any restraint whatever. This instruction to the patient is of the same form as the directive "Ignore This Sign" since, as Haley points out, in being told to be spontaneous the patient is being instructed to be unspontaneous—in other words, to do as he is told.

Beliefs and Their Power in Encounter

What can't be seen are *internalized* instructions (for example, the defense mechanisms dealt with in the last chapter, such as denial and repression, and also such self-instructions as are expressed in the psychosomatic "attitude statements" described in Chapter 10). Impediments to encounter can come from interferences in any component of experience—fixed thought patterns (such as prejudices), sense perceptions that jar the sensibilities (grotesque ugliness of a participant), or drives which arouse internal fear and defense (a passionate yearning for contact and intimacy with another that is forbidden by custom, mores, or one's own unique values). It is easy to fall into a habit of thought in which one of these components is neglected or ignored.

This is the marring fault of an otherwise penetrating study of therapeutic tactics and strategies (see Haley, 1963), and the same flaw pervades the writings of those theorists of therapy who consider only the overt moves of therapy (the "transactionalists" in general). They study and write about psychotherapy as if there were no such things as feelings, beliefs, or plans—as if speech and gesture were adequate to describe therapy. These theorists look at therapy as if it were the same as a chess game, and indeed frequently refer to human relations in the terms of game theory (for example, Eric Berne's recent best seller, *Games People Play*). One can describe chess games by diagrams and conventional symbols. These dry symbols cannot convey the moment of high drama when a chess master such as Paul Morphy (a nineteenth-century virtuoso, still revered in chess circles) pursues an apparently suicidal series of sacrifice moves, only to move in for the kill at the last moment. The old Latin proverb, "Nature, expelled with a pitchfork, always returns," applies even to chess notations: Written accounts of this supposedly cerebral game contain signals which show the "expelled" emotion, such as P-Q4!", meaning that the pawn was moved in a fashion that any knowledgeable chess player would consider noteworthy—even, exclamation point, astounding!

Neglect of the emotional and subjective aspects of encounter is neglect of elements essential for psychotherapy, which can be shown by one example. Haley, a transactionalist who spurns considerations of what one might assume to be going on inside a patient's head, sees the essential elements of therapy as follows: First, a benevolent framework in which change is, by mutual definition of therapist and patient, to take place in the patient; second, encouragement to continue the old behavior; and third, an ordeal which will continue as long as the old behavior persists. (This model fits the type of therapeutic influence called "negative practice" which will be taken up later in this chapter.) Suppose a patient complains of insomnia; one first receives his promise that he will do as he is told by the therapist, and then one prescribes an unpleasant task (such as push-ups or floor scrubbing), which is to be performed whenever he has trouble falling asleep, and preferably for increasing periods— say, one hour the first night, two the second, three the third, and so on —as long as the symptom persists.

There is no mention of feeling in this model of therapy. The cognitive emphasis of this formulation recalls the one Piaget expressed: Without a problem there is no learning. The myopia of this formulation is that it leaves most of the profound experiences of mankind out of account. Many geniuses have undergone profound changes of heart which reversed their life-courses (Tolstoy and Dostoievsky—or Saint Paul). Nor is it only the genius who undergoes massive emotional experience that changes his destiny, with or without benefit of therapy: I once saw a man who had been for years a drunk who would have made Huck Finn's father seem a temperate man by comparison—the day his mother died he had forsworn drink and had remained sober for the 12 years thereafter before I saw him. Beliefs held with strong feeling guide behavior, without any transactional implication. The hermit, the ascetic, the saint, the explorer do not require an audience to transact with—it is their inner convictions, charged with strong feelings, that keep them going on a narrow path in the wilderness. Transactional issues are irrelevant to a St. Francis with his birds.

Encounter at the level of profound feeling has always touched the poet in every man, and writers have used this knowledge to achieve their impact—from Sophocles' Oedipus through Hugo's Jean Valjean in *Les Miserables*, to current depictions of its *failure* in such movies as "The Graduate." Franz Alexander and Thomas French (1946) were, of recent theorists of therapy, most aware of the impact of encounter, using the conversion of Jean Valjean as their model. Valjean's whole life-style and rules of behavior altered as a result of an extraordinarily moving encounter with a priest who gave freely to him instead of seeking his punishment. Religious conversions by the thousands attest the power of changes in internal rules in the guidance of feelings and behavior, quite apart from game-playing manipulations.

The influence of internal expectations and beliefs, the overriding importance of how one feels about the world in one's internalized "mediating system," sometimes assumes extraordinary proportions:

Some 12 years ago I received a phone call from a distraught man in a nearby city. A teacher by profession, a bachelor, this man was unable to travel because of a severe phobia. He suffered attacks of paroxysmal tachycardia, a condition in which the heart's pacemaker is disordered. In these attacks his pulse would rise to such a level as to be uncountable—over 300 beats per minute. The patient was aware that such attacks sometimes ended in death, and was also quite aware that fear can trigger the onset of the attack. In this respect he was in the classical double bind. He could not escape himself, he could not control his condition by commenting on it, but he knew that his fear was likely to provoke the very thing he feared. He had many such attacks and had learned that they could be terminated by the intravenous injection of a sedative, Sodium Amytal. This, of course, required a doctor. He had numerous experiences of trying to find an available physician, waiting in terror until the physician arrived, and of being unable to persuade the physician that he needed immediate help but having to recount his medical history while fighting mortal terror. Usually, the available doctor took convincing. The patient began to limit his sphere of movements to areas in which he knew there were numerous physicians who knew him and could give him quick relief from what he, a former front-line infantryman, felt to be the most agonizing fear he had ever experienced—in his view the most agonizing fear known to man. A vicious circle closed in on the patient inexorably: Fearing an attack if he moved away from hospitals and doctor's offices, he would become ever more frightened—which would set off an attack. He was only able to move around freely if he could arrange to have a physician accompany him. The influence of his faith in the doctor sufficed to prevent attacks, as he never once had to be injected.

The patient had at that time seen five different psychiatrists, none of whom had any success in helping him overcome the problem. Although my schedule book was crowded, the patient sounded so desperate that an initial consultation, with an eye to referral, was arranged (a young resident physician was hired to go and fetch him). In person, he managed to convey the depths of his anguish and despair. A shy person, gifted with considerable literary talents, he managed somehow to express both misery and wry humor in a curious combination that, it turned out, most people he came in contact with found quite winning. He had many emotional problems and conflicts, the most central of which was a fear of death. This fear had a special history for him: He had witnessed, at the age of five, his brother's drowning. Even more, he had been implicated in his brother's death (in his own eyes) because of what he remembered as a curiously deliberate and dilatory search for rescuing adults—he let his mother finish a long telephone conversation before telling her that his brother was floating face down in a nearby creek. More he could not remember.

In this matter, as in all emotionally charged matters, his attempt to discuss his feelings was blocked by the threat of provoking an attack of tachycardia.

He was referred to a skillful colleague who began treating him immediately. Things did not go well. His ability to use any "insight-oriented" treatment was compromised by the ever-present symptom. After working for more than a year with this colleague, the patient withdrew from therapy. One of his former doctors had given him a mild sedative to help him control his panic (at one time or another he had used every tranquilizer then known). The patient became addicted to this drug. His ability to work decreased. His mobility at last diminished to a triangular area bounded by imaginary lines drawn between three local hospitals. As his life constricted, so did his remaining satisfactions, and soon a peptic ulcer added to his misery.

Feeling his life ebbing away and dreading the prospect of permanent hospitalization, he once more consulted me. He was by then out of reach of anything as ephemeral as talk. Something drastic seemed called for. I considered such desperate measures as teaching the patient to give himself intravenous sedation. This was discarded as potentially lethal. Finally, I consulted an anesthesiologist colleague and asked him, "Isn't there something this man can use safely to anesthetize himself and abort an attack?" By happy chance the anesthesiologist, Dr. Sidney Orth, replied that during World War II he had helped to develop a short-acting anesthetic designed to ease the pain of men wounded or burned in armored tanks. Their removal from the tank at the battlefield often required strenuous manipulation and gyrations, and both victims and rescuers yearned for some way to alleviate the ghastly agony involved in such procedures. Inhalation of this nonexplosive anesthetic brings very rapid anesthesia lasting only a few moments; however, the injured man could repeatedly and safely inhale this agent and thus achieve safe surcease from suffering.

After purchasing the necessary equipment (a small portable inhaler), the patient was instructed in its use, and in a gingerly manner, tried it out several times in my presence. He then experimented with it at home. Once he was satisfied he need not fear the helpless state of waiting in terror for the doctor to appear, but could instead influence himself to achieve instant sleep, the change in his life was almost miraculous. Within days he was exploring the countryside, which he had not seen in years, always carrying his trusty inhaler with him. Next came a plane trip to New York to visit a beloved sister, which involved going through the Holland Tunnel. Ironically, he was caught in a traffic jam in the rush hour (a situation he would have avoided at all cost previously—but which he handled with perfect aplomb). Within a month or so he was happily touring Europe. His ulcer healed. He was a man transformed, liberated—and as happy as children at Christmas are supposed to be. He began to explore and work through, in psychotherapy, many of his problems, which had so long been shelved. Five years later, after only brief therapy, though by no means a normal man, he told me his problem had remained solved so that he had had not one attack and most extraordinary of all, that he had not once had to use the inhaler.

Our encounters had not followed Haley's model: I did not force him, through a series of ordeals in our relationship, to change his life style—he discovered by the use of the inhaler that he need not depend on anyone but himself, in extremis. This conviction freed him of his panic and his need for therapy. Had our encounters with each other not involved deep feeling and his belief in my intentions and reliability, however, I doubt that he would ever have dared to test the anesthetic, for he trusted in me that he would safely survive.[1]

Paradoxes at All Levels of Therapeutic Discourse

Barriers to encounter come from several components of thought: sensations, cognitions, and drives. The therapist who is capable of detecting such barriers in any of the possible dimensions is best equipped for his

---

[1] This man's treatment can also be described very neatly as an "in vivo desensitization"—a term used by behavior therapists to describe the deconditioning that life experience accomplishes (when we feel safe enough to engage freely in such experience) in bleaching old patterns of fearful avoidance.

work. A therapist who can deal effectively with only *some* barriers is correspondingly restricted.

In the case of injunctive barriers (those that forbid discussion of the charged matter) simple measures work, as described in the last chapter. Paradoxical barriers must be dealt with by resort to lower or higher levels of abstraction (p. 139). In the conceptual dimension, "Ignore This Sign" messages can be pointed out verbally. But in the feeling dimension, words often fail. For example, if the psychotic avoids verbal contact by incessant chatter, resort to physical contact can produce therapeutic movement. A chattering patient in mania quieted down when one of her co-therapists sat down beside her and calmly placed his feet, crossed comfortably, in her lap. While such maneuvers are for the expert, and may seem to violate professional decorum, manic patients are themselves past words and decorum. Dr. Harrington's gentle and judicious use of belt-and-cuffs with excited patients is another example.

When a patient talks nonsense but acts as if he expects to be attended to, or drones on in an empty barrage of verbiage, the paradoxical discrepancy between his verbal and non-verbal transmission can be broken up by stepping out of the frame and commenting on his behavior, or by withdrawing, as in engaging in side-conversation with a co-therapist. If, in such circumstances, the therapist lets himself fall asleep, he violates a hidden rule of psychotherapy—*of course* a therapist is supposed to keep awake and listen—and such behavior can make more of an impact on the patient's feelings than any number of verbal comments. Highly verbal and intellectual people—a couple coming for therapy because of problems in their marriage—can be brought off their dusty-dry academic discourse by nonverbal means if one of their co-therapists starts a game with them of "hot hand."

The attempt to get past barriers to the feeling component of encounter has gone to extremes in recent years leading to such far-out experiments as therapy in the nude, with all participants immersed together in a warm swimming pool, and to all sorts of nonverbal techniques to break the bonds of language.

The use of nonverbal techniques to remove barriers to encounter risks consequences which anyone knows can ensue from physical contact—combat, seduction, or panic, depending on the preponderance of repulsion, attraction, or fears of same in the exchange. Thus far such techniques have been employed mainly in group settings, or with multiple therapists, where the larger frame of the group's expectations controls the course that individual members follow. Group standards, for example, in nudist camps control the sexual urges of participants. Nudity in the theater is not nudity in the bedroom: The background defines the meaning of the particular behavior. Milgram's studies of influence (1963) showed this: Define a setting as "research," and you lend a meaning to sadistic behavior which is as different from sadism in ordinary life as disrobing in a nudist camp is from disrobing in the public square. He was able to persuade ordinary people to inflict shocks they thought were painful, even potentially lethal, in a "rigged" laboratory situation of "research in learning" in humans.

The taboo on physical contact in the one-to-one type of psychotherapy is still in force amongst those therapists of a medical or psychoanalytic lineage but seems to be bleaching in other circles. Medically trained therapists are no strangers to physical contact with patients. By the time a doctor has finished his internship and psychiatric residency, he has performed innumerable physical examinations which included investigations more intimate than any found elsewhere, and he has learned that such intimacies do not bring sexual arousal either for himself or his patient. Given such experience, one might expect physician-therapists to be less alarmed at physical contact with patients than lay-therapists. The reverse is the case. Two factors have obvious bearing on this paradoxical state of affairs: In the first place, medical training tends to emphasize defensive isolation of feelings toward patients (how can one cut open a belly without such defenses?) and psychotherapy involves confronting feelings in oneself and one's patient that threaten to undo the defensive isolation. Secondly, physicians have had long experience with the hazards of intimate contact—its misinterpretation and hostile exploitation, which unhappy experience led to the evolution of mores which protect both the patients and the doctor (such as the ones which prohibits examining a female except when a nurse or another female is present). Physician therapists tend to deplore the trend toward nonverbal influence and to predict dire consequences for therapist and patient. Time will tell, and it may be that psychologists will have to experience some of the clinical disasters that led to the medical tradition before the proper limits of the use of physical contact in therapy can be found.

The canon prohibiting physical contact with one's patient amongst medically trained therapists has a further justification. Psychotherapists generally have the goal of somehow influencing patients to renounce their yearnings for infantile gratifications so that these patients can find life as adults tolerable. To gratify primitive wishes, such as the need Harlow's monkeys (1969) show for direct tactile contact, seems to many psychotherapists a reinforcement of their patient's regressive avoidance of the problems of adult life. To gratify the need for contact would seem to these theorists to be a perpetuation of, rather than a curative intervention in, the rigid rules of behavior that make trouble for the patient. That master of psychoanalytic theory and practice, Otto Fenichel, however, remarked that reliance on cognitive "insight" to make a difference in the dry-as-dust world of obsessive patients is somewhat like trying to dry oneself with a wet towel. Interpretations for these patients can become more intellectual games, robbed of their reference to feelings.

The search for more vital and vivid influence than words can supply led Wilhelm Reich (1948) many years ago to employ physiotherapy as an adjunct to psychotherapy. He left a mark on the technique of many

Scandinavian psychoanalytic followers, who had been influenced by other nonverbal avenues to encounter, such as Sauna baths and Swedish massage. The laying-on-of-hands has a power rooted in infantile life. It need not necessarily lead to abuse. That patients yearn for physical contact can be seen in the numbers of patients who go to masseurs, or even to chiropractors, and seem to get some benefit from their structured and ritualized ministrations (which licensed physicians fail to supply).

Those who use nonverbal techniques claim remarkable results, as is usual amongst psychotherapists. Currently sweeping the country is a movement toward group experiences using verbal and nonverbal techniques, which is called "sensitivity training."[2] This movement, involving groups called "T" groups, has seized the campuses, considerable portions of the industrial world, and even that bastion of conservatism, suburbia. "T" groups aim at developing and expanding human awareness. Their popularity demonstrates that for much of modern life words have lost their meaning. Conventional channels of discourse have become so conventional as to be empty rituals devoid of meaning. When people resort to charades, psychodrama, nudity, and various types of physical encounter, they discard the paradox-ridden conventional language and begin again to use sensorimotor levels of communication. Actions often speak louder than words, and one needs only a single experience of role playing or psychodrama to feel what these nonverbal therapists and therapies are after. A social-work student who is asked to play the role of client in the first encounter with the social agency expands his awareness of the ingredients that make the exchange vital for the client. For the student, the experience leaps from the shallow textbook world into immediate living reality.

The Genesis of Paradoxical Beliefs

Most problems of paradoxical barriers combine verbal and nonverbal elements. These can assume such complexity as to drive the victim of such messages up a wall—even to madness. Years ago, two child psychiatrists, Adelaide Johnson and Stanley Szurek (1954), uncovered the effect of such messages in the genesis of delinquency in children. Their method was to offer therapeutic interviews with guaranteed confidentiality to these children and to their parents separately—children and parents were both offered the opportunity to be patients. This was an important change in structure from the usual child-guidance clinic encounter which has no fifth-amendment proviso—in the usual exploration of families in such clinics, anything anyone says can be used against him.

Johnson and Szurek's initial studies explored the problem of delinquent stealing. All children steal and normal parents handle the early thefts their children make in a matter-of-fact way: "Jackie—we don't take other

2 The reader who is interested in the avant-garde experiments of the contemporary psychotherapeutic scene can find an enthusiastic account of them in Schultz, 1967.

people's things—go put it back." Children who steal chronically have usually met with another type of parental message on the occasion of their first experiment of stealing: "Jackie—that's terrible—the next time you do that Daddy is going to *really* spank you!"

Children sense the parent's expectation and are caught in a paradox: They hear sounds (sense impressions) which they decode into words which mean "don't steal," but they see facial expressions and sense feelings from the flesh-and-blood mother, behind her facial expression and the sound she is making, which the children decode as "I expect you to steal again." Even the young child can sort out such messages into categories of context variations and intensities of all types—and is inevitably confused. One way out of such confusion is to bet on the feeling-component—that is, to trust the perception of the mother sensed in a mode that goes deeper than mere sounds that can be coded into words (as the babies Bower studied bet on the complete triangle—see p. 18). This bet leads to repetitive stealing, because it follows the message, "I expect you to do it again." Some children, given such confusing messages, bet on the verbal message, "Don't steal," and don't become delinquent. The complexity of the sorting and categorizing problem posed by such messages far exceeds the problems Bower posed to the two-month-old babies, and the solutions children elect are correspondingly variable. All that is sure is that if you want your child to steal, an effective influence toward stealing is one that says one thing in words and another in the language of feelings. The confusion is compounded when the cognitive dimension is itself paradoxical—"stealing is bad" plus the verbal message "I say in words that I expect you to do it again."

Johnson went on to study very disturbed individuals (Johnson et al., 1956). She studied the parents of psychotic patients as well as the patients themselves, and also, with her associates, went into prisons to study murderers. In both groups she found that parents had subjected their children to overt violence—sadistic or sexual—that conveyed an unmistakable perception to the children in nonverbal terms. When a child of two or three years of age is strangled to the point of unconsciousness or beaten to the point of leg fractures, this makes a deep impression. A rule of what one should expect from the world is formed by such experiences. Children learn fast, and one shudders to think what the "battered" children (a syndrome currently recognized and studied instead of ignored, as it was in the past—see Helfer, 1968) will do when they grow up. The murderers Johnson's group studied had been battered. Their internal rules did not contain reliable injunctions against violence, whatever they had been told in words by parents, teachers, or ministers. On the contrary, they were reactively hateful toward the parent who had inflicted the violence and also toward the other parent for failing to intervene. The murders they committed were thinly disguised retaliations for the abuse they had experienced in childhood.

If anyone who murders can be considered sane, Johnson's cases were sane, and were so adjudged in court. Johnson and her associates went on to study insane cases, nonmurderers, those showing schizophrenic breakdowns. These unfortunates had experienced even greater disorganizing influence than had the murderers. They had not only experienced numerous assaults of the battered- or seduced-child variety but had also been asked to deny the evidence of all their perceptual and conceptual capacities. The prototypical experience the Johnson group found was a violent or sexual assault by a parent, capped by a paradoxical verbal statement of the form, "You know I love you and this wouldn't have happened if you hadn't been naughty—I was really trying to be nice to you—*wasn't I!*" At this point the child must make a fateful decision: Either he keeps his sanity and risks losing his parent, or he deserts his sanity and keeps his parent. Those who take the latter course, Johnson pointed out, have a "hole" in their reality testing concerning other people's actions and intentions that can be revived in the exchanges of their later lives. Once having experienced a paradoxical situation, they can re-experience the confusion it engendered. If the exchanges are of sufficient emotional importance and have sufficiently crucial influence, the struggle to cope with unreliably perceived data can culminate in total psychotic disorganization—as in relation to a military superior who reduplicates the sadism and the denial of the soldier's childhood in a situation which the soldier cannot avoid or escape.

Paradoxical Beliefs and Behavior in Interpersonal Situations

Patients bring the confusions and paradoxes of their internal rule structures to the therapist. The therapist's job is to recognize the existence of such confused rules and to try to set them straight. The first phase of this process is the patient's attempt to impose his own paradoxical double binds on the therapist. The patient attempts to establish a climate in the consulting room which reduplicates the paradoxical climate he has incorporated in his efforts to cope in the past. Psychoanalytic theory recognizes this tendency in the concepts of transference and transference neurosis (and their counterparts in the therapist). Dr. Smith's appearance resembles, with his greying temples, one's daddy of yesteryear, and one tends to feel about him the way one felt about one's daddy. The carryover of the *conceptual* operations of the past into the therapeutic situation, together with its paradoxes and binds, has been less emphasized.

The subjective sensation therapists experience in relation to the first phase of the patient's imposition of binds is one best described, if inelegantly, as "being sucked in." The attempt to manipulate the therapist into compliance with paradoxical behavior can begin before the patient actually arrives. It can happen by letter or by telephone and can give the therapeutic relation a particular slant long before the time is ripe for the most usual way of dealing with such manipulations, namely interpretation.

A young lady from another city was referred to me by her former therapist, an old friend. He wrote a letter saying that he hoped I would be able to help this young lady get placed into treatment. I wrote back saying that I would be glad to do so. The next move was a letter from her mother, handwritten on elegant stationery in a rather ornate hand. It arrived on a Thursday and said, "My dear Dr. Lewis, Mr. Brown and I will be arriving on Saturday with our daughter, Kay, and would like an appointment, as we feel this would be mutually advantageous. We will be staying at the Ritz Hotel during our stay in your city." This appeared to me to be a somewhat imperious way of beginning the relationship. Since I had a full schedule that Saturday morning I wrote a note immediately to the mother saying that an appointment would not be possible and mailed it in ample time to get to her. Saturday morning I received a telephone message to call Mr. Brown at his hotel. I did so and the exchange went this way:

> *Dr. Lewis:* "Hello, Mr. Brown, this is Dr. Lewis returning your call."
> *Mr. Brown:* "How are you?" (*Said very unctuously*)
> *Dr. Lewis:* (*Somewhat taken aback*) "Well . . . I'm fine." (*He sounded as if he thought I had been suffering from a long illness.*)
> *Mr. Brown:* "Oh, that's N–I–C–E!" (*I felt as if I had been rescued from the grave in the nick of time.*)

Mr. Brown then pretended that he had not heard from me, although side comments during the brief seconds we talked indicated that his wife was with him in the room and certainly had the letter. He then gave me to understand that my old friend, Kay's former therapist, had assured him that they could expect that I would give them an appointment. Mr. Brown was very short of time and would have to rearrange his plans (he implied move heaven and earth) unless I would see them on Saturday morning. He put every possible pressure upon me to make me feel I was indeed obligated to this busy man of affairs. By this time I was feeling somewhat huffy and simply told him, matter-of-factly, that I would see them the following Monday. When they arrived at my office, the opening exchange involved derogatory comments about the building, the arrangements for people waiting for appointments, the furnishings of my office, and so on. Ostensibly polite, they were clearly hostile, but in the context they could count on my being bound not to confront them with their paradoxical communications. By the time these parents arrived, before I had even seen their daughter, they had already created a reactive set in me—a power struggle was in full sway, and they had already told me a great deal of what their daughter had had to contend with.

Another young lady had also been referred to me by a friend in another city. My first communication with her family was from her mother. She and her daughter had come to get the daughter situated for college. When I returned this mother's call, a charming and gracious lady answered. Within seconds she showed me that she had anticipated every possible reason why it would be an imposition on me, in my exalted status, to give her and her daughter a moment of my time. She realized that it had been thoughtless of her not to have set up some opportunity to talk to me well in advance but added that they had been forced to change their plans by unavoidable circumstances. She immediately showed me that she understood just the sort of annoyances Mr. Brown had been expert in generating, but she so skillfully anticipated these annoyances and drew their sting, that before I knew it I had given her an appointment that afternoon. To do less would, I felt, have been churlish. She had, it turned out, for years occupied a position of considerable responsibility in an international agency where her job was to meet, greet, and shepherd around town various visiting dignitaries. She had raised tact to a fine art and had "read" me, by whatever fragmentary messages must have been given her instant by instant on the telephone, in an astonishingly accurate way.

Both these encounters contained binds, and both were manipulations to gain control of the exchange. Both occurred at a phase in the development of a relationship at which blunt confrontation or interpretation would have been tactless. The arm-twistings involved, by the rules of manners, were not fair game for discussion. The parents of neither of these girls had announced themselves as patients, and to have made interpretations concerning their behavior would have risked their abrupt withdrawal, ending any possibility of therapeutic influence.

The therapeutic relationship is a two-way street in respect to the imposition of double binds, as well as in all other respects. Patients attempt to impose double binds in much the way they were exposed to binds in the past. There is the usual nonverbal message and a "metamessage" in words, going in the opposite direction, denying the first. The therapist can point this out in words, but he can also break up a bind by responding to the hidden implied message. This has been named an "affect flip" by a group of experts in family therapy associated with Carl Whitaker, called in professional circles "the Atlanta Group." The patient presents an expectation that polite but phoney messages from him to the therapist will be taken at face value and meets with a response to the hidden message instead.

Patient: "I'm very grateful for all the attention you've shown me."
Therapist: (*Ignoring the verbal message and responding to nonverbal signs of hostility.*) "The bell just rang, the hour is over."

Such a technique negates the conventional context of therapy, which sets implicit injunctions on the therapist against being rude. Patients expect stereotypical professional behavior from therapists, based on reading, movies, or past experience in therapy. Any sort of behavior which does not fit the stereotype, anything which would seem "unprofessional" to the patient, removes some of the awe and the implied limits to encounter.

When a patient has remained stonily silent for many hours, refusing to communicate verbally, there is an implied defiance of the rule "when you go to a psychiatrist, you're supposed to talk." Sometimes all interpretations of this silence fail in their effect. At this point, a sudden outburst of genuine anger from the therapist may break the log jam. If the therapist intentionally deserts the therapeutic scene by picking up a book and reading it, or by walking out briefly without explanation, or by simply fixing his expression in an artificial frozen smile as if he were made of wax, the stubbornly defiant patient may begin to talk. The Atlanta group has found that telling such a patient any dirty story, as a parable, has the effect of removing injunctions connected with "talking to the Doctor." The aura of the professional office is sometimes so foreboding and carries with it so many threats to the patient that he may refuse to come for therapy. I once treated such a patient, a lady with a severe phobia of leaving her house, to an entirely successful outcome, which first began in her living room. After a few hours of therapy she felt safe enough with me to move to a bench in a nearby park. In a matter of weeks her fears of insanity and of psychiatrists had bleached enough to begin a more conventional office type of therapy, ending in the complete resolution of her phobic symptoms. (This treatment was obviously a form of behavior therapy—"desensitization"—in its early phases, though I could not have so named it at the time.)

A professor coming for couples therapy with his wife sought to double-bind the therapists by politely but pompously droning on as if he were lecturing a class, counting on the compliance and the politeness of the therapists. This went on for quite a time. He showed no sign of running down, but held steadfastly to the floor. When one of the therapists abruptly shouted, "Shut up!" things began to move in the therapy: The professor experienced an orienting reaction of considerable magnitude and began to change his ways.

Patients can resist encounter, as noted above, by employing standard defenses like denial and various forms of resistant behavior like silence, counting from past experience on counterattack from those about them. When the therapist gives them not counterattack but encouragement to *use* these defensive maneuvers the patient is as off balance as the one previously mentioned, who charges at a door to break it down and finds it suddenly opened at the moment of impact. A patient who engages in interminable small talk about the weather or the events of the day is often enticing the therapist into taking a stand and demanding that the patient get down to business. When the patient meets nothing but good-humored small talk from the therapist—even more empty of meaning—his bind is broken up. A defiant young lady who sits silently fuming, finally making a face at the therapist and sticking her tongue out, is taken off balance if the therapist shows acute interest in her tongue and suggests that she stick it out further so he can examine it better. The patient who says he will never get better expects some encouragement with which he can contend, as is usual for him. When the therapist admits that things are probably hopeless and science has failed, that his (the therapist's) powers are exhausted, he takes the patient off balance. A patient who uses his anxiety as a manipulative tool in controlling those around him fails in his effort if the therapist says, "Fine! I hope you'll stay anxious, because that's the only way you'll ever move." The patient who refuses to talk is taken off balance if the therapist says, "It's good for you to be silent, and to share it with me—it's about time you began to take a stand and be yourself!"

Binds that are accessible to verbal interpretation can be broken up by offering, as stated above, a new conceptual framework which removes a pseudo-problem (as in the case of Russellian paradoxes). There are additional elements besides the purely conceptual ones involved in an interpretation which can be used to break up binds. When a silent patient is told "Your struggles against talking to me remind me of what you said about your struggles with your mother—perhaps you are withholding words now just as you withheld feces in your early fights with her," the patient is not only being given a strange new way to look at a piece of behavior, but the behavior in the consulting room is placed in a context which renders his efforts at control ridiculous and therefore empty of any force.

Another type of interpretation skips any intellectual or conceptual step and goes right to the verbal statement concerning the hidden affect expressed:

> Patient: (A scientist who collaborated with his wife, also a scientist, in re- search) "There is no rivalry between me and Joan—why I have the greatest disrespect for Joan's abilities!"
> Therapist: (Ignoring the slip as the object of verbal comment in itself) "That's right! Women have got to be put down, put into their proper place!"

Binds imposed by patients contain not only verbal but also nonverbal elements. The following example comes from a paper published by members of the Atlanta group (Whitaker et al., 1962).

> Technique P: The periodic "Assumption of Omnipotence": This reduces terror in the patient by providing a strong and directive parental image. The therapist communicates his sense of being able to help the patient, his sureness of the relationship and conviction that the patient is susceptible to interpersonal contact.
> Example: (A catatonic patient beginning the interview, snaps his fingers three times.)
> Therapist: "Trying to destroy us, eh?" (Snaps his fingers three times and the patient jumps.)
> "You better be careful or I'll do it the fourth time."

Dreams and Fantasies

The patient's dreams supply an avenue for disclosing hidden verbal and nonverbal binds. While, of necessity, these sources of information have to be reported verbally they begin at nonverbal levels, largely in visual imagery, during sleep. The patient who reports after his first hour in analysis that he had a dream that he was a foreign dignitary visiting the President of the United States, and that a bombing raid took place, suddenly sees his relation to the therapist in a new light when he recognizes that one of the props in the dream, a desk, closely resembled the therapist's desk. The woman who is troubled with vague fears of therapy understands those fears better when she has a dream in which she is being taken to a hospital to see a doctor whose name contains elements of the therapist's name to have her leg amputated. Another woman recognizes the archaic childhood origin of her fear of therapy via a dream in which children around her are being shot down by an army advancing along a railroad track—when she recognizes that the route from her home to the therapist's office involves walking along beside a railroad track. In all these examples the shift of the context of the emotion, fear, from the therapeutic situation to one belonging to childhood, or at least to some marked distortion of the therapeutic situation, helps to break up the injunctions and binds which block the patient.

Dreams provide other invaluable data. Patients often cannot put a finger on why they are upset, either in the therapeutic situation or elsewhere. If they could, they might be able to break up the binds in which they find themselves without assistance. Binds and paradoxes often elude consciousness because of defensive repression, isolation, or denial of one or another of the essential elements of a bind. This can be dealt with via the direct routes of observation, deduction, and inference supplied by the therapist in the techniques already described. Dreams open doors to understanding these defenses. Freud called the interpretation of dreams the royal road to the unconscious: Dreams supply information going beyond defenses and conflicts. Dreams often give glimpses into sensori-motor, preverbal levels of experience. Analysts have reported instances in which dreams have contained references to events in specific places which occurred at a time when the patient was too young to have known more than a few words, but which were susceptible to investigation and verification via independent sources. Marie Bonaparte (1940), for example, reported a woman patient's dream of a traumatic sexual interaction with a gardener working for her parents. The locale was so vivid in the dream that the patient felt some such very early event must have taken place. She went back to this place and gently confronted the gardener. He was abashed, but finally said the dream referred to a real event. One of my patients whose problem was an unaccountable anxiety in the presence of men dreamed of a specific hotel room and sexual behavior on the part of her father. She was able to establish via discrete questions asked her mother that the hotel room pictured in her dream was in reality one in which she had stayed only once in her life, with her father, at the age of two years.

These examples leave one with haunting doubts as to how much the child's imagination contributed to the dreams. Freud himself first accepted such evidence but later came to the judgment that this type of seduction or other traumatization was all in the imagination of the child. Johnson and Szurek's (1954) evidence from the parents' own statements concerning early traumatic events indicates that in this judgment Freud was at least partially in error. Freud did not recognize the way parents can put children in binds and force denials on the child. Instances in which one is placed in the painful position of actually witnessing a traumatic event to an infant and of seeing the subsequent effects are rare.

A physician saw his 18-month-old baby son suffer an accidental amputation of a finger tip when the child slipped around behind the father, who was repairing a water pump in a summer cottage, and grasped a belt running from an electric motor to the water pump. The baby's hand was carried along over a pulley, and the finger tip was snipped off. Attempts by another physician to save the finger tip, in which the father assisted, made that day additionally traumatic for the child. Months later the child had a few nightmares. These recurred occasionally, but even after he had acquired speech the child could never say what the nightmares were about. When he was five years old he saw a movie, "A Tale of Two Cities," the closing scenes of which showed Sydney Carton (played by Ronald Coleman) mounting the steps to the guillotine. The film ends with a long shot of the fall of the knife and the fall of the severed head. The five-year-old appeared undisturbed after the movie, but after the usual bed-time amenities including storytime he fell asleep, only to awaken in a half hour from a nightmare. He was unable to describe his bad dream, as always, but this night a new pattern appeared: He continued to sleep a brief time and to wake in terror until dawn. At four in the morning he was able to tell his distraught parents at last that he could recall his dream: In the dream he was first at the movie and then at the summer cottage, and a huge giant was walking over the hill behind the cottage, crushing all trees and creatures in his path. Only after seeing the movie did he have a vehicle for the expression of his fears and the perceptions he could not integrate at 18 months, and which had eluded his verbal categorizing capacities. The film's action not only recalled visual imagery of his infancy, but also supplied some pattern he could describe in words. The little boy talked about the painful injury with his father, who could supply information about the traumatic day which helped the child comprehend his nightmares. After a relatively brief period of psychotherapy in which the child talked and played out his fantasies and fears with a therapist, the nightmares permanently ceased.

Similar light on old binds comes from waking fantasies.

A professor reacted with feelings of rejection and disconfirmation to an administrative change in his responsibilities in a fashion he recognized as completely inappropriate. He felt sudden and profound depression for no reason, in his own opinion. He experienced many somatic symptoms including continual retching and pain in the upper abdomen and lower chest. His wife's reaction in early co-therapy hours seemed callous—she chided him for his overreaction and shamed him, as if she had been raised by the standards Dr. Levy described as characteristic in Tahiti (p. 109). When he was urged to "make a waking dream" about the pain—to go wherever his fantasies took him —he thought of a huge bird ripping at his entrails, of his terror and wish to escape from this crushing, devouring assault by a quick suicidal death, and then switched suddenly to another subject: He began to talk of his feelings when he was placed in a foundling home for a time when 18 months old, following the death of his father. As he continued to talk, an abrupt change occurred in his nonverbal communication: He had come into therapy appearing to be like the proverbial cigar-store Indian, carved out of wood. Before his depression he had usually presented a casual but jaunty Mississippi River gambler "front." Now, as his fantasy took him back to times charged for him with terror and reactive fury, he began to weep. His therapists felt him hover and waver between abreaction and defensive denial. He first wept, then pulled himself together, speaking of present real problems, then wept again more profusely, then minimized, and so on. One could infer that his wife's coolness stemmed in part from his covert instructions over the years to her to help him reinforce his defensive avoidance of feelings he had *had* to surmount when very young. In the therapy hour during her husband's account of his fantasy a perceptible softening and warming in her attitude took place. The content of the fantasy itself (regarding the rapacious bird) was not examined during this hour at all. The aspects of this man's waking fantasy which brought therapeutic movement were his inner archaic anguish, his struggle to minimize it, and his wife's compliant response to this defensive effort. Via the fantasy, injunctions began to bleach in the therapy.

Negative Practice

The therapist can rob the patient's communications of their double-binding quality by encouraging the symptom from which the patient apparently wants relief. He can encourage the patient to experience his symptoms, but in a new context, either in or out of the therapeutic relationship (as mentioned earlier in this chapter). Behavior therapists, for example, encourage the experiencing of frightening experiences of a phobic nature while at the same time making sure that the patient is in a relaxed state.

The idea of negative practice by which a patient tries to gain mastery of the very thing he fears goes back almost 30 years to the work of Dunlap (1942). There are reports of successful use of this active voluntary practicing of symptoms (which the patient has up to the time of entering therapy experienced passively) in the treatment of tics, phobias, stuttering, obsessions, sexual disorders, compulsive swearing, hysterical aphonia, and even certain cases of schizophrenia. The method goes by various names—"negative practice," "paradoxical intention," "reactive inhibition," and by Haley (1963), "therapeutic paradox."[3]

A rather extreme version of the behavior therapy approach is called "implosion therapy" by its originator, Stampfl (Stampfl and Lewis, 1967) on the model of the contained and forced explosion used to trigger atom bombs. The strategy of this therapy rests on the idea of extinction: The connection between an idea (expressed in words by the patient and, in turn, the therapist), and the disturbing emotional reaction associated with the idea tends to loosen, to bleach out, as it were, when the idea is presented repeatedly in the absence of whatever painful consequences ensued from it originally. Stampfl began with the idea that most neurotic symptoms are avoidance-maneuvers of situations patients believe con-

---

[3] For a summary of the literature in this area and details of the technique see Newton, 1968a, b.

sciously or unconsciously to be painful. Fearful reactions to the sight of blood, Stampfl argues, have their origins in childhood injuries and in the reactions of other persons to these injuries.

Behavior therapists of a conventional stripe might lead a patient, via verbal instruction, through a gradual imaginary confrontation of mild to severely gory scenes. Stampfl plunges right in, suggesting horrendous charnelhouse scenes, horrid mutilations, mangled corpses, and rivers of blood. He reports (and observers confirm) that patients go through intense emotional reactions as he urges them verbally to visualize these scenes in great detail—but claims rapid and lasting success in demolishing such rules as "I can't stand the sight of blood," which have guided patients' behavior for years, by only a few hours of such therapy (10 to 15). The patients protest, show marked physiological reactions, but calm down rapidly—and come back for the next implosion session (Stampfl has had extraordinarily low rates of dropping out of therapy among his patients as compared with control series using conventional therapy). If a patient has beliefs about dirt (called obsessions), and compulsively washes his hands, Stampfl will command the patient to engage in detailed fantasies of wallowing in filth, of falling into an out-house pit, of smearing and eating feces, and so on.

Stampfl follows a sink-or-swim strategy, plunging his patients into what they believe they cannot endure, saying aloud, and with relish, words the patient has hidden in the innermost recesses of his mind. Since the patients discover that the human organism is, after all, quite able to survive such Draconian measures, Stampfl reports their beliefs change, as do the behaviors founded on these beliefs. The handwasher stops fearing dirt. The old maid stops fearing sex after Stampfl has guided her fantasy through an orgiastic night in a bordello a few times. Stampfl watches his patients carefully for signs of anxiety and continues to "implode" them with verbal suggestions until they no longer react with distress.

This type of influence lies hidden in almost every form of therapy, including psychoanalysis, whenever a patient in a safe situation is encouraged to think about things that have frightened him in the past. It is, for example, implicitly hidden in Breuer's and Freud's *Studies on Hysteria* (1955), in which they relate that each and every instance in which a particular symptom occurred was recalled under hypnosis and re-experienced with the greatest possible emotional intensity—108 separate instances of this type, 27 of that, and so on—which is a procedure remarkably similar to the deconditioning procedures used by behavior therapists. Deconditioning, negative practice, or working through are all names for a procedure that in its essential details was in full use in the 1890s, and most likely long before.

These techniques are powerful tools of influence. All require tact, judgment, and an implicit climate of benign concern. Many of them carry with them the risk of provoking abrupt flight or severe emotional disturbance in the patient, should they be misused. Some are of quite recent origin, but others have been studied for years—literature concerning the timing of interpretations, including interpretation of dreams, and the various dangers besetting that mode of influence is considerable (see Greenson, 1967). The inescapable fact is that *whatever* the therapist does in the consulting room will influence his patient, and inaction is not necessarily benign. If he allows the patient's binds to guide the therapeutic relation, he has confirmed the patient's pathology. Any of the measures to improve encounter and to break up old binds is subject to variation guided by judgment in timing and dosage. Though some of them seem to be radical variations from the posture of the movie psychoanalyst or psychotherapist, it must be remembered that classical psychoanalytic technique involved a radical departure from ordinary human behavior, at least until it became widely known. The European analyst who greeted his patient formally at the door of the consulting room, shook his hand, pointed to the couch, and sat down in silence supplied his patient with powerful orienting influences which defined a type of relationship hardly met elsewhere!

Summary

Paradoxical instructions pervade human interactions of all types. These take a form similar to that of a waggish freeway sign, "Ignore This Sign," or of the command "Be spontaneous!" Such instructions pervade not only interpersonal relations but also intrapersonal functions in the form of the self-instructions we label beliefs. Beliefs, and the feelings associated with them, exert powerful control in encounters between people and in the behavior of individuals functioning in isolation from other people, yet beliefs are discounted by many theorists of the processes by which people change. (Haley, 1963, for example). The power of belief and associated feelings showed up in the case of a man suffering several crippling symptoms, which changed radically for the better after he convinced himself he could control his suffering.

Paradoxical rules of behavior often include conflicting sensations, cognitions and drives at all levels, and these emerge in the interpersonal actions of psychotherapy. They can be put to therapeutic use in various ways, some of which necessitate physical contact between the participants because of the multiple levels of paradox. This has its benefits and its pitfalls.

Studies such as those of Johnson and Szurek (1954) cast light on how conflicting beliefs arise in individual development. Parents who force paradoxical rules of behavior upon their children—for example, hateful abuse accompanied by loving words—mar their children in many serious ways. Beliefs of a paradoxical nature implanted in childhood can lead to conflict and confusion in later life—even to the point of psychotic disorganization and murderous behavior.

Less catastrophic examples of paradoxical rules emerge in the processes of interpersonal relations such as psychotherapy. As patients attempt to impose these rules on the therapist, the therapist, in turn, attempts to abrogate these rules and rob them of their power in guiding behavior. These maneuvers begin in the first moments of contact, as shown in two widely differing examples. Unorthodox behavior on the therapist's part has the effect of shattering the expectations that the patient often counts on in his attempts to control the therapist. These take numerous forms but share the feature of novelty. Dreams and fantasies disclose patients' otherwise hidden and archaic expectations and paradoxical rules. A therapeutic use of apparently paradoxical instruction is one that is most often called "negative practice." The patient is encouraged to experience that which he fears, but in a safe setting, and the most vigorous use of negative practice can be seen in a type of therapy called "implosion therapy" by its originator, Stampfl.

16

The Nature of
the Symbolic
Process

If we talk about various types of steering devices for automobiles (rack-and-pinion, worm-and-roller, power-assisted), we have said little about how it is we can jump in our cars and reliably drive from coast to coast, staying firmly on the road rather than flying off into orbit. Thus far the inquiry into influence has considered steering devices almost to the exclusion of the interacting forces which we guide in car driving or in psychotherapy. Before looking at various forms of interpersonal influence, all of which emphasize one or another element of experience, the latter had best be identified more clearly.

Our immediate experience comprises several separable elements which can be categorized in various ways. We customarily distinguish two large classes of phenomena, feelings and thoughts, as the main divisions into which experience can be sorted. In this usage, the class "feelings" lumps together quite different experiences: precise perceptions of objects at a distance (the sight of the morning star), sensations arising within our bodies (the pain of green-apple colic or the pain of an overfull bladder), and passions like love, hate, and sexual lust. The term "thought" covers another broad range of phenomena, from the sorting operations of deaf-mutes or babies playing the peekaboo game, through sensorimotor phases of thought, to the distilled abstract operations of mathematics or philosophical inquiry.

This split will no longer do. "Thought and feeling" is too clumsy a division for the twentieth century, with the knowledge we possess of modern physics and psychology. Alfred North Whitehead, who has been called the twentieth century's first philosopher, welded knowledge of relativity theory into his philosophical system. (Whitehead proposed an alternative to Einstein's theory of relativity at about the same time Einstein announced his own.) This philosophical system is no dream irrelevant to practical affairs; on the contrary, it illuminates the exchanges in such a practical enterprise as the endeavor to alleviate suffering via psychotherapy, and it further illuminates the divisions between various schools—such as conditioning, Zen Buddhism, and psychoanalysis. Only a tiny portion of Whitehead's system can be brought into this inquiry—it is a vast system—but his system offers a clarification of vexing controversies between various theories of influence and their expression in various therapies.[1]

[1] For an introduction and overview, see Lowe, 1962.

Whitehead's View of Time, Causality, and Instinct

The idea of influence involves the idea of causation. Any therapy assumes that there is a present reality—therapist and patient, in a room, for instance—and that a second from now both will still be present in the room, and that what one does will cause some change in the other. It is easy, in looking at causality and time, to overlook the ground upon which the figures of therapeutic action occur. This ground is the continuity of time—the conformation of this moment to the moment which just passed. Reality persists and causes the next moment to have a shape; it does not vanish as a soap bubble vanishes when pricked. Time, Whitehead argued (as had others before him, for example, William James), is at base a continuity rather than a succession of ticks of the clock: The clock remains to tick again, but its sequential ticking is an abstraction from the continuity of the ticking mechanism.

When a therapist makes some move which is followed by a response in his patient, we may say, "The therapist's behavior caused the patient's response." All therapies incorporate such an idea of causality. If causality hinged on mere regularity of association between one thing and another, we should soon find ourselves making primitive conclusions worthy of untutored savages: We should say (as Russell pointed out) that, since day always follows night, night is the cause of day. We urgently require a larger conceptual framework than the day-night sequence in order to arrive at a proper understanding of what "causes" day and night (we need ideas like the conception of the solar system and gravity).

Whitehead supplies such a larger framework in a series of works, but particularly for the purposes of this inquiry in the small volume *Symbolism: Its Meaning and Effect* (1959). The division of immediate experience into "thoughts" and "feelings" does violence to the nature of that experience. Whitehead argues that if we address ourselves to the moment-by-moment process we call reality, we can recognize not just two major factors but three. These three differentiations involve two distinct basic modes of perception and, thirdly, the conceptual elaborations we make in categorizing the data from the two modes into various symbolic representations, whether by gesture, picture, or word.

The Beginnings of the Symbolic Process

Consider the peekaboo game: Bower's observation of human babies (p. 18) reveals a great deal about perception and knowing, and the processes of influence on perception and knowing in any type of psychotherapy: Babies have two modes of perception. One tells them by bright but shallow sense-impression what object might be present at a distance. They also "feel," to judge from their behavior, that someone will really be there, that the signal cube or bar-triangle stand in the place of some real thing, a real person in this case. Whence comes this feeling of the solidity and reality of the other person? It comes from perceptions in another experiential mode, separable from such sense-impressions as photographs or mirror-images. What the baby does is to make bets on whether this or that signal is connected with the "lady-to-come." Whitehead named the deeper knowledge that the lady is there, and will be there again, "perception in the mode of causal efficacy." Some primary perception tells the child that he is not watching a movie or television screen, that the lady is real and can be called back again. This sense of a real, continuous, causally efficacious world containing real persons and objects is the primitive mode of experiencing which guides the behavior of organisms not possessing complex perceptual apparatuses like eyes or ears. Oysters open and close in accordance with the continuous movements of the moon (their feeding cycles correspond to tides) and have the ability to readjust to the moon's movements if transported halfway across a continent—in other words, oysters "perceive" the moon. While this sounds new and strange, it is not: The French astronomer De Marain showed, in 1729, that plants moved into caves in total darkness continued to orient their leaves to the position of the sun outside. In playing peek-aboo, the babies were not reacting to a mere collection of momentary sense-data, but to another sense, like the pull of the moon for the oyster, stemming out of another direct knowledge of the world. This direct mode of perception is poorly localized outside our bodies, but it is impelling—and, as Whitehead pointed out, is connected to "attraction" and "repulsion." It provides our inner certainty that this moment will causally affect the next. We know intuitively that there is a continuity of time—the conformation of *this* moment follows the conformation of the world as it was a second ago. The moon does not "know" the earth in the sense that humans know the intricacies of computers and ways to design lunar modules, but the moon "knows" and affects the earth (our hidden knowledge of this feeling is implied in the word affect, which means both "feeling" and "changes") just as the earth affects the moon.

We couch these "pulls" in the terms of physics, like "gravity" (as if that name told us anything about such a fundamental influence), but the babies' responses to the lady in the laboratory are no less tangible and no more explainable by sense-perceptions like sight or sound alone than are moon-earth relations.

Whitehead traced the fundamental operations of the symbolic process to the kind of behavior the babies showed: They made a cross-reference between a perception coming in by light rays (the sight of the cube or bar-triangle) reflected from afar, and a more direct perception of their own continuous bodily existence, their immediate awareness of their own continuous body and brain functioning, as affected by real objects in the outer world. Whitehead pointed out that perception in the mode of ordinary sensation (he called it "presentational immediacy") is vivid but deceptive: The babies studied by Bower entertained doubt, as shown by the differing number of trials they would make for this or that variant of the bar-triangle. They showed doubt that the symbol △ equals "peekaboo to come." They did *not* behave for one millisecond as though they doubted the young lady's existence, or their own, or their ability to influence her.

The babies confirmed Whitehead in a direct way that adults are less apt to provide: The *picture* of a bar-triangle might fool an adult, in its presentational immediacy, into taking the symbol as the real object it represents, but the baby saw paper as *real* paper (the photograph) and distrusted its causally efficacious connection with the other, prior, real bar-triangle signal. They were not fooled by illusion, as was the dog in Aesop's fable, who dropped a piece of meat to bite at its reflection in a pool of water.

Before relativity theory was such a familiar household commodity, perception in the mode of causal efficacy seemed much more of a strange and hard to grasp concept. Now that we are used to the idea that matter pulls on all other matter, quite without the kind of sensory signalling and conscious awareness we weigh so heavily in our own conscious experience, it does not seem so strange to speak of the moon as "perceiving" the earth. Whitehead's concept of perception of causal efficacy goes far beyond being merely another name for gravity, as might be inferred from the examples given. It includes all connections and relations of any regular sort, those we incorporate in the "laws of physics." The north pole of a magnet "perceives" causally whether another magnet's pole is its south or its north pole. When we walk on a rug in dry winter weather, our finger "perceives" the dry metal doorknob, which doorknob perceives our finger enough to attract an unpleasant spark from it. What we call instinct is merely a special case of the general lawful relation and conformation of objects to each other over time. Conscious, rational, adult thought is an elaboration of the interplay between the two forms of perception, one of which, causal efficacy, humans share with all other objects —rocks and atoms, as well as moons. Sensory apparatuses like the visual or auditory analyzers are analogous to the tracking radars which give precise information about the distant location of a capsule headed for the moon, but the space capsule is perceiving and responding to the gravitational pull of a real moon, a real sun, and a real galaxy of radiating, repulsing and attracting objects. So are the astronauts, at some level of their being.

The Nature of Experience

The Whiteheadian formulation is that our immediate experience combines three components, which are barely separable in any moment of living, but which can be recognized on reflection as distinct.

These are, again, *first,* the data of instinct, the primitive element in our experience—the impact of relativity and interrelatedness of all entities to each other in many ways, usually described in the language of physics (Whitehead argued with Russell that the world is more like a jar of treacle than a pile of shot, as Russell at one time had assumed it was). This concept of instinct is far broader than most—it is not that of the ethologists, involving merely a fixed behavior pattern. It is not quite like that of Freud, which involved qualitatively different energies such as lust and rage and their struggle for possession of the control of behavior—like Stevenson's Mr. Hyde, breaking through Dr. Jekyll's control of himself. (Freud based his theories on a model emphasizing the instinctual mode of experience, but he was hampered by the physics of his university years. This nineteenth-century physical framework tended to give his theoretical formulations a hydraulic or mechanical, rather than a relativistic, slant.)

The *second* contribution to thought comes via our distance-receptors, and in practice, this is fused with the first—as Whitehead remarked, immediate experience is of the nature of "that smelly feeling," and only later do we identify a particular odor as separable from the instantaneous awareness of the emotion-plus-sense impression. It is no accident that he chose smell to make his point—while the sight of something may evoke feeling, the relation of sight to feeling is less direct than that of smell or taste. Proust might have seen dozens of pictures relating to the world of his childhood, but it took the taste-smell of the tea-cake (the Madeleine) to set him off on his nostalgic literary quest.

The *third* component identifiable in moment-by-moment experience is conceptual elaboration—the sorting, classifying, cross-referencing, and indexing humans spontaneously engage in, such as the theorizing which Bower's experiments with babies demonstrate.

Relation to Interpersonal Influence

I once tried elsewhere (Lewis, 1965) to find a simple way to express Whitehead's analysis: Thought as we experience it can be packaged in the formula $T = f(d,s,c)$—thought is a function of drive (d, in the broad sense of "instinct"), sense impression (s), and conceptual elaboration (c). (Consciousness is not essential for this process and applies to only a small fraction of the total thought activity. Oysters, so far as we can now tell, do not consciously adjust to new surroundings. The "mental pole" of their experience is primitive, but adjust they do.)[2] This formula helps when it comes time to examine specific schools, or groups of schools, of psychotherapy, because they differ in the way they emphasize one or another of the terms, in their aims and methods, whether their theorists use such terms or not. Some therapies concentrate on changing the strength of, or control of, feelings. A therapy might aim at the abreaction of hate toward a parent, or perhaps the completion of a process of mourning for a lost love, which had previously been blocked. Another therapy might aim at control of a craving—an addiction or an immoderate lust, for example. Still another therapy might aim at awakening new feelings. All such ob-

---

[2] The clinical vignette in the preface to this volume provides an example of the three components at work—see also, Chapter 10, or Lewis, 1965.

jectives stress the d (drive) element of $T = f(d,s,c)$. The s term, sense perception, comes into the operations of all therapies, but relatively few make this element a major focus (Gestalt therapy being a major exception, in its emphasis on figure and ground and their reversals). Conceptual elaboration, the c element, comes into any therapy, but some schools make their major objective a change in the way their patients conceptualize the world (for example, the school, mentioned earlier, called Rational Emotive Therapy). Conditioning therapies bypass the c element, for the most part.

There is nothing in the symbolic process itself that guarantees the accuracy of any of its phases. This is what keeps therapists in business. The capacity to suppress or ignore some element of the immediate evidence of one's senses lies beneath the whole symbolic process. Symbols necessarily do *not* include all the facts they symbolize—they stand at a higher level of abstraction from what they represent. Abstraction means pulling out certain commonalities from a welter of facts. Some elementary factors are lost. Psychotherapy consists of many operations, most of which can be reduced to efforts to correct errors in the symbolic process: Dr. Jones, the therapist, is not necessarily like all people who have earned titles children revere, like parents, judges, ministers, and the other powerful figures of our childhoods. Patients in psychotherapy learn to discriminate Dr. Jones from the giants of their nursery days.[3]

Psychotherapy concerns itself in part with correcting some of the misjudged, misplaced, and inaccurate leaps people make from the language of gesture (which has many ambiguities) to the language of speech (more ambiguities). It also concerns itself with symbolic errors in connecting objects perceived in the mode of causal efficacy with signals perceived in presentational immediacy. A chair seen in a mirror is not the same as the real chair, and we realize that our senses can mislead us into projecting through the mirror surface an erroneous chair. It is much harder to recognize that a feeling of hate or fear is our own projection of our inner feelings onto some other person's mere appearance. The anti-Semite responds differently to the appearance of a man dressed as a burnoosed Arab than to that same man dressed in the fashion of a rich Jewish banker in New York, but the anti-Semite locates the cause of his feeling as being "out there" rather than in his own inner world.

Lesions of Causally Efficacious Influence

In the consulting room, one sometimes gets the haunting impression that, in attempting to relate to a patient, one is dealing with mere sense-impressions, sham mirror-reflections. The sense of another causally efficacious person, so clear to the baby playing the peekaboo game, is lost under a shimmering pile of verbiage, full of sound and fury—signifying

[3] For an excellent extended account, see Ruesch, 1961.

nothing. For when we perceive emotion—when we hate—it is a real man we hate, not an accumulation of sense data. When we love, or lose a love, we are most aware of causal efficacy. We do not yearn for, nor miss, the pancake makeup of the loved one's presentational immediacy—mere appearance—it is the *real* person who moves our emotions—a photograph will not do. The photograph of a magnet does not attract or repel another magnet. Pictured doorknobs shock no fingertips.

The rule that one takes causally efficacious influence for granted shows up when, in the exceptional instance, such influence is suspended. Try hailing a taxi on a rainy night at dinnertime in New York City. To the taxi driver you are the invisible man. Whenever humans experience inability to influence others, they are reminded of its regular presence and vital importance—its loss produces an eerie and uncanny sensation, whether it occurs in ordinary affairs, as with the inattentive taxi driver, or with the immobile guard standing with fixed gaze outside a palace, or when one tries to reach profoundly depressed patients for whom the world seems to have ceased to exist. Catatonic schizophrenia has become rare since Thorazine and other drugs have become available, but only a few years ago a walk through any ward in any mental hospital housing chronic patients would bring one up sharp in recognition of the ultimate in denial of causally efficacious influence. One saw mute human statues, standing like figures in a wax museum, indifferent as far as one could observe to all events around them, including any overtures made to them. Such a profound breaking of the rules of human encounter by these patients shows the rule: One tends to take for granted the effect on others that one enjoys and employs moment by moment.

To be denied influence is to feel as if one doesn't exist to the other person. The uneasy thought crowds itself into one's mind that perhaps one doesn't exist for anyone. Press further, multiply by many such denials, and one can begin to wonder whether one exists at all, even for oneself. The feeling of being a nothing, a nonentity, goes by various names in its various shades in the psychiatric world—"depersonalization," "estrangement," "derealization." The process by which one person conveys such total denial of another has a currently fashionable name, "disconfirmation," but novelists and philosophers have been aware of it for a long time —William James thought of it as the ultimate torture man can experience.

Major Lesions of Symbolic Reference

The label "schizophrenia" designates a set of behaviors. Eugen Bleuler (1857–1939; see Bleuler, 1950) coined the term to describe a splitting of personality functions. He did *not* mean multiple personalities or mere capriciousness, as popular usage often assumed. He felt a need for a term to describe a state of disorganization: what happens when the relation $T = f(d,s,c)$ is *dissolved,* so that causally efficacious perceptions, precise sense impressions, and conceptual elaboration in symbolic reference between the two proceed independently, largely fragmented from each other—together with their manifestations in behavior. The disorganization Bleuler called schizophrenia is no momentary fragmentation, such as we all suffer, but is lasting, pervasive, and profound.

Suppose one's life experience contains innumerable double binds, paradoxical communications, and denials, and suppose further that one's capacity for integrating and resolving such paradoxes be compromised by some limit imposed by biology (perhaps an enzyme defect such as defective insulin production in diabetics); then at some limit of stress the symbolic process explodes into fragments. The impression this makes resembles that seen in pinball machines, which, when manhandled outrageously, signal back "Tilt" via the lighting-up of a button. Confusion, suspicion, fear of nameless presences or of real persons emerges—pure causal efficacy untamed by clear sensations or clear concepts. Bewilderment, a sense of unreality, paralysis of will (or extravagant possession by *impulse*) occur. Rapid alternations of conceptual elaboration come forth —possible ways of putting together perceptions which are shot through with "Ignore This Sign" characteristics.[4] Even sense-data of an immediate sort do not integrate themselves into an orderly pattern of thought, but pursue a capricious career like a rocket off course, so that the sight of the face of a nurse connects with the memory of a hateful aunt and becomes eventually *defined* as that aunt. The temporary madness of an LSD "bad trip," horrid as it is, is time-limited; the experience I am trying to describe is one continuous nightmare.

Similar disorganizations of $T = f(d,s,c)$ occur not only with hallucinogenic intoxications but also with many febrile and other toxic deliria. Disrupted thought requires a change in the dialogue of the self with the world.[5] Interpersonal relations grind to a halt. Their repair requires clarification, trust, simplification, authenticity, truth. Such reparative maneuvers are involved in some of the techniques mentioned before, those of Rosen (p. 13), Harrington (p. 67), and Roland (p. 65). Tranquilizing drugs help this process. Sometimes a controlled environment—a hospital milieu—is necessary in order to supply these ingredients on a twenty-four-hour schedule. As the confusion diminishes in the patient's mind, one can see the reintegration of thought, feeling, and behavior before one's eyes, as with a child coming awake out of a febrile nightmare.

Summary

Immediate experience of human beings appears different in the light of twentieth-century awareness of relativity. The symbolic process is a cross-reference between a primitive, instinctual mode of perception on the one hand and bright sensation on the other, with conceptual elaborations of the relation between the two modes as the completing element of thought.

4 See Chapter 17.
5 Many moving accounts are available: Beers, 1936; Green, 1965; Laing, 1965.

A. N. Whitehead first showed this to be the case. Experiments with young babies disclose these functions. These same functions pervade the operations of interpersonal influence, such as various psychotherapies, which stress one or another aspect of symbolism. Lesions of the symbolic process affect not only the life of the streets, but also (when profound) motivate the disturbed behaviors that are labelled psychotic (for example, "schizophrenic," or "delirious"), which seem to dissolve the regular relations of thought. *Special* efforts to effect change are required in this state of affairs. The next chapter deals with the variety of modes of influence appropriate to the varieties of disorders of the symbolic process.

17

Influence via Change in Symbolic Practice

Symbolic Practice

The symbolic process, as we have seen, involves several elements organized sequentially in time. It is not a static process, like a photograph, but is more like a videotape. Children learn the accepted modes of symbolizing (language, folkways, mores) for the culture in which they find themselves. They store these patterns in memory for future use in a fashion similar to the way a computer memory-bank stores information and programs for processing that information. (The biblical view that God created man in his own image has a contemporary contrapuntal caveat: Man created computers in his own image, and must be beware lest they become God—a *deus ex machina* if there ever was one.) These modes of symbolizing constitute the habitual symbolic practice of the individual human, and whether theorists of psychotherapy state explicitly that this practice is what they aim to change or not, they must be doing so because of the nature of the organism.

Theorists of various schools seldom refer to "symbolic practice" as such, but their own symbolic practices make it difficult for the student of psychotherapy to reconcile the claims of (apparently) conflicting schools. Only certain elements of leverage for change are mentioned; others are left implicit, ignored, or, as it were, swept under the rug. Each school has its own vocabulary and concepts, its own sequence of operations. This leaves the student to master and compare many different symbolizing and categorizing practices, and confusion often ensues. A general model which any therapy could fit might help the student understand all therapies.

The Concept of "Plans"

Therapy involves the idea of causing a change, whether the condition to be changed is defined as disease, maladaptation, or social tension (this is the definition of psychotherapy in Webster's Third International Dictionary). But what is to be changed? The patient's rules of behavior include some tendency to deal with the world in a particular way which gets him into trouble, as, for example, the phobic man described in Chapter 15 (p. 153). These internalized rules have been dealt with in a variety of frameworks and under a variety of names. (In discussing the work of Bower, the rules of behavior the babies developed were loosely called "theories.") Other terms for the rules of behavior came up in connection with Kagan's and Piaget's work: These authors termed a rule of expectation, including all past experience with, and action upon, the regularities of the environment, a "schema." At other points in the preceding account similar names have been applied—"sets," "neurone-nets," "belief-structures," or, in psychoanalytic terms, "transferences." Pavlovian theory names the regularities which the organism has come to expect in the world "conditioned reflexes."

All of these terms and concepts, with their different shades of meaning, recognize the human capacity to store and to organize information about the world, the self, and the relations between the two in all three components of the symbolic process. All these different ways of naming and looking at this storage capacity imply the continuity of experience—that there is a continual comparative process in the moment-by-moment experience of the individual, matching the new with the old. All these theories and viewpoints recognize that it is novelty, the *mismatch* between the old and the new, which guides attention and makes for change.[1] The ability to compare requires that the individual must possess a series of principles for organizing the world around him.

These organizing principles of thought (with its three elements) are stored from earliest experience. In playing peekaboo, babies at 60 days of age were forming organizing principles. What shall these be called? Kenneth Boulding (1956) proposed the term "the Image," which he meant to include all the knowledge of how the world works that an individual possesses—private, public, visceral, sensory, and so on. Our Image of the world is the stored knowledge, comparable to the memory file of the computer, of all that has happened to us and all we have learned and done. A knotty problem is the question of how some particular item stored in the Image is somehow brought forward and compared with the experience of this movement. A book alluded to earlier, *Plans and the Structure of Behavior* (Miller et al., 1960), addresses itself to this question. Miller et al. applied what was then known of Cybernetics, information theory, computer design, neuroanatomy, and neurophysiology to the study of psychological processes. Central to their discussion is the concept "Plan." A "Plan" (Capital "P") is defined by these authors as "any hierarchical process in the organism that can control the order in which a sequence of operations is to be performed."

Examples of Plans are recipes ("Take two cups of flour. . ."), prescriptions ("Give 30 capsules of one and one-half grains each with instructions to. . ."), golf-instructions ("Keep your head down and your eye on the ball on the back-swing. . ."), road directions ("Go two blocks west after you get to the white church on the right-hand side. . ."), service manuals for any machine ("Keep observing the left upper dial; when it reads 200, turn the right control knob until. . ."). Plans describe sequential processes, organized not like the letter "O" in a span of space which can be grasped

---

[1] See Festinger, 1957.

immediately, but instead, like $T = f(d,s,c)$, organized in time. Plans include any number of subplans, and may reach the degree of complexity exhibited by the well-nigh incredible memory capacities of a Toscanini, who could detect one wrong note in the playing of a long symphony—unnoticeable to most of the audience or even to members of the orchestra playing from scores they watched in front of them—all from memory. Any single symphony was only one of hundreds or thousands of compositions whose Plans he had stored and could recall at will. The motor-operation Plans of the concert pianist's repertoire provide another example—an Arthur Rubinstein *thinks* only about the broad master Plans of all the concerti, etudes, preludes, fugues, and such he has at his command—when he begins to play it is almost as if his fingers had memorized the intricacies of the subplans involved in all the passages of the works he can play, and so it feels subjectively when one learns to play a composition. (Miller et al. point out that there is good reason to think that intricate Plans of motor behaviors are stored ready for use in the cerebellum—ready, like the tape recording of a symphony, for instant use. The rapidity of play required in, for example, the performance of a cadenza of a concerto is such that transmission rates of nerve fibres would not give time for feedback from fingers to brain to guide performance from each note to the next; some prelearned, prerecorded Plan is required that can simply, as it were, be "plugged in" for use.)

These authors explore Plans for remembering, for speaking, for searching and solving problems, for the performance of motor skills and habits, the relation of Plans to values and intentions, and to those "given" Plans, instincts. They provide a fresh perspective on matters neuropsychological. They define a basic unit, which the authors call a TOTE unit, which is a cybernetic feedback-loop explaining neurological functions far better than the traditional reflex-arc model. They apply new insights to many of the considerations thus far discussed, such as hypnosis and therapeutic tactics.

The authors exemplify the TOTE ("Test Operate Test Exit") unit by pointing to the organized operations involved in hammering a nail. Once the nail is started into a piece of wood, the person wielding the hammer observes whether the hammer is raised or not and whether the nail is oriented correctly (he *tests* nail and hammer, "T"), and if the nail is pointing correctly below the raised hammer, he pounds (he operates, "O"). Having hit the nail he observes that the hammer is lowered (another test, "T.") Should the nail be a very small one and should the wood be balsa, the nail might have been driven into the wood so that its head is flush with the wood's surface—in which case, the Plan—"drive the nail till it's fully driven"—would have been completed (the second test, "T," would reveal this fact). The TOTE unit would then be supplanted by another Plan—it would exit from control (the "E" part of "TOTE") Had the person's second test revealed that the nail's head was still above the surface, pounding would have continued. Our behavior is guided by a series of such subplans, Plans and even master Plans (building a complete house—or a life for oneself). The peekaboo game requires a series of Plans, guiding the sequential behavior of the child as he builds Plan after Plan of how to keep the game going. The therapist's behavior in any hour of psychotherapy similarly requires a series of Plans, stored in the Image the therapist has built up of the patient and how he functions, and of how the therapist might help him function differently.

The work of Miller et al. has been relatively neglected in relation to psychotherapy, but the concept of "Plan" seems particularly apt at this point in the discussion of elements of interpersonal influence. The utility of the concept Plan is that it is a dynamic intentionality, like William James' "intention to say something" or Chomsky's sentence-generating rules. It is not a static set of photographic images or remembered words, but expresses the serial ordering in time which is characteristic of psychological processes. Thought is ordered sequentially, as in the unfolding of a sequence of behavior guided by the plans we call instincts, seen in such processes as nest-building, courting, and mating. Plans consist of all three elements of thought—drive, sense perception, and conceptual elaboration—ordered in *time*.

Types of Plans in Interpersonal Influence

Therapists of any school of therapy necessarily give signals to patients that can be divided into two main classes: those that reinforce the Plans patients bring to therapy ("expectations," "conditionings," "sets," "transferences") and those which introduce new variations which do not fit patients' Plans. The classification of "supportive" therapy and "expressive" therapy, which has long been made in the literature of psychotherapy but which may be clearer in the light of the foregoing, is based on this distinction. Those therapeutic influences that reinforce old Plans, that are weighted with the security of good parent-child relations, those that derive from the "kiss-it-and-make-it-well" years, are called "reassurances"—the word itself implies reinforcement of safety Plans. Think of a cat: One can stroke the cat, reassuring it of all the lap-sitting, purring moments of the past—but one can also influence the cat, alerting it to hyperactivity, by inviting it to play by dangling a piece of paper tied to a thread, dragging it along the floor. The latter type of influence, tantalizing the cat, is comparable to the type of influence used in "expressive" or "exploratory" therapies: The patient, like the cat, orients to variations on his Plans which the therapist provides. Residents in psychiatric training have been taught for years that expressive therapy is more stressful than supportive therapy. The former is, in this tradition, reserved for relatively healthy patients, and is to be used cautiously, by therapists who have considerable experience. The cat analogy holds for this distinction: One can entice a kitten into ridiculous and even painful pratfalls by tantalizing it into injudicious orienting moves.

Signals stored by patient and therapist as memory Plans, and the signals given moment-by-moment to each other in therapy, can be divided further into classes of signals according to the level of abstraction of a signal. These classes provide a framework for grouping the different schools of therapy. There are signals that have reference to the relation of objects in the external world to each other. These have the form "the cat sees the rat," and, although most characteristic of schoolrooms, such statements inevitably occur in every therapy. Therapists cannot avoid, for example, setting up some sort of structure in the operations of therapy: "My office is at Fifth and Main Streets," and "Please send your check to the secretary in room 625," or nonverbal gestures indicating "This is your chair and this one is mine." One takes these signals for granted, and they are not even recorded in most accounts of therapy, but they can be powerful influences, as in the earlier example of the European analyst's formal introduction to the couch: Within seconds the structure of therapy had been nonverbally defined. Had he installed a bathtub in his office and directed the patient toward it by gesture, he would have stimulated the patient to an even more powerful orienting response; this would have been a radical departure from his patient's Plans concerning therapy. Another class of signal-groups refers to the relation of the patient's inner world to objects and persons in the environment: "I understand you fear both cats and rats," says the therapist. There are still other statements that refer to events occurring entirely within the patient's head: "You feel your fear of cats and rats is ridiculous and shameful." Within each class of statements there are multiple levels of meaning, specified by supporting signals that involve the therapist's gestures, facial expressions, and feelings, which provoke in turn a multileveled response on the part of the patient. Each of the participants not only signals outwardly but has an inner dialogue at many levels. The therapist's dialogue influences the patient's dialogue and vice versa. All these classes of signal sending and receiving are stored as each moment of therapy passes in the memory Plans of both patient and therapist.

The Lattice of Signalling

The classification of signals leads to the construction of a framework, a sort of lattice-structure at many levels of the symbolic process, in which the interventions with Plans that are characteristic of any school of therapy may be pigeonholed. This lattice might be visualized as resembling a kind of jungle-gym. One can pigeonhole therapies according to what they say they do, though all schools actually cannot avoid some operations in every pigeonhole of the lattice of symbols. Some schools stress signals of one type and neglect to mention the other types. Other schools, *mutatis mutandis,* can be placed on another portion of the lattice of symbolism. The lowest levels of the lattice, in respect to abstraction, are nonverbal sensorimotor ones. Operations at these lower levels can be compared to the type of operation used in analogue computers (those that consist of models or replicas of the object under study—an airfoil in a wind tunnels, for example—the behavior of which permits measurement and inference regarding the original object). The higher levels of the lattice of symbolism operate with a radically different type of information processing, comparable to a digital computer (those that convert information into signals having only some arbitrary relation to the object studied—conventions of mathematics or language, for instance). The signalling processes in any school of therapy involve translations from the analogue-type symbols into higher-level digital-type symbols, and also the reverse translation. The author has devised many diagrams depicting the relations of one type of interpersonal influence to another. Each diagram has its virtues, but the attempt to find a *general* diagrammatic paradigm founders on several intrinsic properties of interpersonal relationships. These are, first, that relations are time-oriented and sequential; hence, a static diagram is inadequate (perhaps fourth, fifth, or sixth dimensions are required). Secondly, a simple diagram (let us say, a cube having three dimensions, perhaps trisected in each dimension according to the intensity of emphasis on a particular dimension) does violence to the nature of experience and of interpersonal influence. One could devise many such "cubes"; experience in fact has many dimensions, and a visual depiction of the necessarily polyhedronal nature of encounter would introduce complicated labels and diagrams that only obfuscate the central fact: therapeutic signalling ($T = f(d,s,c)$ has many categories and emphases. A large honeycomb of cells into which types of signals might be fitted is the more appropriate model. What counts is that all therapies use, at times, all possible categories whether they declare so or not, and some schools emphasize some particular categories as compared with another school's emphasis, even though there are inevitably many implicitly shared categories of signalling.

Lest the complexity of this lattice model seem hopelessly and needlessly elaborate to the reader, let him consider the following caricatures, for demonstrational purposes, of the therapeutic Plans of three broad groupings of schools of therapy—existentialists, behavior therapists, and a third group, the psychoanalysts.

A patient consulting an existentialist might open his account of his problem by verbal signals in the digital mode, saying, "I'm afraid of cats and rats," and simultaneously show cringing and embarrassed nonverbal analogue gestures. These combined messages, expressions of Plans on the part of the patient, could lead to many types of therapeutic interventions, but those chosen by existentialists tend to focus on the aspects of the patient's verbal and nonverbal statements which reveal a Plan, a style of relating his inner world to the world around him. This Plan, as all Plans do, has conceptual elaborations within it. The therapist will comment at a high level of abstraction, calling the patient's attention to a Plan of relating to the world the patient may never have noticed before—a mode, a stance of "being-in-the-world" which has been so pervasive up to that point that it had evaded his attention. The therapist's digital message, "I, too, have felt the terror of nothingness, the fear of death (which of course one sees cats inflict upon rats)," makes a highly abstract inference and leads, when accompanied by reassuring analogue messages implying togetherness, to an exploration of the patient's values, his concepts, and his internal relations with himself—his modes of dealing with the process of moment-by-moment experience. Such a response orients a patient toward previously undiscovered aspects of himself and to new synthesizing efforts. A patient and therapist share in observing their experience of each other and the surrounding world, orienting to new aspects of living. The patient's Plan "cats bring fear" gradually changes to the new Plan, "I *can* stand contemplating my death—cats only reminded me of this problem."

The patient's first message, if heard by a behavior therapist, might lead to questions like, "What *kind* of cats?" and "*When* do you fear rats?"—which questions provide the therapist a list of circumstances and intensities of patient-to-object relationships. Then, without further ado, the behavior therapist might concentrate his efforts on using the authority vested in him by the patient (according to an old Plan which is left implicit in this mode of therapy) to suggest reassuring states of comfort and ease to the patient in the consulting room. Once the therapist is satisfied via analogue signs (muscular relaxation, relaxed expression and position) that this state has been achieved in his patient, the therapist urges the patient to visualize—in other words to revert to sensorimotor internal signals—some least-threatening scenes on the list of rat-and-cat exposures (perhaps cats and rats at a distance) and to signal the therapist by raising a finger (analogue message) at the least hint of fear. Gradually the patient's Plan "cats bring fear" changes to "cats are safe animals."

The existential and the behavior-therapy approaches look very different. Students in any discipline related to psychotherapy are apt to be confused when confronted with therapists whose styles of influence are as discrepant as these stereotypes depict. Given the framework of the lattice of symbolism, these discrepant styles would seem to occupy pigeonholes about as distant from each other as possible. One, the existential style, stresses highly abstract matters—fourth- or fifth-level categories. The other emphasizes reassuring sensorimotor experience on the one hand (via suggestions to relax), combined with dosed exposure to images of external objects—both of these achieved, to be sure, by verbal instruction.

The difference is more apparent than real, once one looks for the way both approaches use the signals they fail to mention. Both styles assume that the patient will receive signals and attend to them. (The rare patient who can talk but who is totally deaf would be considered outside the scope of such therapies.) Neither school takes seriously the possibility that the patient's statement, "I am afraid of cats and rats," is only a meaningless jumble of symbols like those coming from patients called hebephrenic schizophrenics, who often give such cryptic messages (which messages are called, in the trade, "word-salad"). Both styles of therapy assume assurances had been given during the patient's childhood, which the patient has built into his Plans, and which can be used by the therapist for reassurance. Both styles imply that variations offered by the therapist from the patient's Plans will produce orienting responses —an alerting challenge.

Both styles assume a capacity for creative categorizing on the part of the patient, which will allow him to synthesize new Plans of his view of the world. If this were not the case, both styles would be limited to reinforcing and reassuring the old Plans that once gave security, and there would be no point in attempting to introduce variations that would only serve to confuse the patient. There is a shared underlying assumption in both styles of therapy that these new Plans of the patient's worldview will be filed in some lasting form to guide his subsequent behavior —else the therapeutic intervention would be confined to momentary influence. Both therapies assume implicitly that these new Plans will include components, messages, coming from many levels of the lattice of symbolism. These components are both verbal, at many levels, and nonverbal, at many levels (for example, a general component at a high level of abstraction: "Shared encounter is reassuring," or less abstractly "this individual human, this doctor, wants to help and can help me," and even more concretely, "I *can* relax.").

Neither of these caricatured stereotypes of therapeutic Plans, the existential and the behavioral, pays any particular attention to the type of Plans of the patient that other styles of therapy emphasize as the crucial targets for therapeutic influence. All psychoanalytic schools consider the Plans of instinct, and the conflicts of instinctual Plans with the Plans learned in early life, to be vitally important in therapy. Psychoanalysts also consider defensive Plans for dealing with these conflicts essential elements requiring therapeutic influence.

If the patient's Image contains many defensive Plans which prevent access to consciousness of the Plans that nevertheless guide the patient's behavior and get him into trouble, these unconscious plans are not accessible to therapeutic influence. In this connection the value of the concept "Plan" takes on added meaning, since a defense like repression or isolation requires the sequential ordering in time of a process. Any instinctual Plan keeps intruding as time passes. As the vernacular has it, sex rears its ugly head—and repeatedly. The sequential ordering of instinctual Plans requires the sequential ordering of defenses against these, ordered in time. Psychoanalysts' Plans to modify their patient's Plans include the belief that the unconscious must become conscious. "Where there was Id, there must Ego be." This statement is a deliberate oversimplification for the purpose of clarity—analysts are aware that some unconscious Plans can be modified without any conscious effort. They know conditioning influences can allow patients to gain control of and to change even such unconscious processes as heart rate, gastric secretion, or the alpha-waves in the electro-encephalograms of patients (see Razran, 1961). But the contrast between the analytic emphasis on unconscious processes with the behavior therapist's tendency to reluctance to speculate about these processes is the point at issue. For psychoanalysts, the nursery rhyme "Three Blind Mice" says more about human Plans and defenses than does the conditioning of heart rates in the laboratory.

This issue is not handled amongst schools of therapy by a shrug of the shoulders, or by a "there-are-many-roads-to-Rome" type of democratic tolerance. The issue as to whether what the patient says is to be taken at face value, or, on the other hand, whether there are complex underlying conscious and unconscious processes that guide his statement, tends to bring out the polemical tendencies of both analysts and nonanalysts. There is an old story, which can be used as example, concerning the New York Jewish business tycoon who proposed marriage to a chorus girl. On the eve of their marriage the chorus girl said, "Dear, there is something I have to tell you." The businessman replied, "But there is nothing to worry about, my Dear." His fiancée said, "But I have to tell you I am a prostitute." The tycoon answered, "Oh, that's all right, Dear, you go to your church and I'll go to mine." The multiple levels of such an exchange would alert analysts to the deeper levels of the lattice of symbolism; these same messages incite the more extreme behaviorists to a sometimes frenetic objection to their usefulness in the process of therapy. One of the most vociferous of behavior therapists, Andrew Salter (1961), can be heard to say that psychoanalysis is dying and should, like the fabled elephant, drag itself off to some distant jungle graveyard to die. For Salter, dream interpretation is poker with every card wild. (Salter's position is considered extreme even by many behaviorists.) Similarly barbed statements can be heard in conversation with analysts concerning behavior therapies.

A Clinical Example of the Honeycomb of Plans

A glimpse of the complexity and intricacy of the lattice of symbolism with which psychoanlysis attempts to deal can be afforded by a single example, reported by Gerhart Piers (Piers & Singer, 1953). Dr. Piers had a patient who had a problem of losing money in a spiteful and destructive fashion. The patient asked if he could pay Dr. Piers his fee at the close of each session, since the patient felt that he could not trust himself to retain enough money to pay a monthly bill. Several months' discussions concerning the patient's Plans led Dr. Piers to the impression that the patient's request was based on the patient's dim awareness of an old Plan to deprive father, carried out later upon his family, and threatening to guide him in dealing with his therapist, Dr. Piers. Dr. Piers felt that orienting remarks concerning this Plan had called forth enough resynthesizing, Plan-altering efforts from his patient to work a change in the patient. This change seemed sufficient to make it safe to trust the patient to take the responsibility for paying a monthly bill. Paradoxically, this suggestion from Dr. Piers to the patient produced a decided setback. A great deal of analytic material showed the patient was not threatened by guilt at all but rather by shame over being placed in an inferior position by the structure of the therapeutic situation. Paying Dr. Piers each hour had kept Dr. Piers in his place as a hired hand and had repeatedly reassured the patient in his own eyes that he was not what he feared he was—an inadequate male, behaving like a compliant little girl, fawning on her father.

Dr. Piers' account of his interaction with his patient demonstrates the complex effect of patient's Plans on the therapist's Plans and the reverberation between the two. The interchange involved multiple levels of meaning, which both therapist and patient assigned to an apparently simple aspect of the structure of therapy. This example is offered in rebuttal of the position taken by those, like Salter, who take *any* simplistic view of therapeutic dialogue. "I am afraid of cats and rats" can be dealt with at face value in a conditioning therapy. But, around the edges of the inquiries of conditioning therapists concerning a list of feared situations (the hierarchy of anxiety-provoking situations to be tackled by deconditioning influence), all sorts of other operations occur between therapist and patient that involve the Plans of both participants. Therapists may elect to ignore these, but they cannot escape experiencing them with their patients. Ignoring a patient's riposte concerning fees, such as the one made by Dr. Pier's patient, may either reinforce or demolish a Plan the patient possesses. The *lack* of notice by the therapist of this Plan may have an indifferent effect—we do not know, when we receive skeleton accounts of therapeutic dialogue. It is only when therapists like Dr. Piers take note of such side-operations that we can have some inkling of their importance. The initial telephone encounters mentioned above, with the parents of two young ladies (pp. 160–161), fall in the same category. By the time the two young ladies involved came to therapy all sorts of side-operations had set the therapeutic scene. These skewed the communications from the patient to me by Plans set in motion before she ever entered the therapeutic consultation room.

An Attack on Delusional, if Commonplace, Plans

A fourth capsule-stereotype will sketch out a group of therapies that occupy another portion of the lattice of symbolism (or the stored form of same, the patient's Plans). This group concentrates its influence on the internal self-instructions concerning self-to-self relations and self-to-object relations, but at a different level than existential, analytic, or behavioral therapies. The patient's opening statement, "I'm afraid of cats and rats," might meet a statement from such a therapist as "Naturally. Some years ago *most* intelligent people believed the world was flat, and that one would fall off the edge if one traveled far enough in the world. Your fear of cats and rats comes from the days when you were young. You were told that they are to be feared, and you never have examined the premises on which such statements are based. Let's look at your five-year-old logic." One proponent of this type of influence has been mentioned earlier—Albert Ellis (1962), who calls his type of therapy "Rational Emotive Therapy" (RET), but there are many others who examine cognitive processes and their defects—the conceptual elaborations of thought. Many learning theorists concentrate their influence on such faults of cognition as overgeneralization—the assumption that all cats and rats are like other cats and rats. Psychoanlysts hold to this principle implicitly when they interpret transferences (a type of over-generalization). Each interpretation the analyst makes changes an old conceptual Plan. Explicit examination of commonly held false beliefs is not the core of psychoanalysis, except perhaps in the case of one analyst, Camilla Anderson (1957). Attempts to change the patient's conceptual elaborations by an active attack on his habitual modes of thinking take a variety of forms—Thorne's Directive Therapy (1955), Phillip's Assertion-Structured Therapy (1954), and General Semantic Therapy (Korzybski, 1941).

The essential operation in Rational Emotive Therapy is to change the patient's Plans in such a way that he no longer continues to condition himself in the second signalling system, verbal self-instruction, in ways that violate logic, reality, and life with other adults as compared with life with the giants of one's nursery days. Ellis has managed to pick out a collection of irrational ideas held by the general public and promulgated endlessly in the mass media. These certainly have the stamp of the logic Piaget noted in five-year-olds when they concluded that the moon was following them. One of Ellis's convincing arguments concerns one of these: He demolishes the idea that it makes any sense to blame anyone for anything. "Nonsense!" says Ellis. He demonstrates logically that this idea, so generally accepted, is a fatuous continuation of one's childhood omnipotence. When we blame, we are saying in effect, "Things ought to be the way *I* want them to be, and I am entitled to get angry and blame people or things if they don't conform to my wishes!" Ellis attacks this line of reasoning directly with his patients, together with similar plans of the five-year-old variety, by using digital messages that simply call attention to the faulty hypotheses humans are prone to make when young —and to continue to believe into their adult lives.

Therapists of this group restore to respectability the element of thought which for many years seems to have remained under a cloud, the *c* element, conceptual elaboration, of $T = f(d,s,c)$. Freud's dry remark to the effect that the voice of the intellect is quiet but exceedingly persistent somehow was lost in the excitement of exploration of the jungles of our deeper passions—or our glittering sensations. Once our attention is directed to the amount of brainwashing we receive via conversation, books, television, movies, we become aware of the incessant thrust of irrational ideas to which one is exposed.

A Currently Fashionable Delusion

Delusions—defined as fixed false beliefs—are not the hallmark of primitive societies. They are the well-nigh inescapable hallmarks of being human. It is bad manners, and it can be dangerous, to tamper with the religious beliefs of others, or with patriotic and prejudicial ideas, calling all these "irrational ideas" or "delusions." But there are more neutral grounds for showing examples of fixed beliefs that guide behavior ("the world is flat" was one). We smile at the pious acceptance shown by members of primitive (or another) culture to the patently unprovable and irrational ideas put forth by their witch-doctors, medicine men, or priests, but we are like them. One contemporary example can stand for innumerable instances in history: Let one of our fashionable and revered spokesmen, like Tillich, Dobzhansky, or even a sophisticated trio of laboratory scientists, Miller, Galanter, and Pribram (1960) announce (as they do) that "Man is the only creature who knows he is going to die," and our heads nod in assent, just as much in the fashion of sheep as do the heads of members of primitive cultures.

This statement has not a shred of scientific evidence to support it, except the existence of irrational rituals humans have devised to deal with a dead body—which no other animals share, so far as we now know. There is legend aplenty in the other direction—the dying elephant legend, the funeral ritual of an Old Dog Tray. But, since we can't ask animals what their anticipations are with any sensible expectation of an answer, we must rely on their *actions* as indicating whether they know they are going to die or not. The indications from everyday life are that a cornered rat fights for his life. A young cat will leap from a tree to roof-tops at heights which would cause a fatal fall if he missed. An old cat knows better and will stay in the tree all night rather than kill himself. Both cats and rats *appear* to have an idea where things are heading when they engage with each other—especially the cat, who makes bets against the rat's death for the sport of the cat-and-rat game. The scientific evidence indicates that the consciousness of animals includes considerable in the way of anticipatory planning. Chimpanzees collect twigs before they go for a termite picnic (they use the twigs as we use fishing baits). Otters find and use, for an extended fishing period, a stone to break open mollusc shells. Chimps show clear signs, according to Goodall's (1956) observations, of forming strategies and tactics for dealing with intruders (one distracts, via a feint, while the others circle round behind). Animals help each other— Grzimek (Grzimek & Grzimek, 1960) has observed lions, and others have observed elephants, cooperating to feed and protect other injured lions or elephants. How reasonable is it to assert flat-footedly that man is the only creature who knows he is going to die?

Self-Fulfilling Prophecies

Another contribution Ellis (1962) makes is to spell out more directly than other therapists that we *produce* our own emotions by recalling the stored memories (as if replaying computer programs), the Plans associated with events that produced emotions in the past. Ellis recognizes his debt to the history of philosophical ideas—especially to Epictetus— and acknowledges that this is not a new conception. What is new is the central use he makes of the idea in therapy. What is also new is the strong support given this emphasis by the work described above, that of David Graham and his colleagues (1962; Graham et al., 1962a,b), which shows a clear link between attitudes expressed verbally and psychosomatic illnesses. Once this element of influence is recognized, its use is almost embarrassingly powerful, a fact known to all the spiteful gossips of the world, who delight in bringing up painful subjects in order to set off emotional fireworks in other people: "Tell me again what he said when you asked him what he'd been doing at 2 A.M. with his car parked in front of her house. . . ." Ellis also comes in for strong support from the work of Luria (1960, 1969) and his colleagues—the powerful role of speech in the regulation of behavior. Ellis claims rapid and lasting influence toward marked improvement, by concentrating almost entirely on rooting out the irrational self-signalling Plans patients carry around with them, and by supplanting them with reasonable alternatives.

The Influence of Written Plans

Stereotypical capsule-descriptions of therapy do violence to the range of variation in therapeutic influence. Discussion of all the individual schools is unnecessary here since compendia of therapeutic Plans— though they are not so called—are easily available. This is part of the problem to which this inquiry is addressed: Those approaching the psychotherapeutic scene either from the point of view of student or patient face the confusion that results from a plethora of accounts of varying therapeutic styles. The aim of this inquiry is a synthesis at a higher level, not a collection or eclectic description. Fortunately many descriptions are available to the reader.[2]

[2] A clear and concise summary of almost all schools of therapy and their operations can be found in Harper, 1959. Harper's work is some years old, and new variations have appeared since it was written, but he presents a balanced and accurate account. Another less inclusive summary of the operations of various schools is available in the last chapter of Enelow & Wexler, 1966.

By far the most searching of contemporary surveys (see the next chapter) are those of Perry London, in two penetrating volumes (1964, 1969) that supply not only a clear analysis of various schools of interpersonal influence, but also a definitive bibliography for the field.

For a clear summary of methods of changing Plans on the larger scene, that dealt with by social psychologists, see Zimbardo & Ebbeson, 1969.

Mention of books calls attention to another oft-neglected avenue of psychotherapeutic influence, which is the implicit dialogue (at least in some skillful writing) between writer and reader involved in the reading process. To be influenced by another's Plan, his symbolic process, does *not* require the other's physical presence. The influence involved in bibliotherapy is much less personal and immediate, but should not be discounted—many a person's life has been profoundly influenced, his Plans changed, by reading a book. Widely read writers in the psychiatric field like Karl Menninger have received many testimonial letters regarding the therapeutic effect their books have provided in working permanent change. Ellis, to cite just one other example, reports the same experience with his *Guide to Rational Living* (Ellis, 1971) and his other books.

Summary

Any school of psychotherapy is built around a Plan to change the patient's Plans. An overview of schools of psychotherapy discloses that their theorists state explicitly only certain parts of the Plan belonging to a particular school. Other elements tend to be swept under the rug. Such accounts contain a statement of only some of their goals (the objective of a Plan) and only a partial statement of the techniques employed to reach that goal. One is left to infer that certain elements of influence, which theorists fail to mention explicitly, *must* be operating all of the time, since they are implicit in the symbolic process and in the transactions of therapy. But one receives little assistance from these theorists in evaluating how many pounds and ounces of this or that ingredient of influence goes into their therapeutic techniques. Some ingredients which often fail to be mentioned will be examined in the following chapter.

18

Hidden Elements and Pitfalls in Interpersonal Influence

Commonly Disregarded Elements of Psychotherapeutic Influence

Behavior therapists seek (Plan) by a variety of means to alter the behavior of their patients. The basic idea is that if one can be made to feel comfortable and safe in the therapeutic situation, one can think about things which ordinarily would frighten one *without* becoming frightened, and that gradually the connection between the frightening idea or event and one's anxiety response will diminish and finally disappear. Rarely do behavior therapists scrutinize the patient-therapist dimension. Instead they are inclined to euphemistically describe therapy as "an encounter with a kindly professional." Their neglect of the patient's transference reactions, the therapist's countertransference reactions, and the multiple levels of both these experiences has been mentioned. But other elements of influence, such as the phenomenon of identification (and its counterpart in the therapist, counteridentification) are usually left out of account.[1] The sources of the patient's resistance to the therapist's suggestions (and the second-level counter-resistance in the therapist, with the usual multileveled reverberation between the two) are ignored. With their almost exclusive interest in behavior (not as symptoms of something else), behavior therapists often fail to scrutinize some of the influences they unavoidably employ, and in doing so risk failures they might otherwise have avoided or resolved (a strong negative transference can undercut their capacity to help the patient). They thus miss opportunities to assist the healthy growth of patients. Though behavior therapists tend to attack Freudians or existentialists (sometimes savagely it seems), they implicitly hold the existential value that fresh encounter is better than shy, phobic avoidance. They implicitly accept that old Plans exist (transferences, for a Freudian) and that these must be refurbished. But they leave the fourth, fifth, or *n*th level of the experience of encounter with their patients unexamined and ungoverned. And they tend to ignore the identification patients make with their behavior therapists. Recent accounts indicate that behavior therapists have changed from a once-a-week to a three- to five-times-a-week therapy structure: Identification and counteridentification feed upon close and frequent contact between patient and therapist, and such a change in the structure of treatment, one would predict, will force these therapists to recog-

---

[1] For a notable exception, see Sarbin, 1967.

nize these factors. All such influences should be on any therapist's preflight checklist, lest they get out of control before therapy gets airborne and so that a safe landing can be accomplished.

Psychoanalysts' accounts of their work, on the other hand, stress the use of interpretation alone in their therapeutic Plan. The structure of the analytic situation is such, as has been mentioned, that other modes of influence cannot be avoided, such as suggestion, identification, and conditioning of various types.

The third paradigmatic model of contemporary psychotherapy, the existential mode, stresses encounter to the virtual exclusion of other elements of influence. Existentialists seem to be saying that the psychotherapeutic experience strives for something like the fullest participation in, let us say, the enchantment of a musical performance, including the awareness of its imminent finale (the end of this segment of life). Orienting, conditioning, interpretation, identification, the whole symbolic process —these are "givens" of the therapeutic atmosphere requiring no discussion. What counts is a breakthrough—the view shared with another person of some awesome prospect. John Keats ("On First Looking into Chapman's Homer") spoke for the existentialists when he wrote:

> Then felt I like some watcher of the skies
> When some new planet swims into his ken;
> Or like stout Cortez when with eagle eyes
> He stared at the Pacific, and all his men
> Look'd at each other with a wild surmise
> Silent, upon a peak in Darien.

The Impact of Shared Work

These hidden factors of influence are fostered by any lengthy treatment, and there are also atmospheric elements of influence, seldom noted, involved in any school of therapy which continues beyond the first encounter. One of these is shared experiencing, shared common work, which builds up between the participants. This shared work creates affectional bonds—shared memories, goals, even shared fights. The work of a long psychoanalysis, for instance, is a creative venture of collaboration between two persons which has as its announced goal the reduction and resolution of conflicts and unrealistic expectations belonging to the ancient history of the patient (and what remains in the analyst of his own similar distortions). To think that such a monumental effort could fail to make a common bond is to blind oneself—one loves an adopted child as much as one's own, in proportion to the shared experience, the shared investment of understanding and caring that one has made with that adopted child (as a patient said to the writer, "We've been through one helluva lot together.")

While the relation between therapist and patient is a symbolic one early in therapy (the therapist does not feed, clothe, nor house the patient, but only stands in the place of those who once did), successful therapy of any stripe rests on shared work, shared fear, shared learning, and shared success. Even unsuccessful therapy tends toward an investment of feelings shared on both sides, which may go so far as hatred. This real present-day relationship, in contrast with transference fantasies, tends to be relatively ignored in the literature of psychotherapy.[2] Offhand, there seems no particular reason to think of a therapist as being different in kind from one's piano teacher—one develops transference reactions to one's piano teacher, which may or may not ever be discussed—one pays him for his time, and he provides, like the therapist, no material support, yet these facts do not invalidate real affection between student and teacher after years of working together to achieve proficiency.

The Vital Role of Humor

Humor is another ingredient of influence in human relations which seldom finds its way into writings about the Plans of psychotherapy. Yet we all know the crucial importance of a shared sense of humor in the development of a human relationship. Humorless men make poor therapists, whatever the psychotherapeutic school to which they belong. Though the problems bringing the patient to the therapist are often deadly serious in nature, a humorless therapist is crippled in rendering these problems *less* deadly serious. A therapist's sense of humor needs to extend to his view of himself: Children react with fear to austere authority and reject pomposity in adults; the frightened child in the patient reacts similarly. Humor, not wit, expresses the loving aspect of that built-in residue of the canons of one's childhood, the superego, as Freud pointed out: In humor, the loving aspect of parental authority is expressed. A good-humored therapist who can smile at his own foibles and weaknesses, and at those of his patient, can begin in the first hour to rob the patient's ancient ghosts of their power to terrify. The implication is obvious: In choosing one's stance as therapist or patient, value humor.

The Invisible Effects of Culture and Language

The "givens" of therapy only show up when they are violated. It seems quite unnecessary to state in the descriptions of various types of psychotherapies that the therapist keeps his clothes on. It was only after group therapies such as are conducted at Esalon in California (and by now in many other settings) with all participants in the nude, that one noticed this rule. There are many other things that therapists do *not* do. There are injunctive limiting Plans that are part of the mores and folkways of the

---

[2] For a sensitively written exception, see Stone, 1961.

culture in which therapists work. Belching and breaking wind are considered bad manners in most cultures (even these manners have been abrogated intentionally by some of the more "swinging" therapists of late), but there are other taboos which are harder to recognize. Most therapists make no attempt to tamper with the religious beliefs of their patients, but when transported to another culture, they find it difficult to work within the framework of the belief structures (Plans) of their patients. Only recently have psychiatrists in underdeveloped nations learned to use the tribal medicine men to assist them in therapeutic efforts. Even the language used in therapy imposes certain well-nigh invisible limits on one's efforts. One example was given in the case of the Tahitian language (p. 109), but there are others. Modern Russian and Spanish, for example, contain no single word for the process of "becoming" (a word much used by some therapists, for example, Rogerians)—the concept can be used, but with more circumlocution than is needed in English. Until Beardsley Ruml (1933) coined it, English had no word for "homefulness." Ruml, an economist and psychologist, pointed out that the tendency to stay home, or return home ("This is my own, my native land") is the most important single factor for economic and political stability in the world. Without it, there would be chaos—yet we had no name for this powerful feeling until Ruml invented it, and it is still unnamed for most persons. Some bilingual persons, fluent in two languages since childhood, say they can detect subtle differences in their personality functioning depending on which language they use. The larger context supplied by language, custom, and culture inevitably sets limits on the elements of influence.

Dangers Implicit in Techniques of Influence

Invisible influences in psychotherapy are not necessarily indifferent or benign. Though each school tends to police its own area of emphasis, each tends to be oblivious to the unfortunate effects of types of influence which are not explicitly stated in the Plan of that school. Therapists of the school called "client-centered" (Rogerian therapists), for example, by limiting their interventions to reflecting what the patient says, run the risk of reinforcing the kind of five-year-old logic that is incorporated into the verbal self-instructions patients give themselves, which function as conditioned guiding Plans. The encouragement to fantasy and to regressive modes of thought supplied by the psychoanalytic couch has its own implicit dangers, many of which have been pointed out by the analysts themselves. Analysts do not place patients on the couch whose reality testing they judge to be seriously deficient, since the couch posture, with its curtailment of feedback cues, tends to increase the confusion of such patients. The classical analytic structure of four to six hours per week has, however, a built-in conditioning influence which leads to some of the attitudes deplored by those who have listened to psychoanalytic patients and their cocktail party talk—analytic patients sometimes come to have what appears to the outsider to be a sticky dependency on their analysts. These patients imply that every decision, even a minor one, cannot be made independently, but needs exploring with one's analyst. These patients seem to the uninitiated observer to have an exaggerated reverence for the inscrutible Great One, bordering on idolatry. Allen Wheelis, himself a trained analyst, commented wryly that too many people seem to have their backs to the couch instead of their shoulders to the wheel. Some analysts have suspected that the interminable obsessive rumination some patients show, this posture of dependency, is a consequence of the analytic structure. The chief spokesman of this group, Franz Alexander (1953), recommended Plans for interruptions of therapy and for less frequent scheduling of therapeutic sessions. Anyone who has seen patients in therapy five hours a week knows that the process and the possibilities open within it for therapeutic influence are different in character than in once-a-week therapy, but the effects of conditioning influence in that five-hour structure have tended to remain hidden.

The structure of the therapeutic relation subtly changes the process of therapy. If one works in a structure guaranteeing absolute confidentiality, the kind of material patients discuss is different from the material one reads in the records of those who record therapeutic sessions; the tape recorder seems the villain, as one simply never hears the kinds of thoughts, fantasies, or dreams in recorded interviews that one hears when tape recorders are excluded. If one's therapy Plan contains a taboo against treating a man and his wife together, one works only with edited data. The struggles of a patient with his therapist in the encounter may become bleached to the point of virtual disappearance in a successful treatment. The relationship may become serene, secure, and creative between patient and therapist, but the relationship between the patient and his wife may remain of an entirely different character, undiscernible by the therapist until he sees the patient in interaction with his wife in couples therapy. It is a disturbing and disquieting experience to work out most of the problems expressed in the transference over a two- or three-year period and then to see one's patient transformed when his wife is brought into the therapeutic consultation room.

A further invisible influence, by no means always positive, is the self-confirming tendency of subplans contained in one's psychotherapeutic style. Over the years a therapist tends to confirm the preconceptions concerning the structure of the psychotherapeutic relationship he held when he began doing therapy. If he believes that five-hour-a-week therapy is the only type that can achieve results in certain cases, he excludes from his data gathering the very observations that might correct such a position. If he believes that once-a-week therapy is adequate, the same fatal exclusion occurs: fatal, that is, to scientific testing of hypotheses concerning therapy. Rogerian therapists get Rogerian data; Freudian therapists, Freudian data. This subtle effect of conditioning in the therapeutic process appears when one reads the detailed accounts of patients' utterances of therapists working in different schools—patients of Jungian therapists dream Jungian dreams; patients of Freudian therapists dream Freudian dreams. It would appear that the only way to control the pervasive effect of one's therapeutic Plan upon the material and the course of the therapy[3] is to practice in a number of modes oneself, or to explore candidly the work of someone from a different school.

Sectarian and parochial attitudes in the field of psychotherapy tend only to perpetuate distortions of the full range of the patient's combinatory and categorizing potentialities that are imposed by the particular Plan the therapist elects. Again, the work of scientists studying the developmental process, such as Lenneberg (1967) and Bower (1966), gives a wider context: Any *one* therapy taps only a limited pie-segment of a patient's ability to see fresh aspects of the problems he brings to therapy and of new ways to cope with them. In this perspective each school of therapy might be compared to a local dialect of a particular language. The local dialects of all the languages of the world are theoretically innumerable. Each dialect is capable of being used to convey the full range of human thought and none can claim pre-eminence, but each has its peculiar limitations and slants, which lend, for example, the clipped speech of the Yankee a different flavor from the drawl of the Deep South.

The Role of Altered States of Consciousness

One frequently ignored factor in therapy is the alteration of the state of consciousness that occurs as a result of the technique of therapy, whether this alteration is desired or not. Hypnotic therapies, of course, make this factor explicit in their Plans. So do therapies whose Plans include alterations achieved by the injection of drugs ("narcotherapy"), such as that favorite of fictional accounts of therapy, "truth serum" (which involves the intravenous injection of the drug, Sodium Amytal), used to produce a state of fluid thinking resembling dreaming in which repressed memories and experiences can again reach consciousness. Hallucinogens like LSD and psylocybin have been used as adjuncts in formally structured therapy as well as in the informal influences of "tripping."

The influence of the analytic couch is more subtle in altering consciousness. While some therapeutic Plans (for example, hypnoanalysis) include hypnosis, analysts need give no relaxation or sleep suggestions and need make no direct attempts resembling any of the hypnotic induction techniques to alter the level of consciousness of their patients,

---

[3] For a summary of the evidence that patients' values tend to bend and converge with those of their therapists as a result of psychotherapy, see Meltzoff & Kornreich, 1970. Perry London (1964, 1969) has clearly shown that therapists cannot escape influencing their patients goals, values, and morals in the course of therapy, including various efforts aimed at behavior modification.

for an alteration often occurs spontaneously. It is difficult to describe the effect produced by lying on one's back on a couch saying whatever passes through one's mind. Sometimes body-image distortions occur as occurred in one's adolescent years when falling asleep or waking up (these states, bordering on sleep, are called respectively "hypnogogic" and "hypnopompic"). One may feel swollen or shrunken in some part of one's body or feel as if one were floating in the air. In such states one's grasp on the crisp outlines of reality blur, as when one is dozing, and curious sensory experiences can occur which would have pathological significance if they intruded into full waking life. One may have the impression one has heard one's name called, for example, and this carries none of the implications that go with waking hallucination.

Patients drift in and out of such states in the consulting room. Rarely, patients doze on the couch briefly (usually at times when other evidence in their verbal and nonverbal behavior suggests that they are avoiding contact and communication because of a touchy issue), but almost every analytic patient feels a change in his consciousness during some hours. This is most noticeable to the patient as he leaves the hour to return to his everyday affairs. Patients often joke about having to "reassemble the ego," "come off a trip," or some such jocular expression of the feeling of pulling themselves together to face the world, as one does in the first moments of awakening in the morning.

Other therapies than hypnosis or analysis cannot escape employing altered states as an unseen and unremarked element of influence in their Plans. These have an ancient history in the art of healing going back before recorded history, as in the trance and possession states of shamans and their supplicants, the "incubation" of Egyptian and Greek sleep temples, the cures at religious shrines and in encounters with religious relics (Ludwig, 1969). Altered states of consciousness carry with them an increased suggestibility, an increased sense of meaning, a propensity for catharsis, and often terminate with feelings of rejuvenation, which characteristics make the obvious or subtle attempt to exploit such states in therapy of any type almost irresistible. Much of the magic and the ceremony of the world is built on such foundations. The history of mankind's efforts to influence mankind is replete with every imaginable method of altering states of consciousness, so it would be fatuous to assume that these states stay out of the consulting room in any form of psychotherapy.[4] Men seem to have an irresistible hunger for such states —witness the current scene with its LSD and other drugs—and when a form of psychotherapy offers nurture to this appetite it has its place already made. Dostoievsky's insight in *Notes from Underground* applies to all psychotherapies: If mankind were really convinced that Pascal's homunculus, that imaginary little wise man, could, if given sufficient data

[4] This is an assumption Jerome Frank demolishes in *Persuasion and Healing*, 1961. For a fascinating account of the elements of influence in use in primitive cultures today, and the exploitation of beliefs, rituals, and symbols in the service of therapy, see Kiev, 1964.

from the past, predict all future events—if true psychic determinism were to loom on the horizon of Everyman's thought, man would do something totally irrational to prove that he was his own master, not the slave of determinism. Altered states, sought for and secured, give man a control of his own inner life—his consciousness—which proves that he has that mastery of his own experience he so dearly loves.

Altered states of consciousness have been sought in all cultures. Drugs like peyote are not the only route to trance: The hyperalert trance state has been part of religious and tribal ceremonies throughout the ages. "Holy Rollers" achieve altered states of consciousness similar to those of the repetitive tribal dances, and movies of the mass rallies of Nazi Nuremberg reveal a behavior-suggesting trance when the audiences respond to Hitler with a million-throated "Sieg Heil!" Hyperalert states may be part of the appeal of such recent experiments with "marathon encounters," in which groups explore their interactions for 30 hours continuously, eschewing sleep, until some altered interaction, some change in the usual social consciousness, assists them to find a new experience. The malignant bombardment of brainwashing influence, flooding the victim with overwhelming stimuli, has been mentioned; a benign variant is used in the new psychotherapeutic technique called "multiple-impact therapy." In this method, a family sustains the long-continued interventions of assorted therapists of various backgrounds, in combination or singly, whose efforts are directed at breaking up old patterns. These interventions are telescoped into a marathon impact allowing no time for strategic retreat for regrouping on the family's part. A pathological system of family relations often suffers a knock-out blow by the fury of the attack offered by such an experience, and the participants' usual state of consciousness is altered by the incessant barrage over many hours.

Multiple-impact therapy, marathon encounter, and all intentional or spontaneous trance inductions, whether hypnotic or exciting, disclose again the hidden aspect of influence, involving the orienting reflex. This is, that *any* intervention by the therapist is bound to act, assuming it has been received and attended to (a big assumption), as an interference with the ongoing course of the patient's life. Any intervention whatsoever is like a signal to a moon-rocket, changing its course, whether by .003 degrees or by 30 degrees. Every word the therapist utters has this potentiality, every shift in his posture, or change in his expression. His is a position, a role, that prevents him from having *no* influence —he cannot be the stranger in the subway sitting quietly five seats away reading his newspaper, or the unnoticed bystander at a subway station, although schizophrenics frequently go far toward treating therapists in such a fashion. The conditions under which patients enter therapy —whether under their own volition or under coercion—place the therapist in the spotlight so that *no* response can be as much an instruction to the patient as *any* response. The analyst's silence has been mentioned: Classical psychoanalysis aims at minimal interference with the patient's spontaneous stream of consciousness, yet some signalling is unavoidable. A fixed, wax-figure smile can be as potent an influence as a slap in the face. And further, these smiles can influence at levels *below* ordinary alert consciousness, at ordinary levels, or even at super-ordinate levels of the highest abstraction human consciousness can comprehend—all of them intermingled. Absence of any reverberation between patient and therapist at all levels is as powerful an influence as positive reverberation: One way to drive a five-year-old (or a 50-year-old) to panic is for the therapist to behave as though he no longer could see the patient. Carl Whitaker pointed out conversationally that there is no more vivid example of William James' idea of the ultimate torture—disconfirmation—than to say to a child of five: "Johnny! Where *are* you?" (Fumbling motions in the child's vicinity) "You were here just a second ago!" (More fumbling motions and ignoring of verbal and nonverbal signals from the child).

Unmentionable Dimensions: Devotion and Commitment

The final element of influence, which often remains invisible in the written descriptions of therapy, is the dimension of devotion, and its reverse, indifference, detachment, and renunciation. Therapists of any school can, like the parents Escalona studied (p. 11), either neglect or smother. Early on, in most therapies, ground-rules come up and are defined—such as appointment hours, contact outside the office, fees, freedom to telephone the therapist. Often some of the structural ground rules are described in the literature, but therapists hold more rules than they announce, and vary even those they describe in ways that are as capable of influencing patients as were Mr. Von Osten's cues to Clever Hans. How to describe the tone of one's voice when changing an appointment time? Or the effect of being seen by one's patient at the theater? Such factors influence the patient's assessment of how devoted one is, or how indifferent. Psychoanalysts have written the most about these matters, since they concentrate attention on transference (the minute scrutiny of the unrealistic expectations patients derived from earlier parental devotions), but such subtle variations on a theme, the Plan of therapeutic structure, seldom find their way into the literature of other schools of therapy.

Many levels of meaning pervade even apparently simple comments concerning the structure of therapy. "I'll see you next week" can convey affection, anxious concern, indifference, disgust, or anger. Such tones have an instructional influence that is independent of the informational content of the message. A message may have a "hard-boiled" content at the verbal level, but may simultaneously convey concern and devotion by the analogue signals which accompany its spoken words. These complexities make the evaluation of written or even tape-recorded records of therapy a questionable procedure indeed.

Therapists of any school convey to their patients impicit objectives, limits, and commitments, which may be at wide variance from what these therapists say in words. As in all other dimensions, the patient also conveys to the therapist complex messages of the same sort. This implicit dialogue about unspoken Plans often governs the degree of dependency, the intensity of commitment, and the movement toward termination of the relationship. Animals carry on rather complex transactions governing dominance and submission, aggression and its inhibition by infantile behavior or by "humility signs," and territorial rights.[5]

Human beings have not lost their heritage of communicative ability, and this type of dialogue goes on in the consultation room, whether or not it is described in the literature. How do patient and therapist deal with the problem of ending therapy? Usually written descriptions speak of such indicators as loss of symptoms, better integration, freedom of expression, increased enjoyment of life, work, and love. Patient and therapist discuss such developments from time to time in most types of therapy, but an additional nonverbal dialogue concerning whether or not it is time to terminate therapy occurs.

This second dialogue has its counterpart in the rather complex transactions animals engage in as their young mature. Some forcibly eject them from the nest. Some chase their young away—mother bears cuff their cubs about until the cubs go up a tree to get out of harm's way, whereupon mother bear runs away before the cubs can get down the tree and find her. Other species—seals and lions, for example—rely on the male's harem-building tendencies to disperse young animals throughout the territory available to the species, a trait which some see as having survival value.

Human babies cannot survive such treatment, but there are marked and discernible differences in how human mothers deal with the dependent clinging as contrasted with the exploring tendencies babies show (Rheingold, 1966). Summarized with crude brevity, studies have shown that socioeconomic factors affect the ways mothers handle babies, and that the sex of the child makes a big difference. Girls are generally encouraged to cling, boys to explore. The best learning and development occur, as Escalona (1968) observed, when mothers neither smother nor reject, but let the child struggle with problems at least part of the time. There are signs that humans do better if some equivalent of being pushed out of the nest is given by their mothers: The distinguished researcher in child development Harriet Rheingold (1966) calls this "de-tachment" and is currently studying what looks to her to be an essential for development —the mother's active discouragement of the baby's clinging.

[5] These have been described in detail by Lorenz, 1952, his student Tinbergen, 1951, and others— see Ardrey, 1966.

Clinging in infants is an extraordinarily persistent schema which can be seen in the behavior of primates in extreme form under experimental conditions. The babies whose monkey mothers had been raised as total isolates show clinging to a degree not seen in human affairs (Harlow, 1963). These mothers are inadequate in *all* social relations, including motherhood. It takes extraordinary ingenuity and patience on the part of investigators even to devise ways of impregnating such animals, as they are unable to respond to sexual advances in any of the ways usual for monkeys. Even the most practiced, energetic, and determined monkey Lotharios frequently fail with these poor creatures. The behavior shown after these mothers deliver their babies—a travesty of motherly behavior —even goes as far as grinding the infants' faces into the wire mesh of the cage. Many monkey infants, treated thusly by their mothers, just die. But Harlow points out an extraordinary coda to this testament to the force of the clinging schema: The second time around, the behavior of even an infanticidal monkey mother is characterized by almost adequate treatment of her second baby. The perished baby had left a mark on his murderous mother's Plans: He had taught her how to be a mother.

The attenuated transactions of the consultation room are faint echoes of processes that stand out so starkly in the nursery, laboratory, or jungle. Yet when Ellis (1962) responds to a plaintive comment from a patient by directing him to do more homework in systematically teasing out and correcting defective Plans—writing them down, examining their premises—he is actively pushing the patient toward autonomy. This is a mother-bear type of maneuver, which Ellis recognizes as such. At the other extreme, also recognized as a planned tactic, was the indefatigable and indomitable effort of the late C. P. Oberndorfer, who tried to search the limits of traditional psychoanalytic influence: For 27 years he treated a man hovering on the edge of schizophrenic disintegration.[6] Oberndorfer concluded that the treatment influence had stabilized this man at an obsessive-compulsive level as compared with the total chaos which overtook his patient whenever interruptions occurred in the treatment. In the mid-range between these two extremes of devotion and detachment, some therapists leave it to the patient to decide whether to continue therapy (and how often) without any comment as to the reasons guiding the patient's decision. Other therapists (especially analysts) take the patient's attitude toward the structure of therapy as grist for the interpretive mill. Termination or continuation can express long-standing Plans on the patient's part, and analysts do not take attitudes about termination at face value. They look for evidence in free associations, dreams, and such, to help evaluate what the patient is trying to express by whatever position the patient takes toward therapy. Analysts ask themselves whether their patients are expressing rebellion, dependency,

[6] Personal communication, but see Oberndorfer, 1943.

inertia, or avoidance. They look at such attitudes from a higher level of abstraction, placing them in a larger framework of meta-Plans.

Devotion and detachment in therapeutic influence receive less emphasis in writings about therapy than they deserve, judging from the evidence that these are potent influences throughout the animal kingdom. These factors have a way of insinuating themselves into the side-operations of therapy—those taken-for-granted exchanges not considered part of "Therapy-Proper"—in a way that mostly eludes description. (A partial inventory: phone calls; trappings of the consultation room; contact outside the consultation room; frequency and availability of therapeutic sessions; gossip about therapy, or the therapist; implications of the therapist's degree—D.D., M.D., Ph.D., M.S.W.; endorsement by enthusiastic adherents).

An Even More Unmentionable Dimension: Money

Whatever the therapist's choice on the dimension of devotion, his behavior weights the scale of what matters in therapy in ways left out of written accounts of therapeutic influence. Take the matter of fees. Far from being purely a matter of local professional convention, this element of influence has all the subtlety and richness of the peekaboo game, and more.

Every school of therapy has its pecking order. This order, like the barnyard ordering of hens and roosters, depends on seniority, power, prestige. Senior therapists select those patients they wish to influence. Every therapist who starts a practice experiences a sort of professional bachelorhood like that of young lions or seals, during which he is treated by senior therapists as a loner, out of the tribe, garnering what he can from the therapeutic pickings of older and more accepted therapists. Rich and powerful people insist on seeing famous therapists, chairmen of academic departments, or therapists fashionable amongst their friends ("no one else will do"). The market place invades the consultation room to the extent that referring therapists have described patients to me as if a fee-per-hour were a price-per-head. Such communications remind one of the obscene atmosphere of a slave market: "She is a $35 patient." Ugly as this is, it must be honestly faced as an element of influence, guiding the choice of treatment structure (the frequency of interviews, the place on the waiting list, and the duration of therapy). And what happens when a patient comes a cropper financially? The dimension of devotion re-emerges at such times. Therapists vary enormously in their views of what to do about the financial vicissitudes their patients undergo. Some regard these as the patient's problem; others fall back on the oath of Hippocrates and stay with the patient through whatever ill-times befall him. Patients can hardly fail to note such differences in stance in their therapists, whether or not one posture is prudent in the long run as compared with another.

The way a therapist regards the dimension of devotion has further consequences for the process of therapeutic change. A way to limit one's observations about psychotherapy is to limit one's practice by insisting on fees which few patients can pay. Unfortunately there are innumerable rationalizations available for selecting patients in psychotherapeutic practice. Some common ones hinge on and point to a patient's lack of motivation, lack of readiness to change, inclination toward a death-struggle for power, or some other factor, some Plan operating in the patient that excuses the therapist from responsibility to secure a viable relationship. A therapist can determine what sort of practice he wants by paying attention to what he feels he can handle in the way of patients' demands. Those therapists who follow the mode of the devoted general practitioner (the bearded father-figure of the familiar painting, sitting by the sick child's bedside while the child's parents hover in the shadows) will predictably have lives of discomfort. Those who take a forthright position that the patient's life is his own to manage may sleep long and (perhaps) well. This is a decision that depends upon the therapist's Plans, his tastes and values, rather than upon tested results.

Emissaries from each extreme camp on the issue of devotion can adduce evidence that the other side is soft-hearted, soft-headed, or at least ineffective. Followers of the hard-line position do not have to contend with the patients who leave their cold, austere northern domain for more tropical, acceptive climes; followers of the soft-line position are blocked in discovering how much their patients could have endured and learned from meeting frustration. The available evidence tends to confirm the followers of the soft line more than the hard line, because the soft-line practitioners' patients come back again and again and provide evidence that these therapists' efforts are necessary, whereas the hard-line people, however much they use the "He wasn't ready" or "They seem to be functioning" argument, lack any data regarding follow-up (an enterprise woefully lacking in *any* school of psychotherapy). It is also self-evident that those patients who cannot grapple with a hard-line position will automatically tend to gravitate toward more immediately relieving therapeutic atmospheres, in which the therapist supplies the mother-surrogate type of efforts to force change.

If a therapist believes that a proper psychotherapeutic structure requires four hours a week, he automatically (though invisibly) restricts his practice to those who can afford such a structure. If a patient cannot afford four hours per week at the usual fees, the therapist either refers him to a therapist who will charge less, works in another structure, or reduces his fees. Interpretations of motivations on the patient's or the therapist's part on this dimension are only limited by the imaginativeness of the observer.

Like other feedback mechanisms which are built into the structure of therapy, this emphasis upon factors which skew the sample with which the therapist works has pervasive influence upon his opinions about all manner of factors in the psychotherapeutic process. Build yourself a practice, in fantasy, on one of many existing views regarding fees: You will have a different opinion in ten years depending upon which stance you take regarding the influence of money. Captains of industry whose fees are paid by their companies (as part of fringe benefits for executives) respond to the whole therapeutic structure in a fashion differing from similarly gifted individuals who subsist on the usual professorial incomes. The children of wealthy parents are usually indifferent to fees, working as well in therapy for low as for high fees, feeling little guilt about missed hours or other delinquencies except what has been taught them regarding ritual observances of all kinds.

People have a way of approaching their obligation to pay for the therapist's time that is a product not only of their psychopathology or individual needs, but also of the cultural milieu in which they are immersed. A cultured clergyman, independently wealthy, approaches fees differently than a Messianic ascetic fundamentalist. This is not limited to patients belonging to one profession: The same range of attitudes in the approach to therapy and its cost can be seen in United States Senators who come for treatment. Nor is the range of variation of the influence of fees specified by considering the therapist's demands on the patient. Some patients have such an overwhelming awe of the therapist's stature that they regard their obligation as patients beyond all sense and reason. This is yet another invisible factor in therapy: Many an experienced therapist, having set up the therapeutic agreement, has discovered several years later that the patient had implicitly set up an irrational exaggeration of that agreement: It comes as a surprise that some patients (and especially those who pay a reduced fee) do not feel free *NOT* to come to an hour, do not recognize that they have leased time, and no more, and hence repeat a compulsive ritual in the process of being treated for their symptoms. An enormous gain in maturation, a marked change, can come when such a patient discovers he or she is not required to appear—instead, merely expected to pay for the time.

The Invisible Force of the Therapist's Values

The therapist's beliefs regarding devotion affect sharply his stance regarding not only his own relation to his patient, but in the larger arena, what personal commitment means in any relationship—including marriage, parenthood, and friendship. If a therapist believes that most marital conflicts can be resolved, his stance toward a husband complaining of a wife's faults will be guided by the intent to find some barrier blocking the relation between the man and his wife. He will try to change the barrier. If the therapist has had an unfortunate experience with marriage, and has come to believe that such an intense relation is hardly worth the trouble, his interpretations may well be directed toward the "sick" reasons guiding his patient which keep the patient in an unrewarding search for what the therapist believes to be only an illusory Holy Grail, marital bliss. This is quite inescapable.

Patients, and patients' spouses, approach therapy armed with a colorful set of prejudices garnered from cocktail-party gossip, reading, and various mass-media depictions of therapy and its effect on marriage. Spouses generally fear the dissolution of their marriages as a consequence of the treatment of their partner. A lively set of prejudices influences prospective patients. These are of two sorts: Therapy is popularly supposed to do two, quite opposite, things—it will either improve the relationship between husband and wife, or it will dissolve the relation and lead to divorce. The former is a hope, the latter a fear, and the writer has encountered both for many years. These two views are not mythologies of patients; they are shared by those who are themselves therapists when approaching their own personal therapy.

Facts bearing on such an issue are very hard to come by. They require a considerable time-lag in which to follow up outcomes of therapy. All sorts of extraneous factors are involved—social set, Zeitgeist, religion, to mention a few. There are, after all, also bad marriages which ought to be dissolved. The reader who is approaching either becoming a therapist or a patient must at this point just take his chances since no scientific data is available. The writer's own experience has been that the overwhelming majority of marriages are improved by the therapy of either partner (which one announces that he or she is a "patient" is relevant to problems in the marriage but irrelevant to the final outcome) and that only a small number of marriages dissolve as a result of therapy. The number of patients treated in the last 25 years who have divorced their spouses as compared with those who stayed married make a ratio which is a tiny fraction of the average national rates for divorce (the sample was admittedly biased—all these people wanted their marriages to improve and were not coerced). The main trend is toward improvement, expansion, and enrichment of the relation. The small handful of exceptions to this rule the writer has known were like the relationships Maugham so vividly described in *Of Human Bondage*—and when the divorce occurred, the subsequent course for both parties seems, over the years, to have been a great improvement.

Devotion, commitment, or detachment, then, can be important influences, operating almost invisibly in the structure of therapy (as expressed in fees, the frequency of therapy hours, and other peripheral determinants). Many long-lasting therapies end at times having little to do with the state of progress of the patient—the end of an academic year or the therapist's vacation time, for example. Even disregarding such external determinants, the matter of termination of therapy depends on unmeasurable values and goals (Plans) of both therapist and patient.

One of the most sensible and modest objectives, stated to the present writer by Dr. Lawrence Kubie—"enough change to make more change possible"—is scarcely subject to quantitative measure. The Plans of therapists seem to follow the fashions of the time. Behavior therapies once were scheduled on a once-a-week basis, but of late have tended, as mentioned previously, toward much more frequent timing and a much more prolonged course as yet more subtle hierarchies of anxiety-response are discovered. Training analyses in Freud's day were brief and often casual (conducted while Freud took his daily constitutional stroll), but have tended to lengthen with the passage of each decade. Thirty years ago, a 200- to 300-hour analysis was common; in recent years a thousand hours is the more common figure.

Whatever theorists of psychotherapy say in writing about what they and their colleagues do in therapy, it must by now be evident that the nature of the process is such that these therapists must inevitably be doing a great deal more than they can set forth in words, even if the operations they seek to describe are in the forefront of their awareness. Plans for therapy, as set forth in the literature of psychotherapy or the spoken accounts of therapists, must be regarded as the roughest of sketches. They are hardly more accurate than the varying reports of eye-witnesses to other complex events—they are inevitably slanted and incomplete. This state of affairs brings frustration to those who wish to understand the process of therapy, but this frustration may be balanced by comfort in the thought that what theorists fail to mention are the elements of influence which make all therapies more similar than different.

Summary

Interpersonal influence involves elements which frequently fail of mention. This overlooking of hidden elements marks the literature about psychotherapeutic influence. Behavior therapists tend to ignore transference, identification, and the counterparts of these developments which occur in therapists. Psychoanalysts neglect discussing other inevitable developments in the analytic process, such as suggestion, conditioning, and identification. Existential therapists in turn neglect the mechanisms stressed by other therapists—conditioning, interpretation, suggestion, and identification. Other hidden elements of interpersonal influence are the emotional impact upon the participants of their work together (realistic affectional bonds), the vital role of humor in interpersonal relations, and, even more subtle, the context given by language and culture. Different structures of treatment and type of intervention carry within themselves implicit risks, such as conditioned dependency or reinforced pathological self-signalling.

Alteration of states of consciousness occurs in many therapies and is sometimes sought specifically ("hypnotherapy" and "narcotherapy"). In other therapies, altered states of consciousness are a hidden influence.

Some change in the level of awareness, however, occurs spontaneously as a result of such maneuvers as the psychoanalytic practice of placing the patient recumbent on a couch. Such changes in conscious alertness involve changes in the orienting response, as described in Chapter 4.

Devotion, commitment, or its lack in the therapist is the least discussed of all hidden influences, most especially as expressed in that aspect of relationships which is sure to bring out the uglier motives of human beings, namely, money.

19

L'Envoi

advice to those approaching interpersonal influence

This inquiry has centered on higher-level interventions with the symbolic process. These seek to secure change for the better via the words and gestures of the interpersonal process. But the symbolic process is a continuum which extends from molecules and cells, through glands and organs, to the abstract operations of thoughts, values, and language.

There are many ways to influence pathological or other unfortunate processes in humans. Diabetes or arterial hypertension can be influenced for the better by many routes, such as drugs, diet, exercise, change in the level of stress in the family. We are not disenchanted with the efficacy of medical practice when we learn that a change in jobs can reduce the pains of ulcer, or that frequent feedings also work, or that severing the nerve which controls acid secretion in the stomach *also* works. So we should hardly be surprised that many different psychotherapeutic interventions work in regard to our total functioning. There are psychiatric equivalents for what insulin does in diabetics—for example, manic-depressive psychosis is almost totally controllable by the drug lithium carbonate. Considerations of space, however, make a discussion of the type of influence supplied by drugs outside the scope of this inquiry.[1]

Assuming that processes requiring the services of a general practitioner or some specialist have been safely attended to, the problem of selecting a therapist or therapy depends in turn on the nature of the problem requiring therapy.

Is the problem the psychiatric equivalent of a splinter in a thumb? A phobia of cats can be a nuisance or it can reach major proportions, but, given favorable circumstances such as the possession of great wealth, it is possible to avoid all (or nearly all) the cats in the world. Or, without wealth, one can undertake a limited deconditioning of one's anxious responses to a harmless animal. Granted that anyone can profit from a hard look at himself with the help of an experienced analyst, it seems foolish to prescribe psychoanalysis for the relief of the more or less trivial preferences, irrational beliefs, or fears most humans carry around.

Or is the problem a profound and pervasive one? A depressive outlook which pervades one's life constantly and deepens into agonizing despair

---

[1] There is a current trend to abandon the "illness" model of personality and behavior disorder. This may well assist progress in areas in which calling a person "sick" cramps efforts toward favorable modification of his condition. It seems likely that some major disorders will always fit the disease model best.

at intervals is a serious—even a life-threatening—illness. Even less serious conditions can have remarkable rigidity requiring powerful intervening force to achieve change—certain marital problems, for example, give the observer the impression that both partners move on tracks like the figurines in a Swiss clock, and their movements do not change even after many years of mutual dissatisfaction. Various addictions—gambling, racing, drugs—seem to have a life of their own, like cancerous growths feeding on a healthy body, and measures to influence these sinister Plans need to be decisively potent.

One's first step should be to seek an appraisal of the problem by a professional whose training and experience is wide enough to equip him to advise which type of intervention is most appropriate. These choices are multiple, as must be obvious from the foregoing, since human problems are not unidimensional, like the length of a line, but instead multifaceted, like a complex polyhedron (the volume of a cube can be changed by change in any one of its sides). The experienced professional will consider various dimensions of the problem and weigh whether a particular variety of influence (in psychology and psychiatry, for example: group therapy, behavior therapy, family therapy, intensive individual therapy) is most likely to make the most effective and economical intervention with old Plans.

If one intends being a client or a patient, how does one find such a professional? Ask several lawyers or doctors in the community, preferably experienced ones, to whom they would send their wives, or whom they would themselves consult. A doctor's doctor is apt to be good. The test of a therapist is to endure in the free market place, and doctors are free to get the best in the market place of therapeutic practice. Doctors see results of therapy over the years in a way unavailable to the laity. Their own successes and failures make them skeptical of the results of others in the healing arts. While they have their own trade-union prejudices, doctors will know a senior professional—perhaps a senior psychiatrist—who can appraise a problem. In many centers known to this writer, this psychiatrist is less apt to be burdened by medical fraternity bonds than a surgeon or a general practitioner (M.D.'s refer to M.D.'s). He will be more ready to refer a patient to professionals equipped to supply a particular service who may not be physicians (a psychologist expert in behavior therapy, for example).

Other ways of finding such an appraiser are via professionals who have occasion to brush with therapists in the course of their work. Ministers, lawyers, judges, and social workers tend to be knowledgeable about who is a good appraiser, and often who is a good therapist. On the average, the senior members of university departments of psychiatry or psychology can be relied upon for appraisals and referrals.

Once one has the names of several possible appraisers, it is well to get collateral information about them. The nation regards the selection of Supreme Court justices as a matter worthy of careful scrutiny. The same prudent regard is appropriate to an enterprise as intimate, important, and expensive as psychotherapy. No knowledgeable person wants mediocrity on the Court nor mediocrity in his therapy, and methods of assessing the person making an appraisal of one's personal problems and their therapeutic resolution are not different in kind from methods of appraising a candidate for the Court. The appraiser may (and probably will) refer one to another professional, and his judgment of the qualifications of the professional he recommends is a function of his wisdom: Do not let the appraiser off lightly. Any data about his past, present, public, and private life are fair game.

Anyone should suspend politeness when he looks at the appraiser and the person to whom he is referred and not hesitate to shop around. Doctor-shopping may have its drawbacks—we run the danger of confirming our own narrow prejudices, as in lawyer-shopping. If we look for a lawyer who will merely advise what we already had decided as the proper course of action, we have wasted our money. But the content of psychotherapy does not abrogate ordinary social experience quite as much as the content of legal problems does. Shopping around is appropriate in looking for a therapist: One is picking a friend as well as a method of influence. If a therapist strikes one on a first visit as being a pompous ass, then one should head for the hills. Another exploration another day will find a more compatible person with whom to work.

But, it might be said, therapy is a strange undertaking and perhaps personal evaluation of a therapist cannot distinguish between the person and the method. Nonsense. Every bit of evidence the writer has (and it is, to his sorrow, more meager than he would wish) is that a therapist's behavior in therapy is not appreciably different than his behavior, judged by ordinary social standards, outside the consultation room. If a therapist is a boor at a cocktail party, he will be a boor in the therapeutic situation. If he greets one in an urbane fashion, empathically making the first five minutes easy, this is an excellent indicator of what is to come later.

While nobody but the participants know for sure what goes on between two people behind a closed door, there are opportunities to obtain glimpses of how a therapist relates to his patients that are available to a practitioner. The writer has watched many colleagues interview and treat patients as part of their teaching of medical students. Another chance to calibrate social with therapeutic behavior comes from working as a co-therapist with a colleague in couples or family therapy. A third source is the account of a patient who had formerly been in therapy with a colleague concerning that colleague's strengths and weaknesses. Finally, supervision of the way junior colleagues conduct therapy, and the psychotherapeutic treatment of practicing therapists for their personal problems both offer insight into how these colleagues deal with patients.

There are few exceptions, in the writer's experience, to the rule that a man is the same man in or out of the therapeutic role. These are, first, that some people who are quite shy and inhibited in social circumstances can warm up and be relaxed and intimate as therapists. Secondly, some people who are gentle, genial, and considerate in their lives outside the consultation room can be, in their professional work, incisive, provocative, and even brutal by ordinary social standards; however, the writer has never seen such a therapist at work who failed at the same time to convey to the patient in a larger context the therapist's usual social tact and warmth, which supplied a vital framing for his ostensibly "cruel" confrontations. Patients perceive the warm smile behind the obscene epithet.

One should trust one's immediate reactions. The above remarks hold for all schools, all ages and experience, of therapists the writer has known. Generally, therapists are most rigid and doctrinaire in the first few years of their practice, whatever their training. As they mature the rough edges of their styles soften, almost as do vintages of wine or spirits. What study there has been shows that mature therapists of any school are more alike in their work than are youthful ones. There is no firm evidence against the proposition that, in picking a therapist, his experience and maturity is more important than the school he came from or espouses. There are excellent therapists in every school, and inept ones, too. There are good male therapists and bad ones, good female therapists and bad ones. Some therapists whose degree is an M.D. are good—some aren't. Some therapists who hold the Ph.D. degree are better than some M.D.'s. There are probably more gifted therapists holding neither degree than those holding either Ph.D. or M.D. If trade gossip from colleagues and patients can be credited, therapists who have themselves had therapy, been patients, tend to be better therapists than those who haven't (in the writer's opinion, it is legitimate to ask, as part of a general inquiry into qualifications and training, whether a therapist has had therapy or not). One's best guide is how they come across in person. The battle is the payoff in military affairs, and so it is in the highly charged encounters of psychotherapy. To paraphrase General Omar Bradley, a second-class Plan in psychotherapy, beautifully executed, is better than a first-class Plan poorly implemented.

Once into therapy, candor regarding its progress or lack of progress is definitely called for. All injunctions against criticism ought properly to be suspended. If comments critical of the process bring no improvement (they will of course be interpreted in some way or other by the therapist) then switch to another therapist. Marriage and parenthood carry with them obligation to see it through. Therapy should provide one an arena in which, no holds barred, one can at last discover *how* to see it through— but should therapy bog down to a stalemate, it is time for a consultation (along traditional medical models) with another therapist, who may be able to assist one's therapist in breaking up the stalemate.

If one is approaching interpersonal influence from the other side of the encounter, all the preceding maxims should be taken for granted as being part of the client's or the patient's Bill of Rights. For example, it is silly to be coy about any personal information that a patient might obtain concerning the professional's private life by a visit to the local newspaper's files, or from a biographical directory of one's professional organization. To assume a cloak of professional anonymity about these matters is fatuous. If a patient asks if one is married it is perfectly proper and sensible to tell him, and then use it as best one can, in exploring why the question arises.

The beginning appraisal from the therapist's side rests on sizing up the patient's Plans at all levels of his functioning, and looking for conflicting Plans, paradoxical Plans, and in general for those which went awry at a phase of development tinged with the arbitrary logic of "the-moon-is-following-me" variety. Gaps and avoidances are important to find, and injunctions, vital. These gaps may be described in other terms, like repression, denial, or projection, but the essential element is that something is missing, or at least misplaced.

Once the therapist has some idea of where the trouble lies, he has the option of using various procedures to repair bad or ineffectual Plans. A fear of cats can exist in relatively healthy and effective mature adults, and might call for deconditioning therapy and no more. But if the only string the therapist has to his therapeutic bow is behavior therapy, he will not be able to offer change in all levels of personal life, which other therapies afford—such ephemeral changes as are described as "enrichment," "expansion," or just plain "growth." The implication is rather obvious: One should as a therapist be happy to use any and every tool he can put his hand upon. Therapists should explore and become expert in all forms of influence, even though they may elect and prefer a particular form.

The basic paradigm of "Plans to change Plans" lifts one above consideration of purity of technique versus a tasteless and uncritical eclecticism. One should be equipped to hypnotize, to analyze, to manipulate, to see individual, couple, family, or extended group at will and with a clear conscience of committing no heresy. If the defective Plan hinges on a belief in witches, a cognitive attack on this Plan is appropriate. If the defective Plan hinges on an ancient connection between bodily processes and linguistic symbols, a systematic correction of such connections is called for, just as Breuer and Freud undertook successfully long ago. If the defective Plan stems from some inability to resolve confusions and paradoxes at high levels of abstraction (Russellian paradox, Zen dilemmas), still other interventions are appropriate. Therapists may narrow what they wish to do, but they are responsible for knowledge of the law, in therapeutic as well as in daily life, and in both cases ignorance is no valid excuse.

The Soul thereby by synthesis creates a new fact which is the Appearance woven out of the old and the new—a compound of reception and anticipation, which in its turn passes into the future. The final synthesis of these three complexes is the end to which its indwelling Eros urges the soul. Its good resides in the realization of a strength of many feelings, fortifying each other as they meet in the novel unity. Its evil lies in the clash of vivid feelings, denying to each other their proper expansion. Its triviality lies in the anesthesia by which evil is avoided. In this way, through sheer omission, fewer, fainter feelings constitute the final Appearance. Evil is the half-way house between perfection and triviality. It is the violence of strength against strength.

Alfred North Whitehead
Adventures of Ideas

20

A Summing Up

the argument in a nutshell

The central element of influence is that patients come, attend, and respond to the therapist, whether they come of their own will or are coerced. To influence is to sway another, whether for the moment or for life. Patients come for therapeutic influence because some of their Plans have gone awry. Those who come of their own free will still have a belief —A Plan—that another human may have something to offer of value to them. Therapists can at least count on the use of this remaining Plan to supply leverage to alter the faulty or conflictual Plans which have caused suffering for the patient. Yet even those coerced into therapy can be influenced. This seems less of a mystery today than formerly. Some of the elements of influence in both cases are: the orienting reflex, the combinatory and categorizing capacity of the human mind, and the special expression of this faculty in linguistic processes. These basic elements combine into the more complex influences, such as those named suggestion, identification, and interpretation. The problem of levels of abstraction in each of these arises, since differing levels give many opportunities for conflict and paradox.

Plans, whether those of the patient or the therapist, intimately involve the life of feeling, to the depths of our nature. We share some of our most primitive Plans with the animals—these we call instincts or instinctual drives—we eat when hungry and we avoid pain whenever we can. Animals, taught to respond to one signal, a square, as meaning "food will come" and to another, a circle, as meaning "pain will come" thereafter have two Plans. One Plan guides the animal toward pleasure; the other leads away from pain. When such an animal is presented a new series of signals in which the original square signal is gradually altered to resemble a circle, the animal's Plans come into conflict, and strong unpleasant feelings appear to develop. In these circumstances the animal shows signs of distress and confusion which look like what humans call anxiety. Young animals which have developed Plans concerning mothering (from the experience of being mothered) show what looks to humans like depression when their mothering Plans are rendered inoperative through separation from their mothers. Animals like monkeys, taught to push a lever in order to receive food, show what look like temper-tantrums when the Plan the monkeys had developed fails to be confirmed—when it is arranged or it merely happens that no food appears when the lever is pushed. Animals like rats, which have instinctual orienting Plans that guide their survival efforts in situations of grave danger, will give up and die when the operation of these survival Plans is interfered with. (Rats swimming in water drown much faster if their vibrissae, the feelers around their muzzles which only signal the rat of his position with respect to objects and do not help him swim, are clipped off.)

Human Plans can suffer all these types of confusions and disconfirmations, and all these types of painful feelings result. But humans suffer many additional types of conflict given by their more complex symbolizing capacity. Influence in psychotherapy aims at correcting the confusions, disconfirmations, and errors of the patient's Plans. The desired end result for the patient is the possession of more reliable, more zestful, more loving and creative Plans.

All psychotherapists (by definition of their role as distinct from practitioners of brainwashing) aim for the patient's good. They seek an increase in his ability to synthesize contrasting feelings and ideas, an increase in his awareness of himself in his fullest being, and a decrease of his tendency to trivial and fearful avoidance of aspects of himself and others. Therapists seek creative advance, not the destructive clash and retreat of paranoia or of suicide—they try to foster confident mastery in the place of the panic and flight of phobia. They want patients to be able to experience joy *together with* sorrow, rather than disengagement from the world in the anguished turmoil of depression. The therapist sways his patient toward encounter, not alienation and apathy. All therapists hold such goals in common, although one therapist may prize some of these goals above others, and although the varieties of influence they employ may appear to be very different.

All therapies involve Plans to change the patient's Plans. These therapeutic Plans employ all aspects of the symbolic process, including perceptions coming to the patient in the mode of sense presentation of distant objects, the more primitive mode of perception of bodily processes and urges, and the conceptual elaborations of both of these in thought processes. The Plans to change the patient's Plans rest on the tactics and strategies of communication at all levels of abstraction, from nonverbal levels to highly abstract ones. Poetry is as much in place as is practical necessity in therapuetic Plans.

Recent studies of the preverbal roots of influence in infancy have shown quite surprising sophistication of the infant's information processing and of the mutual influence between baby and adult. Fifty-day-old babies are now known to behave almost as if they were adult scientists, testing complex hypotheses about the nature of the world. They are also, mammals that they are, controlled in part by Plans they bring with them into the world, among which is one which has scarcely been noted in accounts of therapeutic influence. This is the reflex which automatically guides the baby to attend to any mismatch (but especially *slight* mismatch) of his perceptions of the present with any Plan he was given by his biological makeup, uterine experience, and his life up to the present. This reflex is called the orienting reflex, and it now appears to be intimately involved in every tactic of psychotherapy.

Studies of the beginnings of verbal influence in childhood have confirmed the importance of what Pavlov named the "second signalling system" in humans, powerful in its role in regulating all behavior. This is speech, whether vocalized or silently rehearsed in thought. Other studies of those who do not possess, or have lost, verbal regulation of behavior (those, for example, whose congenital deafness has denied them language, or those who have suffered brain damage) have supplied more light on this form of influence.

Verbal and nonverbal influences interact in ways previously unsuspected in processes intimately involved in illnesses. Study of this interaction discloses the profound effect of the two signalling systems in the life of feeling and of bodily processes, normal and pathological. Ulcers of the stomach seem clear manifestations of illness; tears and blushing are not so named. The second signalling system, verbal processes, regulates bodily functions, as when someone weeps in recounting a loss. The name "illness," on the other hand, poorly differentiates ulcers from tears: This is one of the many errors of the symbolic process.

The symbolic process is subject to errors deriving from many sources, inescapable because of its abstractive function. Some of these involve paradoxical and pathological confusions between various levels of verbal and nonverbal influence ("first" and "second" signalling systems). These have been scrutinized in recent years in studies of family interactions. Such paradoxical influences can be put to therapeutic use. They have also been used to produce not only therapeutic results, as in the confusion technique of hypnotic induction, but also attitude changes, as in brainwashing.

Therapeutic influence is a process, the complex interaction of two Plans. It is the sequential interaction of two Plans ordered over time. This occurs in all human interactions. In the concert hall, Arthur Rubinstein emerges from the wings, takes his place at the piano, and plays a series of works. His audience, in the next period of two hours, is moved to tears as a result of the presence of the Master and a series of sounds he causes the piano to produce. They rise and shout, "Bravo!" The complexity of influence in this process in the concert hall and in the process of therapy comes from multiple levels of the symbolic process operating in time. Simplifications of this process, made by every school of therapy (in order to be able to describe it at all) are achieved by ignoring some of its aspects. Very simple formulations of any variety achieve their simplicity by massive editing of the facts. The truth seems to be that we need all possible ways to understand and utilize the elements of influence (including understanding of those unfortunate consequences which attend any misuse of an item of our psychotherapeutic armamentarium) to assist synthesis, to resolve the violence of strength against strength, and to promote creative advance.

This inquiry has sketched many processes in humans, young and old, in instinctual, perceptual, conceptual, linguistic, and transactional areas. If one bears in mind the processes shown in the behavior of 50-day-old babies, acting in the fashion of adult scientists; four-year-old children, speaking as accomplished linguists; and 50-year-old dreamers, creating anew like a Picasso—the richness and variety of the psychotherapeutic scene may seem less mysterious. The contentions of various schools relate to the superficial appearance of their operations rather than to fundamental differences.

References

Alexander, F. Psychoanalysis and psychotherapy. *Journal of American Psychoanalytic Association,* 1953, **2**, 722–733.

Alexander, F., French, T. M., et al. *Psychoanalytic therapy.* New York: Ronald Press, 1946.

Anderson, C. *Beyond Freud.* New York: Harper & Row, 1957.

Ardrey, R. *The territorial imperative.* New York: Atheneum, 1966.

Bateson, G., Jackson, D. D., Haley, J., & Weakland, J. Toward a theory of schizophrenia. *Behavioral Science,* 1956, **1**, 251–264.

Beadle, M. *A child's mind.* Garden City, N.Y.: Doubleday, 1970.

Beers, C. *A mind that found itself.* New York: Doubleday, 1936.

Bell, R. Q. Developmental psychology. *Annual Review of Psychology,* 1965, **16**.

Benjamin, L. S., & Graham, D. T. Unpublished manuscript, University of Wisconsin Medical School, 1967.

Bettelheim, B. Individual and mass behavior in extreme situations. *Journal of Abnormal and Social Psychology,* 1943, **38**, 417.

Birdwhistell, R. L. *Kinesics and context.* Philadelphia: University of Pennsylvania Press, 1970.

Blauvelt, H., & McKenna, J. Capacity of the newborn for orientation. In B. M. Foss (Ed.), *Determinants of infant behavior.* Vol. I. New York: Wiley, 1961.

Bleuler, E. *Dementia praecox, or the group of schizophrenias.* New York: International Universities Press, 1950.

Boas, F. *Race, language, and culture.* New York: Macmillan, 1940. Paperback ed., Free Press, 1966.

Bonaparte, M. Time and the unconscious. *Journal of the International Psychoanalytic Association,* 1940, **21**, 427.

Boss, M. *The analysis of dreams.* New York: Philosophical Library, 1958.

Boss, M. *Psychoanalysis and daseinanalysis.* New York: Basic Books, 1963.

Boulding, K. *The image.* Ann Arbor: University of Michigan Press, 1956.

Bower, T. G. R. The visual world of infants. *Scientific American,* 1966, **215**, 80–92.

Breuer, J., & Freud, S. *The standard edition of the complete psychological works of Sigmund Freud.* Vol. II. *Studies on hysteria.* London: Hogarth Press, 1955.

Buber, M. *I and thou.* New York: Scribner, 1958.

Cassirer, E. *The Philosophy of symbolic forms.* Vol. I. *Language.*

New Haven, Conn.: Yale University Press, 1953.

Chase, S., in collaboration with Chase, M. T. *Power of words.* New York: Harcourt, 1954.

Chomsky, N. For a survey of his work, see Lenneberg, E. *Biological foundations of language.* Appendix A. New York: Wiley, 1967.

Chomsky, N. *Syntactic structures.* The Hague: Morton, 1957.

Davis, I. E. *Recovery from schizophrenia: The Roland method.* Springfield, Ill.: Charles C Thomas, 1957.

Dunlap, K. The technique of negative practice. *American Journal of Psychology,* 1942, **55**, 270–273.

Ellis, A. *Reason and emotion in psychotherapy.* New York: Lyle Stuart, 1962.

Ellis, A. *A guide to rational living.* North Hollywood, Calif.: Wilshire Book Co., 1971.

Enelow, A. S., & Wexler, M. *Psychiatry in the practice of medicine.* New York: Oxford University Press, 1966.

Erickson, M. H. *Advanced techniques of hypnosis and therapy.* In J. Haley (Ed.), *Selected papers of Milton H. Erickson, M.D.* New York: Grune & Stratton, 1967.

Escalona, S. K. *The roots of individuality.* Chicago: Aldine, 1968.

Festinger, L. *A theory of cognitive dissonance.* New York: Harper, 1957.

Fisher, C. Subliminal and supraliminal influences on dreams. *American Journal of Psychiatry.* 1960, **116**, 1009.

Frank, J. *Persuasion and healing.* Baltimore: Johns Hopkins Press, 1961.

Freud, A. *The ego and the mechanisms of defense.* New York: International Universities Press, 1946. (Originally published in 1936.)

Freud, S. *Collected papers.* Vol. II, pp. 285–404. London: Hogarth Press, 1949.

Freud, S. Project for a scientific psychology. In M. Bonaparte, A. Freud, & E. Kris (Eds.), *The origins of psychoanalysis: Letters to Wilhelm Fliess, drafts, and notes, 1887–1902.* New York: Basic Books, 1954.

Freud, S. *The standard edition of the complete psychological works . . .* Vol. X (1909). *Two case histories.* London: Hogarth Press, 1955.

Fromm-Reichmann, F. Basic problems in the psychotherapy of schizophrenia. *Psychiatry,* 1958, **21**, 1–6.

Glasser, W. G. *Reality therapy.* New York: Harper & Row, 1965.

Goodall, J. New discoveries among wild chimpanzees. *National Geographic,* 1956, **128**, 802–831.

Grace, W., & Graham, D. T. Relationship of specific attitudes and emotions to certain bodily disease. *Psychosomatic Medicine,* 1952, **14**, 243.

Graham, D. T. Some research on psychophysiologic specificity and its relation to psychosomatic diseases. In R. Roessler & N. S. Greenfield (Eds.), *Physiological correlates of psychological disorders.* Madison:

University of Wisconsin Press, 1962.

Graham, D. T., Kabler, J. D., & Graham, F. K. Physiological responses to the suggestion of attitudes specific for hives and hypertension. *Psychosomatic Medicine,* 1962, **24**, 159.

Graham, D. T., Lundy, R. M., Benjamin, L. S., Kabler, J. D., Lewis, W. C., Kunish, N. O., & Graham, F. K. Specific attitudes in initial interviews with patients having different "psychosomatic" diseases. *Psychosomatic Medicine,* 1962, **24**, 257.

Graham, F. K., & Jackson, J. C. Arousal systems and infant heart rate responses. In L. P. Lipsitt & H. W. Reese (Eds.), *Advances in child development and behavior.* Vol. V. New York: Academic Press, 1970.

Green, H. *I never promised you a rose garden.* New York: Holt, Rinehart and Winston, 1965. Signet paperback.

Greenson, R. R. *The technique and practice of psychoanalysis.* Vol. I. New York: International Universities Press, 1967.

Grzimek, B., & Grzimek, N. *Serengeti shall not die.* London, 1960. Reported by W. H. Thorpe, Ethology and consciousness. In J. C. Eccles (Ed.), *Brain and conscious experience.* Pp. 470–505. New York: Springer-Verlag, 1966.

Haley, J. *Strategies of psychotherapy.* New York: Grune & Stratton, 1963.

Haley, J. The art of being schizophrenic. *Voices,* 1965, **1**, 133–147.

Harlow, H. F. Motivation as a factor in the acquisition of new responses. In M. R. Jones (Ed.), *Current theory and research in motivation.* Lincoln: University of Nebraska Press, 1953.

Harlow, H. Motivation in monkeys and men. In F. L. Ruch (Ed.), *Psychology and life.* Glenview, Ill.: Scott Foresman, 1963.

Harlow, H., and Harlow, M. The young monkeys. In *Readings in psychology today.* Del Mar, Calif.: C. R. M. Books, 1969. Pp. 139–145.

Harlow, H., & McClearn, G. E. Object discrimination learned by monkeys on the basis of manipulation motives. *Journal of Comparative and Physiological Psychology,* 1954, **47**, 73–76.

Harper, R. *Psychoanalysis and psychotherapy.* Englewood Cliffs, N.J.: Prentice-Hall, 1959.

Hayakawa, S. L. *Language in thought and action.* (2nd ed.) New York: Harcourt, 1949.

Helfer, R. E. *The battered child.* Chicago: University of Chicago Press, 1968.

Ingle, D. Reported by H. L. Teuber in J. C. Eccles (Ed.), *Brain and conscious experience.* New York: Springer-Verlag, 1966.

James, W. *The principles of psychology.* Vol. I. New York: Holt, Rinehart and Winston, 1890.

Johnson, A. M., Giffin, M. E., Watson, E. J., & Beckett, P. G. S. Studies in schizophrenia at the Mayo Clinic II, Observations on ego functions in schizophrenia. *Psychiatry,* 1956, **19**, 143–148.

Johnson, A. M., & Szurek, S. A. Etiology of antisocial behavior in delinquents and psychopaths. *Journal of the American Medical Association,* 1954, **154**, 814–817.

Joos, M. Language and the school child. *Harvard Educational Review,* 1964, **34**, 203–210.

Kagan, J. Christopher: The many faces of response. In *Readings in psychology today.* Del Mar, Calif.: C. R. M. Books, 1969.

Kellner, R. The evidence in favor of psychotherapy. *British Journal of Medical Psychology,* 1967, **40**, 341–358.

Kiev, A. *Magic, faith and healing.* New York: Free Press, 1964.

Klein, G. S. Consciousness in psychoanalytic theory: Some implications for current research in perception. *Journal of American Psychoanalytic Association,* 1959, **7**, 5.

Klein, G. S. On hearing one's own voice: An aspect of cognitive control in spoken thought. In N. S. Greenfield & W. C. Lewis (Eds.), *Psychoanalysis and current biological thought.* Madison: University of Wisconsin Press, 1965.

Kluckhohn, R. *Mirror for man.* New York: McGraw-Hill, 1967. Fawcett Premier paperback.

Kol'tsova, M. M. The rise and development of the second signal system in the child. *Trudy Inst. Fiziol. im Pavlova,* 1949, **4**, 49.

Korzybski, A. *Science and sanity.* Lancaster, Pa.: Science Press, 1941.

Krauss, R., & Sendak, M. *A hole is to dig.* New York: Harper & Row, 1952.

Laing, R. D. *The divided self.* Baltimore: Penguin Books, 1965.

Leiter, R. G.: *Leiter international performance scale.* Chicago, Ill.: C. H. Stoelting Company, 1936–1965.

Lenneberg, E. H. *Biological foundations of language.* New York: Wiley, 1967.

Lenneberg, E. H., Nichols, I. A., & Rosenberger, E. F. Primitive stages of language development in Mongolism. In Association for Research in Nervous and Mental Disease, *Research publications.* Vol. XLII. *Disorders of communication.* Baltimore: Williams & Wilkins, 1964.

Lewis, W. C. Structural aspects of the psychoanalytic theory of instinctual drives, affects, and time. In H. S. Greenfield & W. C. Lewis (Eds.), *Psychoanalysis and current biological thought.* Madison: University of Wisconsin Press, 1965.

Lewis, W. C., Wolman, R., & King, M. The development of the language of emotions. *American Journal of Psychiatry,* 1970, **127**, 1491–1497.

Lind, J. (Ed.) Supplement 163. *Acta Paediatrica Scandinavica.* Uppsala: Alqvist and Wiksells, 1965.

London, P. *The modes and morals of psychotherapy.* New York: Holt, Rinehart and Winston, 1964.

London, P. *Behavior control.* New York: Harper & Row, 1969.

Lorenz, K. Z. *King Solomon's ring.* New York: Crowell, 1952.

Lowe, V. *Understanding Whitehead.* Baltimore: Johns Hopkins Press, 1962.

Ludwig, A. Altered states of consciousness. In C. Tart (Ed.),

Altered states of conscious-ness. New York: Wiley, 1969.

Luria, A. R. *The role of speech in the regulation of normal and abnormal behavior.* New York: Liveright, 1960.

Luria, A. R. Speech development and the formation of mental processes. In M. Cole & I. Waltzman (Eds.), *A handbook of contemporary Soviet psychology.* New York: Basic Books, 1969.

Lyublinskaya, A. A. *Essays on the mental development of the child.* Moscow: Akademy of Pedagogic Science Press, R. S.F.S.R., 1959.

Margolin, S. Address inquiries to Sydney Margolin, M.D., Department of Psychiatry, University of Colorado, Medical Center, Denver, Colorado.

May, R. Contributions of existential psychotherapy. In R. May (Ed.), *Existence.* New York: Basic Books, 1958.

Meers, D. R. Communist child care programs: Innovation and Pandora's box. In H. P. David (Ed.), *Child mental health in international perspective.* Washington, D.C.: Joint Commission for Mental Health Care of Children. Harper & Row, 1968.

Meltzoff, J., & Kornreich, M. *Research in psychotherapy,* New York: Atherton Press, 1970.

Menninger, K. Theory of psychoanalytic technique. *Menninger Clinic Monograph Series,* No. 12. New York: Basic Books, 1958.

Milgram, S. Behavioral study of obedience. *Journal of Abnor-mal and Social Psychology,* 1963, **67**, 371–378.

Miller, G. A. The magical number seven, plus or minus two. *Psychological Review,* 1956, **63**, 81–97.

Miller, G. A. Galanter, E., & Pribram, K. H. *Plans and the structure of behavior.* New York: Holt, Rinehart and Winston, 1960.

Mussen, P. Early socialization: Learning and identification. In *New directions in psychology.* Vol. III. New York: Holt, Rinehart and Winston, 1967.

Mussen, P. H., Conger, J. J., & Kagan, J. (Eds.) *Child development and personality.* New York: Harper & Row, 1969.

Newton, J. R. Considerations for the psychotherapeutic technique of symptom scheduling. *Psychotherapy: Theory, Research and Practice,* 1968, **V**, 95–103. (a)

Newton, J. R. Therapeutic paradoxes, paradoxical intentions and negative practice. *American Journal of Psychotherapy,* 1968, **XXII**, 68–81. (b)

Nodine, J. H., & Moyer, J. H. *Psychosomatic medicine: The first Hahnemann symposium.* Philadelphia: Lea & Febiger, 1962.

Oberndorfer, C. P. Results of psychoanalytic therapy. *International Journal of Psychoanalysis,* 1943, **24**, 107–114.

Ogden, C. K., & Richards, I. A. *The meaning of meaning.* New York: Harcourt, 1926.

Papousek, H. The development of higher nervous activity in children in the first half of life. *Society for Research in*

Child Development Monographs, 1965, **30**, (2).

Pavlov, I. P. *Conditioned reflexes.* London: Oxford University Press, 1927.

Pfungst, O. *Clever Hans (the horse of Mr. Von Osten).* New York: Holt, Rinehart and Winston, 1911.

Phillips, E. L. *Psychotherapy: A modern theory and practice.* Englewod Cliffs, N.J.: Prentice-Hall, 1954.

Piaget, J. *The language and thought of the child.* New York: Humanities Press, 1951.

Piers, G., & Singer, M. B. *Shame and guilt—A psychoanalytic and a cultural study.* Springfield, Ill.: Charles C. Thomas, 1953.

Piers, G., & Piers, M. W. Learning theories and the analytic process. Paper presented at the Annual Meeting of the American Psychoanalytic Association, Chicago, May 1957.

Razran, G. The observable unconscious and the inferable conscious in current Soviet psychophysiology: Interoceptive conditioning, semantic conditioning, and the orienting reflex. *Psychological Review,* 1961, 68 (2), 81–147.

Reich, W. On character analysis. In R. Fliess (Ed.), *The psychoanalytic reader.* New York: International Universities Press, 1948.

Reik, T. *Listening with the third ear: The inner experience of a psychoanalyst.* New York: Grove Press, 1948.

Rheingold, H. L. The development of social behavior in the human infant. *Society for Research in Child Development Monographs,* 1966, **31** (5).

Richmond, J. B., Lipton, E. L., & Steinschneider, A. Observations on differences in autonomic nervous system function between and within individuals during early infancy. *Journal of the American Academy of Child Psychiatry,* 1962, **1**, 83–91.

Rogers, C. R. *Client-centered therapy: Its current practice, implications and theory.* Boston: Houghton Mifflin, 1951.

Rogers, C. R. (Ed.), with the collaboration of Gendlin, E. T., Kiesler, D. J., & Truax, C. B. *The therapeutic relationship and its impact.* Madison: University of Wisconsin Press, 1967.

Roheim, G. The symbolism of subincision. *American Imago,* 1949, **6** (4), 3–10.

Rosen, J. N. *Direct analysis.* New York: Grune & Stratton, 1953.

Rosenthal, R. Introduction to *Clever Hans (the horse of Mr. Van Osten).* New York: Holt, Rinehart and Winston, 1965.

Rosenthal, R., & Fode, K. L. The effect of experimenter bias on the performance of the albino rat. *Behavior Science,* 1963, **8**, 183–189.

Ruesch, J. *Therapeutic communication.* New York: Norton, 1961.

Ruml, B. "Homefulness." Address presented at the annual scientific meeting of the American Psychological Association, Cleveland, Ohio, 1933.

Russell, B. *The autobiography of*

Bertrand Russell. Boston: Atlantic-Little, Brown, 1967.

Salter, A. *Conditioned reflex therapy: The direct approach to the reconstruction of personality.* New York: Putnam, 1961. Capricorn Books paperback.

Sapir, E. *Culture, language and personality.* Berkeley: University of California Press, 1956.

Sarbin, T. R. Hypnosis as a behavior modification technique. In L. Krasner & L. P. Ullman (Eds.), *Research in behavior modification.* New York: Holt, Rinehart and Winston, 1967.

Schutz, W. C. *Joy.* New York: Grove Press, 1967.

Sechehaye, M. *Reality, lost and regained, autobiography of a schizophrenic girl.* New York: Grune & Stratton, 1951.

Sechehaye, M. *A new psychotherapy in schizophrenia.* New York: Grune & Stratton, 1956.

Sokolov, E. N. *Perception and the conditioned reflex.* New York: Macmillan, 1963.

Spiesman, J. C. Autonomic monitoring of ego defense process. In N. S. Greenfield & W. C. Lewis (Eds.), *Psychoanalysis and current biological thought.* Madison: University of Wisconsin Press, 1965.

Spitz, R. A. *The first year of life.* New York: International University Press, 1965.

Spitz, R. A., & Wolf, K. M. *The smiling response. Genetic Psychological Monographs,* 1946, No. 34.

Stampfl, P. G., & Lewis, D. J. Essentials of implosive therapy: A learning-theory based psychodynamic behavioral therapy. *Journal of Abnormal Psychology,* 1967, **72**, 496–503.

Sternbach, R. A. *Pain—A psychophysiological analysis.* New York: Academic Press, 1968.

Stone, L. *The psychoanalytic situation: An examination of its development and essential nature.* New York: International Universities Press, 1961.

Stratton, G. M. Vision without diversion of the usual usage. *Psychological Review,* 1897, **4**, 341–360.

Strupp, H. H., & Bergin, A. E. Some empirical and conceptual bases for coordinated research in psychotherapy. *International Journal of Psychiatry,* 1969, **7**, 18–40.

Thomas, A., Birch, H. G., Chess, S., Hertzig, M. E., Korn, S., et al. *Behavioral individuality in early childhood.* New York: New York University Press, 1963.

Thorne, F. Directive and eclectic personality counselling. In J. L. McCary & D. E. Sheer (Eds.), *Six approaches to psychotherapy.* New York: Dryden, 1955.

Tinbergen, N. *The study of instinct.* Oxford: Clarendon Press, 1951.

Vygotskii, L. S. *Thought and speech.* Sotsekqiz, 1934. For summary see Sokolov, E. N. Studies of the speech mechanisms of thinking. In M. Cole & I. Maltzman (Eds.), *A handbook of contemporary Soviet psychology.* New York: Basic Books, 1969.

Watzlawick, P., Beavin, J. H., & Jackson, D. D. *Pragmatics of human communication.* New York: Norton, 1967.

Wexler, M. The structural problem in schizophrenia: The role of the internal object. *Bulletin of the Menninger Clinic,* 1951, **15**, 21.

Whitaker, C. A., Felder, R. E., Malorie, T. P., & Warkentin, J. First stage techniques in the experimental psychotherapy of chronic schizophrenic patients. In J. H. Masserman (Ed.), *Current psychiatric therapies.* Vol. II. New York: Grune & Stratton, 1962.

Whitehead, A. N. *Symbolism: Its meaning and effect.* New York: Putnam, 1959. Capricorn Books paperback.

Whitehead, A. N., & Russell, B. *Principia mathematica.* Cambridge, England: Cambridge University Press, 1910. 3 vols.

Whorf, B. L. *Language, thought and reality.* J. B. Carroll (Ed.). New York: Wiley, Technological Press, 1956.

Wittgenstein, L. *Tractatus logico-philosophicus.* New York: Humanities Press, 1951.

Wittgenstein, L. *Philosophical investigations.* (3rd ed.) New York: Macmillan, 1958.

Wolman, P. A. "Affective" spelling. Unpublished paper, Harvard University Medical School, 1969.

Wolpe, J. *Psychotherapy by reciprocal inhibition.* Stanford, Calif.: Stanford University Press, 1958.

Wynne, L. C., & Singer, M. T. Thought disorder and the family relations of schizophrenics: I. A Research Strategy. *Archives of General Psychiatry,* 1969, **9**, 191–198.

Yngve, V. H. A model and an hypothesis for language structure. *Proceedings of the American Philosophical Society,* 1960, **104**, 444–466.

Zimbardo, P., & Ebbesen, E. B. *Influencing attitudes and changing behavior.* Reading, Mass.: Addison-Wesley, 1969.

Index